Saint Lucia
Simply Beautiful

Edited by Arif Ali

HANSIB

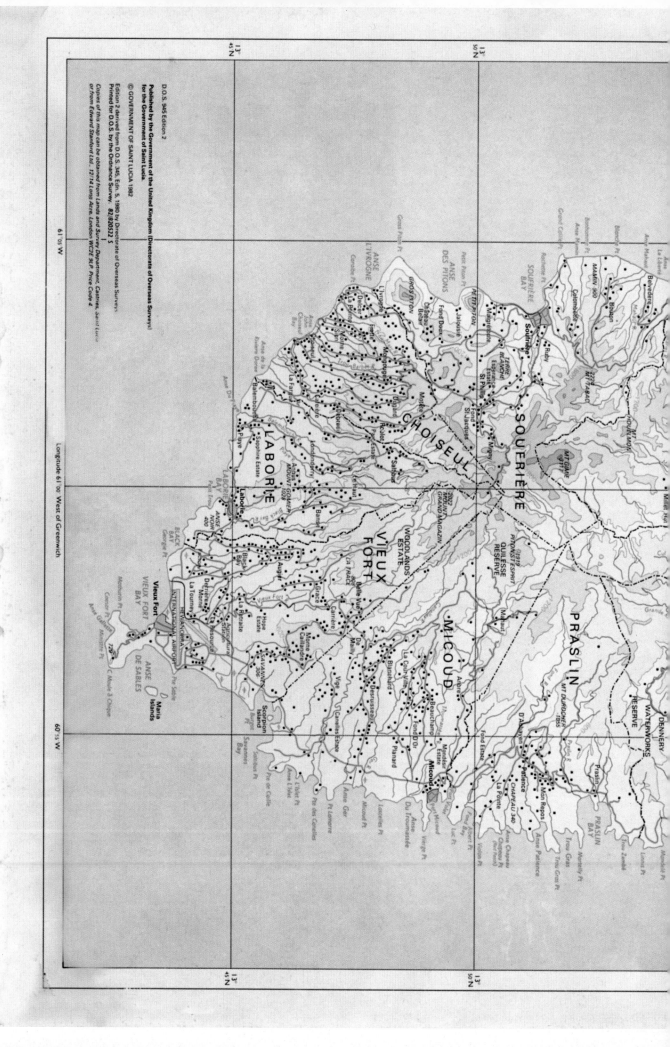

D.O.S. 945 Edition 2

Published by the Government of the United Kingdom (Directorate of Overseas Surveys)
for the Government of Saint Lucia

© GOVERNMENT OF SAINT LUCIA 1982

Edition 2 derived from D.O.S. 345, Edn. 5, 1980 by Directorate of Overseas Surveys.
Printed for D.O.S. by the Ordnance Survey.   82/820522 S

Copies of this map can be obtained from Lands and Survey Department, Castries, Saint Lucia
or from Edward Stanford Ltd. 12/14 Long Acre, London WC2E 9LP Price Code 4

SAINT LUCIA

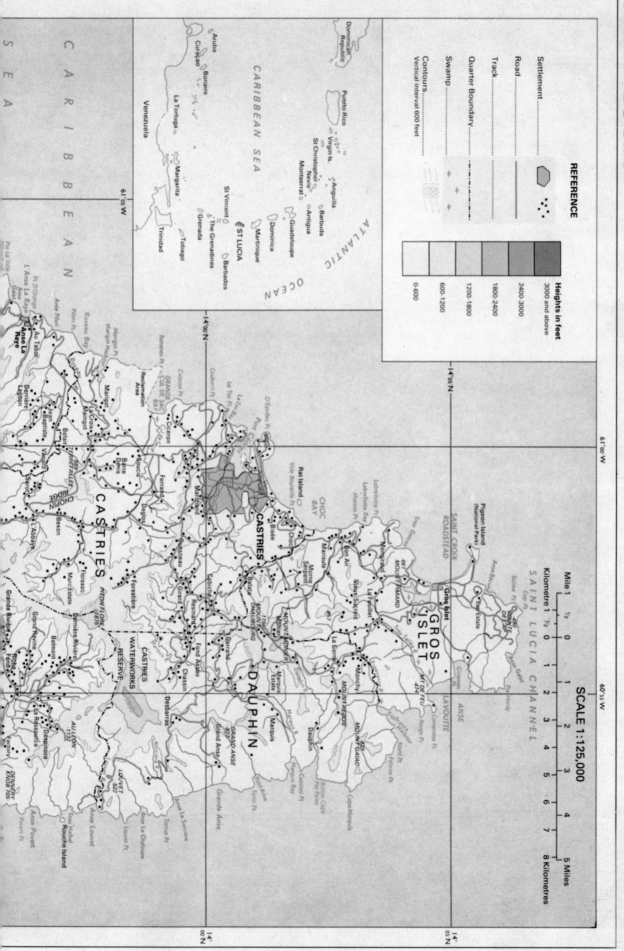

REFERENCE

Settlement	
Road	
Track	
Quarter Boundary	
Swamp	
Contours	
Vertical interval 600 feet	

Heights in feet

3000 and above	
2400-3000	
1800-2400	
1200-1800	
600-1200	
0-600	

SCALE 1:125,000

Mile 1   ½   0   1   2   3   4   5 Miles

Kilometre 1 ½ 0 1 2 3 4 5 6 7 8 Kilometres

Pitons

Marigot Beach Resort

Marigot Bay:
Situated on the East coast. A British
Admiral once launched an ambush from
this picturesque bay by camouflaging
his fleet with palms. Today, a yacht
haven, Marigot Bay remains one of St
Lucia's most beautiful spots.

Southeast Coast

Published in 1997 by **Hansib Publishing** (Caribbean) Limited
PO Box 2773, St John's, Antigua, Westindies

Distributed by **Readers Book Club** (Books Direct) Third Floor, Tower House, 141-149 Fonthill Road, London N4 3HF, UK

Telephone: 44 (0) 171 281 1191
Fax: 44 (0) 171 263 9656

Editor: **Arif Ali**

Project Manager: **John Hughes**

Bulk Photographs: **Angus Thompson**

Colour Origination by **Graphic Ideas Studios Limited**, London

Printed in the United Kingdom by **Caledonian International Book Manufacturing**, Glasgow, Scotland

Copyright Hansib 1997

British Library Cataloguing in Publication Data

A catalogue record for this publication is available from the British Library.

ISBN - 976 8163 07 0

PUBLISHER'S NOTE: Readers unfamiliar with Hansib's publications may note the use of 'Westindies' (not 'West Indies'). This has been used in all Hansib publications since 1973 in a tribute to the formation of the Caribbean Community (CariCom) at Chaguaramas, Trinidad, on 4 July 1973 and as an appropriation of the name given by the "discoverers" to assert the region's united, unique and distinctive identity.

Acknowledgements

Producing a book of this nature is inevitably a collective effort, requiring the support and cooperation of many people.

In my Foreword, I pay tribute to successive governments, diplomats, overseas compatriots and businesses in Saint Lucia who have consistently and enthusiastically backed and encouraged this project, and without whose support this book would not have been possible. Thank you once again.

I am equally indebted to my core team in London: to **John Hughes, Keith Bennett, Robert Govender, Isha Persaud, Victoria Elkington BA, and Sam Rajah**, as well as to various members of my family and our Saint Lucia representative, **Claudia Jean Baptiste**.

In addition, I must thank the following:

For articles - **Robert J Devaux CBE, Maria Grech, John McCormick, Carleen Jules, Jacques Compton, Cedric George, Lindsay Harrison, Dunstan St Omer, Gregor Williams, Milton Branford, Marie-Ange Louis, Dr Maria-Louis Felix, Father Anthony, June King-Frederick, Guy Ellis, Chris Jackman**, and **Jonathan H Everett**.

For photographs and graphics - **Angus Thompson, John Hughes, Carleen Jules, Robert J Devaux CBE, Marios Modeste, Danielle Devaux, David Cummings, Linda Molloy**, and the **Saint Lucia Government Information Services and the Saint Lucia Tourist Board.**

Grateful mention must be made of the **Saint Lucia Tourist Board, the Ministry of Tourism, Cable & Wireless, Cassius Elias, Pamela Murtagh, Jean Mighall, Verena Calderon, Agnes Francis, Felix Finnisterre, Marie Fowler, Patricia Charles, Lydia Cox, Joan Alexander, Roger Joseph, Tracey L Warner, P Hillary Modeste, Phyllis Regis, Donna Philip, Frank Noville, Jeremy Palmer-Martin, Kennedy 'Boots' Samuels, Margot Thomas, Bernard Johnson, Nicholas Pinnock, Vaughan Charles, Edward Lionel, Dexter Mondesh, Alice Bagshaw, Harold Beansolul, Avril Edwin, Lyndon John, Anita James, Earl Huntley, Jim Spark, Anne Marie La Nasa, Caroline Popovic, Milton Branford, Dr Michael Louis, Phyllis Roberts, Vino Patel, BWIA airline, the Auberge Seraphine Hotel, Sandals La Toc Hotel, National Car Rental, Saint Lucia Helicopters, Unicorn Tall Ship, George Odlum, Camilla Joseph, Brian Lousisy, David Jordan, Darrel Montrope, Lancelot Arnold, Fenna Williams, Jane Tipson, Michael Fedee, Thecla Joseph, Jennifer Norville, Coletta President-Aruoma, Herbie George, Lancelot Arnold, Clarina Philip, Chris Huxley, Martina Labadee, Mervin** (our pilot with Saint Lucia Helicopters), **Dr Michael Louise, Brian Louise, Jimmy Curnell, Ianthe Charlamaine, Hayden Antoine**, and **Reema Harracksingh**. In their many and varied ways, their help has been invaluable.

Special thanks must go to Graphic Ideas, our designers and typesetters, and to Caledonian International Book Manufacturers, our printers. As always, they have done everything possible to accommodate our schedules and demands.

Finally, deepest thanks to those good people who helped quietly and with devotion, but whom I forgot to mention. Along with all the people of the simply beautiful island of Saint Lucia, I hope they can take pride in this book as a real expression of my gratitude.

AA
Hansib Publishing

Saint Lucia - *Simply Beautiful*

Contents

Foreword

The idea of producing a book to capture the beauty of Saint Lucia in all its forms began life some three years ago.

With the assistance of the country's High Commissioner in London, HE Aubrey Hart, a letter was sent to then Prime Minister Sir John Compton, who expressed interest in the proposed project, enabling a very enthusiastic Ramanus Lansiquot, the then Minister of Tourism, to actually commission the project, with the help of what was appropriately dubbed "seed corn money" from a generous Cable & Wireless.

Our two Saint Lucian colleagues, Michael Clerice and Simon Augustine were very helpful in our early negotiations, and a special word of thanks must go to Manny Cotter, who has been supportive, helpful, and frankly indispensable throughout.

Everything was in place to begin work in 1996. However, Saint Lucia then became preoccupied with other pressing matters and later its general election.

We were, however, delighted that the new government, which emerged as a result of that election, earlier this year, promptly welcomed our proposals as something that would be beneficial to their country. Indeed, we have received support and encouragement not only from the present Minister of Tourism, the Hon. Philip J. Pierre, but also from his Prime Minister, the Hon Dr Kenny Anthony, who has given blessings, advice and cooperation. Throughout all these stages, special thanks are due to Percy McDonald, whose presence as Permanent Secretary in the Ministry of Tourism has been a constant and consistent source of encouragement and support.

This is the eighth volume in Hansib's Nations series, which has so far embraced countries in both the Caribbean and Asia. According to feedback we receive from the countries themselves, they have been considered a boon by both the public and private sectors, who use them as corporate gifts as well as for their own information purposes.

We would hope, in particular, that, in the face of the present economic crisis afflicting Saint Lucia and some of its neighbours, regarding the export of bananas to the European market, **Saint Lucia - Simply Beautiful**, will prove a constructive tool for the promotion of economic diversification, particularly in terms of tourism, the most readily available option, as well as in other areas of investment promotion.

In this, we are at one with Prime Minister Dr Anthony, who addressing a meeting, sponsored by Hansib Publications on the topic 'Crisis in the Caribbean - Labour's Way Forward', at the 1997 Annual Conference of the British Labour Party , declared:

"We have not remained complacent, begging for protection, while our competitors leap ahead of us and eat our dinner. We are determined to increase the competitiveness of our industry and to diversify our agricultural sectors and our economies generally."

Any visitor to Saint Lucia, from the moment of arrival to that of departure, cannot but be overwhelmed, not only by the grace, hospitality and kindness of its people, but also by the sheer wealth and variety of what this small country has to offer: from luxurious beaches to luxuriant rainforests and waterfalls; from unique flora and fauna to fascinating history and culture.

Indeed, Saint Lucia is simply beautiful. If this book manages to convey this to the reader, it will have served its purpose.

Arif Ali
London
October 1997

Message from the Prime Minister

WELCOME TO SAINT LUCIA

A Country that is Simply Beautiful

By opening this book, you are taking the first step to experiencing one of Nature's real treasures - an island paradise that we have come to describe as 'Simply Beautiful'!

It is my hope that every page of this book will serve as a beckoning finger, enticing you toward taking the final step, that is, to set foot on Saint Lucia's shores.

There can only be one Saint Lucia. Its beauty is truly unique and unsurpassed. Ask the British and the French. History has witnessed and recorded these superpowers fighting over this little piece of God's earth for nearly 200 years, exchanging 'ownership' of it fourteen times in the process!

But Saint Lucia is about more than just sheer natural physical beauty. The people, its greatest resource, are the most generous, warm and creative you will ever come across. And you will find them - when you do visit Saint Lucia - ever willing to share with you, the comforts of their homes.

The Government of Saint Lucia places significant emphasis on the promotion of tourism and tourism development generally. But we do not want you to think of St Lucia only as a great place to visit - we want you to know too, that it is a great place for business investment. We have been seeking, in recent times, to expose the rest of the world to that which Saint Lucia has to offer. It is our hope that this book will contribute in a tangible way to this process.

Take the first step...and remember we are waiting to welcome you, in person.

Hon Dr Kenny D Anthony

Prime Minister

Message from the Hon. Philip J. Pierre, Minister for Tourism, Civil Aviation and Offshore Financial Services

Congratulations to Hansib on the publication of a comprehensive book:
Saint Lucia - Simply Beautiful.

This book highlights the factors that contribute to make Saint Lucia a unique island that offers all visitors a truly different and enjoyable holiday:

A walk in the natural rainforest, where rare species of wildlife can be seen, or a diving expedition to the coral reefs; a drive to the majestic Pitons, or a quiet day on the beach, are all available for families, friends, or honeymooning couples who want to relax and romance after a wedding in a truly tropical paradise.

The new government of Saint Lucia is committed to the development of sustainable tourism as a means of economic empowerment for the benefit of all stakeholders.

This publication offers an accurate and concise analysis of all aspects of life in Saint Lucia and will serve as a valuable reference tool as we prepare to deal with the global competition of the new millennium.

I am sure that the colourful, artistic and imaginative pages of this book will captivate readers with the hospitality and friendliness of the people of Saint Lucia.

The Government and people of Saint Lucia are proud to be involved in this venture.

Saint Lucia At a Glance

Saint Lucia is Simply Beautiful.
Saint Lucia is 27 miles long and 14 miles wide.
Saint Lucia is located 60-61 degrees West longitude and 13 degrees North latitude
Saint Lucia is four hours from New York by air and eight hours from London

Airports: St Lucia has two airports. Hewanorra International Airport at Vieux Fort - some 40 miles south of the capital Castries and Vigie Airport, five minute from the centre of Castries.

Visa/Entry Requirements: Valid passports are necessary for persons entering St. Lucia, except for citizens of the Windward Islands the UK, US and Canada who possess valid return tickets and who are on a visit not exceeding 6 months. Visas are not required if the visitor is a citizen of the US or a Commonwealth country, or if the visitor is a national of a country which has an agreement for exemption of the Visa requirement.

Vacination: No vaccination is required, unless transiting or coming from an infected area within six days of arrival.

Business Hours: Government
8.00 am - 12.30 pm; 1.30 pm - 4.00 pm Monday to Friday.
Banks: Monday -Thursday: 8.00 am - 3.00 pm and Friday 8.00 am 5.00 pm.
Commerce: 8.00 am - 4.00 pm Monday to Friday. 8.00 am - 12 pm Saturday

Population: 140,000 . **Capital:** Castries (population) 53,000

Driving: Local temporary driving permits are issued by the immigration office at both airports on presentation of a foreign or international licence at a small fee. Car rental companies can assist obtaining driving permits. driving is on the left-hand side of road. St Lucia has an extensive road system and the main roads Saint Lucia are among the best in the Caribbean.

Climate: Annual temperatures range between 70*F and 90*F and cooling breezes guarantee a natural 'air conditioning'. Rainy season is June to early December. When the rains come, it is generally short, heavy showers.

Clothing: Summer wear year round. Summer sweater for cool evenings. Casual resort wear during the day, some restaurants may require jackets or ties for dinner.

Communications: Cable and Wireless (West Indies) Ltd fulfils island's telecommunications needs, including overseas direct dialing and prepaid phone cards

Currency: St Lucia uses the Eastern Caribbean dollar. EC$ 2.71 = US

Drinking Water: Water is safe for drinking.

Language: English is the official and working language, however most St Lucian's speak a local French-based patois.

Electricity: Generally 220 volts 50 cycles, with square three-plug. Converters/adapters are available at major hotels. A few hotels offer both 220 volts 50 cycles and 110 volts 60 cycles.

Religion: 85 - 90 per cent of St. Lucians are Roman Catholic. Other religions include: Anglican, Methodist, Baptist, Seventh Day Adventist, Pentecostal, Bethel Tabernacle and Jehovah Witness.

National Emblems

THE FLAG

The official description of the flag is as follows:-

1.   On a plain blue field, a device consisting of a white and black triangular shape, at the base of which a golden triangle occupies a central position.

2.   The triangles are superimposed on one another; the black on the white and the gold on the black. The black ends as a three pointed star in the centre of the flag.

3.   The width of the white part of the triangle is one and a half inches on both sides of the black. The distance between the peaks of the black and white triangles is four inches.

4.   The triangles share a common base, the length of which is one third of the full length of the flag.

MEANING OF THE FLAG

1.   Cerulean blue represents fidelity. This blue reflects our tropical sky and also our emerald surrounding waters - the Caribbean Sea and the Atlantic Ocean.

2.   Gold represents the prevailing sunshine in the Caribbean Prosperity.

3.   Black and white stand for the cultural influences - the white part, the white culture, the black part, the black culture - two races living and working in unity.

4.   The design impresses the dominance of the Black culture vis a vis that of Europe, against a background of sunshine and the blue sea. This symbolises the three Pitons.

5.   The triangle, the shape of which is an isosceles triangle, is reminiscent of the island's famous twin Pitons at Soufriere, rising sheer out of the sea, towards the sky - themselves a symbol of hope and the aspirations of the people.

National Emblems

Old badge of St Lucia
1833 - 1936

Saint Lucia Parrot
Amazona Versicolor
The National Bird of
Saint Lucia

DIMENSIONS OF THE NATIONAL FLAG

The dimensions of the national flag shall be in the following proportions: 6' x 3' and 9' x 4.5'.

How to display the flag:

1. The flag should be at regulation appearance. It should not be faded or bleached, and a torn flag should be repaired before being hoisted.

2. The flag-mast, when erected on land, should be placed upright and should be in a central or conspicuous place. On buildings, however, the flag-mast may either be placed in an upright position on the roof or fixed at an angle on the front of the building or from a balcony.

3. The flag-mast should be painted white.

4. No other flag may be flown above the Saint Lucia flag. When several flags are flown on one halliard the Saint Lucia flag is placed at the peak. When the flags of two or more nations are of the same height and of the same size, the flag of one nation should not be displayed above that of another.

5. No other flag, colour, standard, ensign or other emblem should be displayed above or to the right of the national flag, i.e. to the left of the observer while facing it.

6. When two flags are placed against a wall with crossed staffs, the Saint Lucia flag should be at the right (i.e. the observer's left facing the flags) and its staff should be in front of the other flag. When a number of flags are grouped and displayed from staffs, the Saint Lucia flag should be at the centre at the highest point of the group.

7. When the national flag is flown with other flags, it should be the first to be hoisted and the last to be lowered. It should never be lowered while the other flags are flying or being hoisted.

8. The flag may be displayed flat above and behind the speaker in a church or in an auditorium. If on staff, it should be at the right of the speaker as he faces the congregation or audience. Other flags should be at the speaker's left, if the flag is displayed on a staff elsewhere than on a platform or chancel, it should be at the right of the audience or congregation as may face the speaker. It should not cover a speaker's desk or be draped in front of the platform.

9. Except on a day of special significance, the national flag shall not be flown on a motor car without the permission of the Minister.

10. Where the national flag is flown on a motor car, it shall be affixed to a small staff erected on the right front fender of the motor car so that the flag should be above the bonnet of that motor car.

11. A citizen may fly the flag on a day of special significance provided he flies the flag from an upright staff on or in front of his dwelling or place of business.

WHEN TO DISPLAY THE FLAG

1. The national flag will be flown every day from the public buildings from 6:00 a.m. to 6:00 p.m. It may be flown daily from government buildings, from schools when they are in session, and from places of business.

2. The national flag should not be flown after 6:00 p.m. except inside a building. On important ceremonial occasions, however, the flag may be flown in the open after 6:00 p.m. when it should be floodlit, if possible.

THE FLAG IN A PARADE

When carried with other flag or flags, the flag of Saint Lucia should be held on the marching right or in front of the centre of the line of flags. When the flag is passing in a parade or in a review or during the ceremony of hoisting or lowering the flag, all persons present should face the flag and stand at attention.

THE FLAG AT HALF-STAFF

1. The national flag is flown at half-staff in times of mourning.

2. When flown at half-staff the flag should first be raised to the peak and then lowered to half-staff. The flag should again be raised to the peak before it is lowered.

3. By half-staff is meant lowering the flag by its own depth from the peak of the staff.

The decision on the occasions on which the flag should be flown at half-staff would rest with the Cabinet.

PROHIBITED USES OF THE FLAG

1. The flag should not be dipped to any person or thing, except in accordance with maritime practice.

2. The flag should not be displayed on a float, motor car or other vehicle or on a boat, except from a staff or masthead.

3. The flag should not have placed on it or attached to it any mark, insignia, letter, word, figure, design, picture or drawing.

4. The flag should never be used as a receptacle. It should not be used to cover a statue or monument.

5. The flag should never be used for purposes of adornment or advertising. It should not be printed on, or reproduced on, articles of clothing or furniture.

6. The flag, when on display, should not be allowed to touch anything beneath it such as furniture, floors, trees, plants, vehicles, buildings, water, or the earth.

National Emblems

NATIONAL ANTHEM

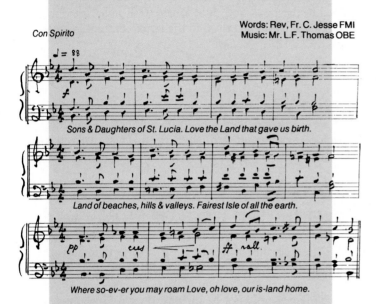

ST LUCIA'S NATIONAL ANTHEM

Con Spirito

Words: Rev, Fr. C. Jesse FMI
Music: Mr. L.F. Thomas OBE

Sons & Daughters of St. Lucia. Love the Land that gave us birth.

Land of beaches, hills & valleys. Fairest Isle of all the earth.

Where so-ev-er you may roam Love, oh love, our is-land home.

Gone the times when nations battled
For this 'Helen Of The West'!
Gone the days when strife and discord
Dimmed her children's toil and rest
Dawns at last a brighter day
Stretches out a glad, new way.

May the Good Lord bless our Island
Guard her sons from woe and harm!
May our people live united,
Strong in soul, strong in arm,
Justice, Truth and Charity
Our ideal love forever be!

1. Whenever the National Anthem is played, all civilians present should stand at attention, men with bared heads. Persons in uniform should act in accordance with instructions.

2. Normally one verse only will be played. It shall consist of the first twelve bars of the anthem unless otherwise stated.

The National Anthem shall be played:-

(a) for the purposes of a salute on ceremonial or official occasions, on the arrival and departure of:

i. the Governor-General;
ii. the Sovereign or a member of the Royal Family;
iii. a foreign Sovereign, Head of State, or member of a reigning foreign Imperial or Royal Family;
iv. Governors-General of independent Commonwealth countries;
v. Governors of the OECS States;
vi. Governors, High Commissioners or Officers administering the Government of a dependent territory within the Commonwealth; and

(b) at the beginning of all public performances in a cinema house.

3. The National Anthem may be played:-

(a) at the completion of any public function, or
(b) when toasts are proposed at official functions.

4. The National Anthem should not be parodied in verse or in song, neither should it be played in any tempo other than officially recognised. In particular, the tune should not be used as a dance number for the purposes of advertisement.

5. When more than one National Anthem is played, the Saint Lucia National Anthem should be played last.

COAT OF ARMS

The emblems of the Coat of Arms and what they represent are:

'The ROSE which you see on the coat of arms tells us about England. At one time England was our "mother" country because she was in charge of our affairs. Another flower, the FLUER-DE-LIS, makes us remember that we belonged to France as many as seven times. Two pieces of bamboo form the cross of the shield. The Bamboo is our national plant. The LITTLE STOOL on the cross is an African stool. It is there to help us remember the first black people in our country came from Africa. To light us on our way, we have a TORCH which is held up high. The PARROT is our national bird and there is one each side of the Coat of Arms. Our Motto "THE LAND, THE PEOPLE, THE LIGHT", is printed at the bottom of the shield.'

The Coat of Arms of Saint Lucia is the official seal of the Government. It may not be used or reproduced in any form without Government approval.

The Democracy

CONSTITUTION AND ADMINISTRATION

The Saint Lucia Constitution came into operation on February 22, 1979, the date on which St. Lucia attained independence from Britain.

Supreme Law Alteration

The Constitution is the supreme law of St. Lucia and any other law which is inconsistent with it is void. Provision is made in SECTION 41 for the alteration of any of the provisions of the constitution. A bill to alter this section must be supported by the votes of not less than three-quarters of all the members of the House. To alter any of the other provisions of the Constitution, the support of two-thirds of the members are needed. Certain provisions may also be changed by referendum based on the majority of the votes validly cast.

Constitutional Provisions

The Constitution makes provision for, among other things: the protection of fundamental rights and freedoms; the establishment of the Governor General; the composition of Parliament and the Senate; the House of Assembly; the procedure to be followed by Parliament; the delimitation of constituencies; the establishment of commissions; and the establishment of the office of Parliamentary Commissioner

GOVERNMENT

The way in which St. Lucia is to be governed is also set out by the Constitution. Government consists of the Executive, the Legislature and the Judiciary, based on the separation of powers principle.

Carrying the Mace at the

The Governor General

The Governor General represents Her Majesty the Queen, the official Head of State. His functions are mainly ceremonial, and include the important duties of opening the House of Assembly on an annual basis by delivering the Throne Speech, and assenting to Bills passed by the legislature.

Parliament

In addition to the Office of the Governor General, a two-house system of Parliament exists. It is made up of a Senate and a House of Assembly. The Senate consists of eleven nominated members. The House of Assembly consists of seventeen elected Members.

Administration

A Prime Minister is appointed by the Governor General from among the members of the House of Assembly. This is the person who appears to the Governor General likely to command the support of the majority of the members of the House. In practice this person is usually the leader of the political party which controls the majority of the seats in the House of Assembly.

The size and composition of the Cabinet is in the prerogative of the Prime Minister. He may choose to add, alter or to reshuffle the Cabinet in any manner he deems fit.

The Democracy

Legislation

Bills are passed into law upon receiving the support of the majority of the Members of each House of Parliament. Usually Bills begin their debate in the House of Assembly and get their final approval in the Senate before being sent to the Governor-General for his assent.

The Judiciary

The lowest arm of the Judiciary is the District Court. There are two District Courts in Castries which are served by magistrates. In the out districts, District Courts are set up which are usually served by magistrates once a week. A Traffic Court and a Family Court are also in existence.

There is a High Court located in Castries which has jurisdiction in criminal and civil matters and also issues of a constitutional nature.

Appeals from the High Court are heard by the OECS Court of Appeal which serves countries in the Eastern Caribbean. This is a circuit Court which moves from territory to territory. Final appeals are heard by the Privy Council, which sits in England.

House of Assembly

St Lucia Government Buildings overlooking the Port of Castries.

Constitutional Development

The first civil governor of St. Lucia was Brigadier General George Prevost, commissioned on April 15 1801. General Prevost was assisted in the Civil Administration by a "Conseil Superieur composed of 12 of the most respectable inhabitants in St. Lucia."

In 1802, when the island was briefly occupied by the French, the Civil Administration continued, although with some minor changes. It was fully restored by the British in 1803.

A form of Crown Colony system of government was adopted for St. Lucia in 1808. It allowed for continued "home rule through Orders-in-Council", by which means legislation was imposed upon the colony.

The Civil Government of St. Lucia was reorganised in 1816, with instructions issued by the Prince Regent in Council to Major General Richard Seymore, Governor of St. Lucia. The Governor issued an Ordinance on December 15 1816, outlining "the principal features of the new Privy Council composed of five of the leading proprietors of the recast Conseil Superieur". The Conseil Superieur was now strictly confined to its function as a Court of Appeal. The President of the Court of Appeal was authorised to preside at the Privy Council in the absence of the Governor.

The Privy Council was abolished in 1832. Two separate Councils were then formed: the Executive Council, composed of the Governor, Colonial Secretary, Attorney General, Colonial Treasurer, and Protector of Slaves; and the Legislative Council, composed of the Chief Justice and the above named, together with five of the principal proprietors of the island. The new arrangement was inaugurated in April that year, under the auspices of Major General James Farquharson. The "official" members holding office took precedence over the "unofficial" members without office. They were all nominated under the "sign manual" and were now to be addressed as "Honourable", a title which was first used in October 1818.

From 1838, St. Lucia was included in the General Government of the Windward Islands under a Lieutenant-Governor, with headquarters in Barbados. The post of Resident Governor in St. Lucia was replaced by an Administrator, subordinate to the Governor of the Windward Islands. The Administrator now had a seat on each council.

Minor changes to the councils were effected in 1844 and by Royal Letters Patent dated March 17 1885, the Windward Islands seat of Government was transferred to Grenada.

In 1922, the Wood Commission visited the Windward and Leeward Islands with terms of reference "to ascertain if the people were ready for some form of political development". Several influential persons, including Dr. Edwin, C. Beausoleil, Emelius D. Cadet, George Cooper, George S. Gordon, Louis A. McVane, George H. Palmer and Thomas G. Westwell, led a deputation to plead St. Lucia's case before the Wood Commission. These "political pioneers" formed a "Representative Government Association with a view to agitating for political reforms". A public meeting was held on Columbus Square and McVane read out the association's manifesto. He then presented Lord Halifax, Chairman of the Wood Commission, with a copy.

By Letters Patent dated March 21 1924, provisions were made for the first Legislative Council under the new partially elected principal. The first elections were held on March 9 1925, with three electoral districts. The first three members elected to the Legislature in St. Lucia were Hon. Thomas G. Westall (North), Hon. George H. Palmer (East), and Hon. Thomas B. Hull (West). The inaugural meeting of the new Council was held under the auspices of Governor Sir Frederick S. James on May 1 1925. In addition to the three elected members, the Council was made up of the Administrator or Colonial Secretary presiding, Attorney General, Treasurer, Registrar of the Royal Court, Chief Medical Officer, and Inspector of Schools. The three nominated members were George Barnard, William Degazon, and Gabriel LaFitte. By Order-in-Council dated October 29 1936, the Governor was given "reserve powers for ensuring the passage of legislation which he considered expedient in the interest of public faith or good government".

The three elected members in 1925 were voted into office with very little campaigning. Indeed, two were unopposed. In 1928 the three candidates ran without campaign or opposition. However, by 1931 the story

Government House, Morne Fortune

was different. Although McVane ran unopposed in the North, Belmar and DuBoulay conducted a lively and heated campaign in the West. Also in 1931, provisions were made to allow women to enter the political arena and become either elected or nominated members of the legislature. The minimum voting age was set at 21 years.

The Constitution of the Executive Council was regulated by Royal Instructions of 1936, 1939 and 1945. When present in St. Lucia, the Governor presided at meetings; in his absence, the Administrator presided.

A new Constitution was granted to the Windward Islands in 1951, the year adult suffrage was granted to the Lesser Antilles. New constituencies were added to those already existing in St. Lucia, bringing the elected members up to eight. There were still three nominated members. The second general election in St. Lucia under universal adult suffrage was held in September 1954.

Letters Patent dated February 15 1956 made provisions for the establishment of a Ministerial system of government in St. Lucia. The first three ministers were declared on March 15 1956. They were Hon George F. Charles, Minister of Social Affairs; Hon. Herman B. Collymore, Minister of Communications and Works;

and Hon Dr. Karl G. Lacorbiniere, Minister of Trade and Production. However, responsibility for financial matters still remained with the Governor, through the Financial Secretary. Under this new Constitution, the Executive Council was recognised as the policy making authority and consisted of a Chairman, three official members, four elected members and one nominated member. The Legislative Council consisted of a President, two official members, three nominated members and eight elected members, of which three were ministers. At the General Elections held in September 1957, the St. Lucia Labour Party won seven of the eight seats. During this election campaign, an appreciation of the concept of party politics began to be displayed in the country.

A Federation of the West Indies was attempted in 1958 and Dr. Lacorbiniere became a member of the Federal Parliament, attaining the post of Deputy Prime Minister. The post of Governor of the Windward Islands was abolished in December 1959. St. Lucia was granted a new Constitution on January 1 1960. The Administrator became Her Majesty's Representative in St. Lucia. This new Constitution provided for a Chief Minister and three other Ministers appointed on his advice. It also provided for two more elected seats in the Legislature, bringing their number

Constitutional Development

up to ten, and for two nominated members instead of three, with the Crown Attorney as the only official member of the Legislature. The Administrator was no longer President of the House. A speaker was to be elected from inside or outside the Legislature. On January 7 1960, Hon George F. Charles became St. Lucia's first Chief Minister responsible for Treasury, Inland Revenue and Medical and Public Relations; Hon. John G. Compton became Minister of Trade and Industry; and Hon. Martin Jr Baptiste became Minister of Communications and Works. The Executive Council was still the decision-making authority of Government.

The St. Lucia Labour Party won nine of the 10 electoral seats at the General Elections held in April 1961. The Federation collapsed the following year, when Jamaica opted out. The controversial Banana Bill caused the St. Lucia Labour Government to fall in 1964, after two members resigned their seats. The Administration dissolved the House on April 6 1964. The newly formed United Workers' Party won six of the 10 electoral seats at the General Elections held two months later. Hon. John G. Compton became Chief Minister, with four other Ministers, one without portfolio.

St. Lucia attained Associated Statehood on March 1 1967, which allowed it full control of its internal affairs, with Britain responsible for Defence and Foreign Affairs in consultation with the Government of St. Lucia. The Executive and Legislative Councils were abolished and replaced by a Cabinet and a House of Assembly. The post of administrator was abolished and replaced by a local Governor as the Queen's representative in St. Lucia. The first Governor under the new status was Dr. (later Sir) Frederick J. Clarke and the Chief Minister Hon. John G. Compton became the first Premier of St. Lucia. The Cabinet comprised the five Ministers, the Attorney General, and the Secretary to Cabinet. The House of Assembly comprised a Speaker, the ten elected members, three nominated members, and the Attorney General.

In 1969, the voting age was reduced to 18 years. In 1974 seven new constituencies were added to the existing ten, bringing the number of elected members up to seventeen.

Sir John Compton the first Prime Minister of independent Saint Lucia

On February 22 1979, St. Lucia obtained total independence from Britain. St. Lucia's Parliament now comprised Her Majesty's representative, the Governor General; a Senate; and a House of Assembly. The decision-making body of Government remained the Cabinet of Ministers. The first Governor General under the new status was Sir Allan Lewis, and Premier Hon. John G. Compton became the first Prime Minister of independent St. Lucia.

The Senate presently comprises 11 Senators, six appointed by the Governor General on the advice of the Prime Minister, three on the advice of the Leader of the Opposition, and two by the Governor General on the advice of the general community. The House of Assembly comprises 17 elected members and a Speaker, who may be elected from outside the House. The Cabinet comprises the Prime Minister and such other Ministers as he may consider necessary. The post of Attorney General ceased to be a public one in 1979.

The Legal System

The Law

The criminal law of Saint Lucia is largely governed by the Criminal Code of Saint Lucia (1992). Provision is made therein for offences and the procedure to be followed in prosecuting them.

Offenders

Offenders are broadly categorised into: offences affecting public policy and rights. Examples of particular offences include: forcing or compelling a person to marry someone (article 199); impersonation (article 272); consulting an *obeah man* (article 281); and vagrancy (article 664).

Offences are either tried summarily (that is before a magistrate) or indictably (that is before a judge and jury). Some offences are triable either way, for example those relating to the possession and trafficking in dangerous drugs (illegal narcotic and psycotrophic substances).

Bail

Provisions are made for bail in most instances. Applications are usually made to a magistrate who has a discretion to grant or refuse bail. In some instances, where the offence is of a summary nature, the police may also grant bail. No bail is granted, however, in murder cases.

Procedure Hearing

The majority of criminal matters are heard before magistrates at the District Courts. These Courts are opened year round, interspersed by short breaks.

Queen Elizabeth II visits St Lucia

Sentencing and Pardons

Crimes of a serious or indictable nature are heard by the High Court before a judge and jury. Assizes are held in February, June and October. Types of sentences which can be given include: jail terms; fines; corporal punishment; community service; and capital punishment. Capital punishment is enforced by the State. Death by hanging is pronounced on persons guilty of murder and treason. Death sentences may in some cases be commuted to life sentences. The Constitution makes allowances for pardons to be given by the Governor General to any person convicted of an offence. Also, under the Constitution, a Committee on the Prerogative of Mercy is established, which may grant a pardon or commute to a life sentence a person convicted of an offence who has been sentenced to death.

National Honours

THE ORDER OF ST. LUCIA

What is it?
A Society of Honour with Her Majesty The Queen as its Sovereign Head, established in 1986 for the purpose of according recognition of citizens of Saint Lucia and other persons for distinguished, outstanding or meritious services, or gallantry.

AWARDS OF RECOGNITION ARE MADE IN SEVEN GRADES:

Grand Gross (GCSL)
Made only to a person appointed to the office of Governor General of Saint Lucia. The holder is also empowered to use the title of "His (or Her) Excellency" for life.

Saint Lucia Cross (SLC)
Bestowed on a person who has rendered distinguished and outstanding service of national importance to St. Lucia.

The number of persons holding this high honour cannot exceed twenty-five at any time.

Citizens of St. Lucia awarded the St. Lucia Cross are authorised to use the title "The Honourable" before their names.

Medal of Honour (SLMH)
This Grade of the awards is divided into two Classes (Gold and Silver)

It may be awarded to persons who:

(a) have rendered eminent services of national importance; or

(b) have performed outstandingly brave or humane acts to a national of St. Lucia or other country.
When an award is made in the second category it shall be in Gold only for acts of conspicuous courage in circumstances of extreme peril.
For acts of bravery in hazardous circumstances the award shall be in the Silver class.

Medal of Merit (SLMM)
Awards of this Medal are made in classes of Gold or Silver to persons who are considered to have performed long and meritorious service in the Arts, Sciences, Literature or other such fields.

Les Pitons Medal (SLPM)
Awards in this Grade of the Order of St. Lucia may be made in Classes of Gold, Silver or Bronze, for long and meritorious service tending to promote loyal public service, national welfare or inculcate and strengthen Community spirit.

The National Service Cross (NSC)
An award of this honour can only be made to:_

(a) an officer of the Royal St. Lucia Police Force not below the rank of Assistant Superintendent.

(b) an officer of the Fire Service not below the rank of Deputy Fire Chief; or

(c) an officer of the Prison Service not below the rank of Deputy Prison Officer who has rendered loyal and devoted service beneficial to St. Lucia.

The National Service Medal (NSM)
Like the National Service Cross, this may only be awarded to Members of the Royal St. Lucia Police Force, and the Fire and Prisons Services, as well as to a Commissioned Officer of a Cadet Corps.

Appointments to the Order are made only once a year - on Independence Day on the recommendation of the National Awards Committee, which is appointed under the statutes of the order.

The National Awards Committee makes its recommendation from nominations submitted by any persons or organisation, except for awards of the National Service Cross and Medal, which are made under specified provision in the Statutes.

Investitures of the Order of St. Lucia are made in the name of Her Majesty by the Governor General, who is Chancellor of the Order.

Police Service

Police parade in ceremonial uniform

The St. Lucia Police Force is headed by the Commissioner of Police. The Commissioner is appointed by the Governor-General acting in accordance with the advice of the Public Service Commission upon consultation with the Prime Minister.

The headquarters of the Police Force is on Bridge Street, Castries. Mainly administrative duties are carried out here. These include dealing with matters of immigration, traffic and public relations.

Central Police Station, located on Jeremie Street, serves as the hub of everyday police activity in the city. Most criminal matters are dealt with here. A Special Services Unit and the Police Training School are located at La Toc, Castries. Also a Marine Police Unit is located at Pointe Seraphine, Vigie, Castries.

A police station is found in every district. Approximately 600 officers are enlisted in the Police Force. Since there is no army or defence force, the Special Services Unit are sometimes called upon to play a paramilitary role.

PRISONS

Her Majesty's Prison for Male Offenders is located at the southern end of Bridge Street in the city of Castries. It was built in 1837 to accommodate 62 inmates. On September 7, 1997 its population was approximately 307 inmates.

Her Majesty's Prisons for Female Offenders is located at Tapion in Castries. On September 7, 1997 its population was seven inmates.

The prison population consists of prisoners on remand awaiting trial and those convicted. They are housed apart as space permits.

Marriage

1. The Law

Marriage in St. Lucia may be performed by a minister of religion or by a marriage officer authorised by law. Marriages may be celebrated by license of the Attorney General, or after the publication of banns or notice in the case of religious marriage, or after the publication of notice in the case of civil marriages.

For visitors and locals alike, a marriage license may be obtained upon application by petition to the Attorney General. This petition must be lodged at the Attorney General's office at least two days before it is required. However, the Attorney General may, if he thinks fit, consent to the petition being lodged within a shorter period.

Marriage in St. Lucia may be celebrated between sunrise and sunset.

2. Procedural Guidelines

A marriage license will only be issued to persons under 18 years where there is consent in writing by parent or guardian.

Where either party has changed their names by deed poll, or otherwise, the relevant document must be produced.

Marriages may be made in Heaven - but St Lucia makes them more worldly, being the Number 1
'Wedding and Honeymoon'
destination in the Caribbean

Education System

The formal education system in St. Lucia is run almost entirely by the state, through the Ministry of Education, Culture and Labour. All educational institutions falling under the administration of this Ministry (infant up to and including senior secondary) are non-fee paying.

The stipulated compulsory school age in St. Lucia is 5–15 years. It is estimated that 95–98% of the primary school cohort and 45–50% of the secondary school cohort are actually enrolled in these institutions.

The formal educational system is as follows:

PRE-SCHOOL EDUCATION

Pre-school education is generally provided for children between the ages of two-and-a-half to five years. There are currently 150 pre-school centres, all of which are privately owned. There are also 30 Day Care Centres, 8 of which are run by Government through the Ministry of Community Development, Social Affairs, Youth and Sports. Total enrolment is currently at 7,200.

Since 1985, the Ministry of Education, with the establishment of a Pre-School Unit, has undertaken the responsibility of supervising the activities and the facilities at all of these centres. The Ministry provides assistance in training the pre-school teachers and in supplying basic materials needed to run the centres.

The Pre-School programme helps to develop each child's ability to obtain knowledge and information which will be useful in future educational pursuits.

PRIMARY EDUCATION

This is made up of infants, junior primary, and senior primary. The infant level incorporates the first three grades of public schooling. The junior department includes grades four, five, six and seven and the senior division caters for grades, eight, nine and ten. However, this may vary somewhat from area to area.

SENIOR PRIMARY PROGRAMME

The Senior Primary School programme caters for students who fail to gain entry into the secondary schools via the Common Entrance Examination. While the majority of these students continue to receive tuition at the primary schools, some are enrolled at the three Senior Primary schools on the island. In 1992, enrolment at these three schools totalled 1,275. Following three years of tuition at these schools, the students are given another opportunity to gain entry in the secondary schools at the form 3 level by sitting the Common Middle Examinations.

SECONDARY EDUCATION

Secondary Education is provided at the age of 11+ and up to the age of 17+. Secondary schools admit students in the 11–13 age range from the primary schools, on the basis of performance on the National Common Entrance Examination (CEE). Of the 4,728 students who sat the examination in 1992, 2,015 (43%) were assigned to secondary schools. The assignment rate has increased steadily from about 30% just five years ago.

Over the last decade the Ministry has embarked on a programme of upgrading Junior Secondary schools to full Senior Secondary school status.

Four of the Secondary Schools: Castries Comprehensive, Soufrière Comprehensive School, Vieux-Fort Comprehensive School and Leon Hess Comprehensive School, provide a wide choice of technical/vocational subjects in addition to regular academic options.

Education System

POST SECONDARY AND POST-COMPULSORY-SCHOOL AGE

The major post-secondary education thrust in St. Lucia since the 1970s, has been through the Morne Educational Complex. The Complex comprised an 'A' Level College, Teachers College, and a Technical College. The process of integrating these institutions into a single institution, began with the appointment of an officer to undertake preliminary studies into the feasibility, cost, implications of, and possible approaches to integration.

In January 1983, the Minister of Education appointed a nine-man task force under the chairmanship of Dr. Vaughan Lewis, current Secretary General of the Organisation of the Eastern Caribbean States (OECS), to study and report on integration of the complex into a single College. Committee submitted its report in January 1984, arguing that the Morne Education Complex should be integrated into an autonomous open Comprehensive Community College, providing education services to persons of post-compulsory school age, able and willing to avail themselves of the resources of the new College.

In 1984, Cabinet approved the name "Sir Arthur Lewis Community College" in commemoration of the St. Lucian born Economics Nobel Prize winner.

The College began operations in September, 1986 and currently comprises:

Three Main Divisions:

(a) Arts, Science, and General Studies;

(b) Teacher Education and Education Administration;

(c) Technical Education and Management Studies.

Four Departments

(a) Nursing Education

(b) Continuing Education

(c) Health Sciences

(d) Agriculture

A Computer Based Learning Centre

EXPANSION

Under the OECS Regional Vocational and Technical Education Project, funds were provided to expand the training capacity of the Division of Technical Education and Management Studies of the college. This included a new building, provision of new furniture and equipment, fellowships, training for staff, and consultancy services.

The college has expanded its service to include two centres in the south of the island:

(a) The Business Education Centre; and

(b) The Distance Education Centre.

The former is geared towards meeting the education training needs of small business owners and managers, while the later is designed to meet the training needs of persons in Clerical and Secretarial fields.

Former military barracks converted into a community college

A yacht racing scene off the coast of Pigeon Island

La Sport Cap Estate

St Lucian Profiles

NOBEL LAUREATE WEEK

Although St Lucia is a small society with limited resources, many of the country's best known poets have published their books locally, for example MacDonald Dixon, John Robert Lee, Kendel Hippolyte and Jane King. For painters and sculptors, there are several small galleries. The internationally known Llewellyn Xavier operates his own gallery, as does the island's leading sculptor, Joseph Eudovic. A School of Music has been established and the popular annual Jazz Festival provides opportunities for local musicians like Luther Francois, Emerson Nurse and the band Third Eye to play with personalities like Wynton Marsalis and George Bensen.

In 1979, St Lucian economist Sir Arthur Lewis was awarded the Nobel Prize in Economics. In 1992, after much anticipation throughout the Caribbean and the international literary world, St Lucian poet and playwright Derek Walcott won the Nobel Prize for Literature. Not since T S Elliot in 1948 has a poet from English-speaking world been the recipient of the coveted award.

Within a few hours of the announcement from Stockholm on October 8, 1992, then Prime Minister John Compton invited Mr Hunter J Francois to head a committee to advise the Government on the most appropriate ways to honour Derek Walcott.

The major suggestion that emerged was the establishment of an annual Nobel Laureate Day on January 23, the birthday of both Laureates. The Day was to be the highpoint of a proposed Nobel Laureate Week. By the time this first Week had got underway in January 1993, the intellectual and artistic achievements of Sir Arthur Lewis and Derek Walcott had become a focus around which St Lucians would celebrate Caribbean thought, art and culture.

For that first week, art exhibitions, lectures, symposia, evenings of poetry, drama, folk music and dance were successfully organised, with numerous distinguished guests from throughout the Caribbean.

In the course of this week, Derek Walcott announced plans for the Rat Island Foundation, to organise an international centre for the arts on the small island just off the north-west coast of St Lucia. The US edition of Omeros, Walcott's book length poem, carries a painting, by the poet, of the island on its cover. In honour of the late Guyanese, James Sonny Rodway, Walcott's old teacher, he launched the annual James Rodway Memorial Prize for Poetry, open to all CARICOM writers. The Walcott Studies Association was formed as an initiative of the St Lucia Folk Research Centre to support studies of Walcott's work, as well as that of his generation and other St Lucian creative writers, artists and cultural activists.

Since that first Nobel Laureate Week, an annual festival has been instituted. Walcott himself is present and reads new work. The work of Sir Arthur Lewis is brought to a wider public through the Sir Arthur Lewis Memorial Lecture, organised by the Sir Arthur Lewis Community College. The first lecture was delivered by Dr Andrew Downes of the Institute of Social and Economic Research of the University of the West Indies.

The Derek Walcott Lecture was inaugurated in 1997, by Rex Nettleford, the deputy Vice Chancellor of the University of the West Indies.

SIR WILLIAM ARTHUR LEWIS

Nobel Laureate, Economist

William Arthur Lewis KT was born in St. Lucia on 23rd January 1915, the fourth son of George Ferdinand and Ida Louisa Lewis nee Barton. George and Ida Lewis were teachers. They were the proud parents of Stanley, Earl, a psychiatrist, Allen Montgomery who was knighted by the Queen, became the first Governor General of St. Lucia and the first President of the St. Lucia Labour Party, William Arthur records his indebtedness to his father: "My progress through the public schools was accelerated. When I was seven I had to stay home for several weeks because of some ailment, whereupon my father elected to teach me so that I should not fall behind. In fact he taught me in three months as much as the school taught in two years, so on returning to school I was shifted from grade 4 to grade 6."

Arthur was seven, when his father died, leaving Ida Louisa with the responsibility of bringing up five sons alone and unaided.

In 1979, Professor Sir Arthur Lewis was awarded the Nobel Prize for Economics.

At seventeen, Arthur won a St. Lucia government scholarship to a British University. He enrolled with the London School of Economics for a Bachelor of Commerce degree. In 1937, age 22, he graduated with a first class degree in commerce. Arthur not only topped the class in the final examination but did so with distinction. This earned him a scholarship to do a Ph.D. in industrial economics. He got his doctorate in 1940. He had joined the teaching staff of the London School of Economics in 1937 he remained there until 1947, the same year he married a Grenadian educator Gladys Jacobs.

In 1948, at 33, he was appointed the University of Manchester's Stanley Jevons Professor of Political Economy. From 1960 to 1982, Arthur Lewis was Princeton University's Professor of Public and International Affairs, and later James Madison Professor of Political Economy. During this period Sir Arthur published about seventy-five (75) articles, monographs, books etc. He was knighted in 1963. After he retired from Princeton in 1983, he was elected President of the American Economic Association. Sir William Arthur Lewis MA., Ph.D., LHD., LLD died on Saturday June 15, 1991.

The Pitons

St Lucia parrot - Jacquot

JOHN GEORGE MELVIN COMPTON

Mr Compton has already earned for himself a secure place in St. Lucia's history. He was born in Canouan, Saint Vincent on April 29, 1925, but left at an early age for St. Lucia, the island over whose destiny he has presided for the past three decades. There were two central figures in the life of this distinguished and much loved statesman - his doting mother, Ethel, who encouraged her son to work hard and to be an achiever, and his uncle, Mailings Compton. Both profoundly influenced his moral, spiritual and intellectual development inspired by their own unswerving loyalty to the Protestant ethic with its emphasis on discipline, diligence and duty.

Uncle Mailings' loved the sea, was a fine captain and also a skilled shipbuilder who inspired his own employees by example. They were a contented workforce, rewarded properly and treated with respect.

Mailing' equally conscientious nephew also embraced the success and service ethic with equal fervour. He was punctual and productive when he worked in the Curacao oil facility, a conscientious law student at the University of Aberyswyth in Wales and a very bright scholar at the prestigious London School of Economics. John Compton was called to the St. Lucia Bar on August 7, 1951.

CHEF HARRY JOSEPH: Chef Harry, experts claim, is the best chef in the Caribbean. Having mastered the complex art of Caribbean cooking, he decided that he would try his hand at European dishes. But no half measures with this fastidious master of the Caribbean kitchen. He journeyed to London and joined the famous master chefs of the even more famous Dorchester Hotel, where he effortlessly attained Cordon Bleu standard.

Back in St Lucia he bought a restaurant, The Green Parrot, set imperiously above the Castries and the Caribbean Sea. That was 24 years ago. Today the Green Parrot is one of the great restaurants of the Caribbean with a world famous reputation for its rare delicacies.

HONOURABLE ALLAN BOUSQUET: The enterprising and energetic representative of the Babonneau area of Castries has helped, in partnership with its forward looking people, to turn it into one of the most attractive and thriving communities in the island.

WINVILLE KING: This model civil servant set a most worthy example with his honesty, high sense of duty, industry and fairness. This long serving official could say with the late President Kennedy of the US: 'Ask not what your country can do for you, but what you can do for your country.'

LETON THOMAS: The Principal of the pace-setting Sir Arthur Lewis Community College, has successfully impressed on intelligent minds that education is not an end itself but an instrument of social, cultural and economic progress for the whole of society.

OWEN KING: An efficient, caring and highly skilled surgeon who has left an indelible mark on the history of medicine in St. Lucia. Despite his many burdens he has also found time to organise an efficient health service administration.

HUNTER FRANCOIS: A former Minister of Education with clear and well defined ideas on how education can help speed up development, and how development programmes in turn, score an own goal when they do not give the proper priority to curricula more relevant to the specific historical and cultural needs of their islands. Mr Francois conceptualized the Morne Educational Complex and founded the Saint Lucia Music School.

TEDDY THEOBALDS: Belongs to a long line of original and creative intellectuals and thinkers committed to the improvement of the quality of life for formerly colonised people. A brilliant engineer, Mr Theobalds worked unobtrusively, away from the glare of publicity, in the solution of infrastructrural problems. He played an important role in the extraction and provision of potable water.

RICK WAYNE: 'Mens sano in corpore' - a sound mind in a healthy body - is a revered ideal in the island. There has been no greater role model in the realm of physical fitness than Rick Wayne who spectacularly bagged the coveted Mr World, Mr America and Mr Universe titles.

RODDY WALCOTT: Twin brother of the world famous Nobel Laureate, he is a prolific playwright and an outstanding director of drama. His exemplary contribution to the Caribbean theatre is much appreciated by a people proud of the highly developed state of drama and literature in the islands.

AMBASSADOR EDMUNDS: St. Lucia's Ambassador to the United States for more than a decade. His engaging personality won him a wide circle of friends in the Administration and in Washington diplomatic and media circles. Unsurprisingly, he became the Doyen of the Diplomatic Corps in the American capital.

DUNSTAN ST. OMER: An artist of international stature, he began his career in Harry Simon's Studio where another master of a different art, Derek Walcott, also painted. The young St. Omer was directed by his guru, Harry Simon, to paint the island landscape in all its stunning and

Roseau Valley

diverse beauty. He did so with unsurpassed skill. Like most great artists, St. Omer, had his share of frustration, disappointment and penury, but he stuck to his palette through thick and skin, gloriously enriching art and the vibrant art movement in the Caribbean. His greatest service to art and historiography - the first of the decolonised thinkers of the Caribbean -was the creation of a new tradition of Creole religious art, rejecting the Euocentric concept of Christ and Christianity with its misleading representation of the Middle Eastern Son of God as a European. St. Omer put the case for a Christianity liberated from cant and hypocrisy in words that still reverberate both in the art world and in the cathedrals of the world: "If Christ is not black, he is of no use to us." Strong black saints and beautiful dark skinned Madonna's also restored credibility to a Christian historiography tainted by the falsifiers.

THE RT. HON. SIR VINCENT FLOISSAC: Chief Justice and President, Court of Appeal, Eastern Caribbean Supreme Court. Never a bookish man, though a learned one, Sir Vincent, in the finest tradition of the consummate all-round scholar, was at home on the playing fields as he was in courts of law, shining particularly in soccer and tennis. After winning the Open Island Scholarship in 1948, he went to England where he enrolled at Grays Inn and also joined London University. He completed his LLB in 1951, his Bar finals in 1952 and obtained a Master of Laws in 1953. He had a highly successful and dazzling 37 years at the St. Lucian Bar, one of the most subtle and penetrating legal minds in the entire Commonwealth. He was appointed Queen's Counsel in 1969 and became a member of the Seychelles Court of Appeal in 1998.

In 1991 he was appointed Chief Justice and President of the Court of Appeal of the Eastern Caribbean Supreme Court in 1991. He was invited to join the Judicial Committee of the Privy Council in 1992, and the same year he became an Honorary Bencher of Grays Inn.

GEORGE ODLUM: This master orator was a mere 25 when he took on the best minds of his generation at Bristol University, bagging every single debating trophy in his stay there. He was singled out for post-graduate studies at Magdalen College, Oxford, but went reluctantly, after making sure that this would not dilute his strongly held Pan-African views.

There was, he said, some virtue in an Oxford education: it enabled him to think deductively and incisively. Odlum returned to St. Lucia and was promptly appointed Permanent Secretary in the Ministry of Trade. He joined the Commonwealth Secretariat in London as an economist. He returned to the Caribbean in 1967 as the Executive Secretary to the Council of Ministers of the West Indies Associated States. This brilliant economist had another side to his modest and charming character, he was not only a lover of the arts but also a theatrical producer of considerable ability. His production of Lorca's 'The House of Bernarda Alba' won a Festival award. One of the organisational wizards behind National Production EXPO '69, Odlum rekindled an interest in folk art

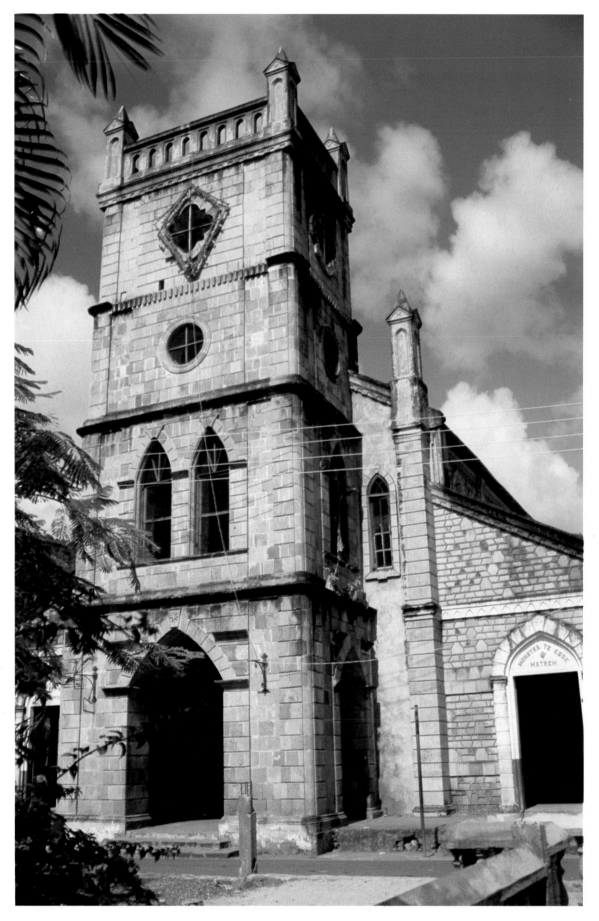

Soufriere Catholic Church

Capturing a St Lucian sunset

and the Creole language. He was also one of the men of influence and achievement with the Walcott brothers in the Saint Lucia Arts Guild, and became St. Luciaís Ambassador to the United Nations, an appointment welcomed enthusiastically by the islanders.

GEORGE FREDERICK LAWRENCE CHARLES:
Trade union leaders are not often regarded as virtuous beings. The very nature of the bargaining and negotiating process, with its cut and thrust, is not a respecter of the Marquess of Queensberry rules. Charles is probably one of a select number of the virtuous, labeled Ti Jesie (little genius).

This warm, kindly man in some ways embodies the Trade Union Movement of the early Forties. A doughty fighter for the working people, he courageously attacked the bastions of a privileged oligarchy. While he was patient, gentle and sympathetic, he fought for his members with passion and conviction.

HAROLD FITZSIMMONS:
The Father of St Lucian Culture he occupies an honoured place in the island's hall of fame. Born in St. Lucia on December 4, 1914, Harold Fitzsimmons took to painting while still a pupil of Saint Mary's College, St. Lucia's leading school for boys. Like most artists of ability, he was diffident about his own talents and went to work in an office. Six years later, he took the plunge and became a full time, professional artist. His work was much admired at home and abroad, particularly in Canada and the United States. He taught painting and one of his students was Dunstan St. Omer. Another famous 'graduate' of his class was the literary genius Derek Walcott, also a gifted water colourist.

He was the founding member of the St. Lucia Archaeological and Historical Society, and his famed versatility extended to botany. He wrote intelligently about local plants and their usage.
Harold Fitzsimmons died on May 6, 1966.

JOSEPH QUINTIN CHARLES:
Born in 1908 in Soufriere. In 1920, aged 12 he won a scholarship to St. Mary's College. After school he joined a wholesale and retail provisions merchant as an apprentice. He was a conscientious worker who immersed himself thoroughly in his work, because even at that age he had larger commercial ambitions. Soon he launched his own business, exporting fruit and vegetables to Canada. He worked late into the night typing out his invoices on a battered old Remington typewriter. A strong, silent man he was famous for keeping his own counsel. He neglected the pleasure principle for the much more rewarding work ethic. He expanded his overseas business, and locally he moved astutely into the confectionery, hardware and tobacco trade. He did not drink and led a Spartan existence. JQ pulled off a master stroke by buying the whole of Choc Estate for the large sum of £8000 (sterling). The islanders marveled at the audacity of a young black businessman forging ahead so spectacularly on his own, especially at a time when commerce was firmly in the hands of white planters and traders.

JQ was one of the founders of St. Lucia Cooperative Bank, a director for forty three years and a President for a decade. It was a 'penny bank' but from modest beginnings, it played a crucial role in the development of St. Lucian commerce, when the white-owned banks openly discriminated against local people.

DEREK WALCOTT: He is one of the world's greatest writers, admired universally for a genius, which while authentically and marvelously St. Lucian transcends frontiers, oceans and mountains. Not many Nobel Laureates are acclaimed without dissent. Walcott is one of the few, because of the sublimity of his prose and poetry, the awesome, majestic power of his thought, his magnanimity of spirit and his remarkable humility.

MARIE CLEPHA DESCARTES: Marie Clepha Descartes, better known as Sesenne of Patience, was born on March 28 1913 at La Pointe, Mon Repos, Micoud. Sesenne's father was the overseer on the Patience Estate in Micoud area. He was the local King of La Rose, her mother La Reine, was Queen of La Rose. Sesenne married, had nine children and was a baker.

Sesenne began to sing when she was 6. At 18, she became the Chantuelle of the La Rose Society, of which her parents were King and Queen. Sesenne also excelled as a dancer, her favourites being the Debot, Kontwidance, Knot, La Comette and Belair.

In 1967 she was chosen to represent St. Lucia at the Carifesta celebrations in Grenada, where her song "Manmay-la-di-Why" was a big hit. Sesenne has been honoured with many awards, with special pride in the British Empire Medal (BEM) in 1984.

She taught the people of St. Lucia to appreciate the importance of their own traditions. In Amelle Mathurin's words: "Sesenne could have been a millionaire and have all of us as her servants, but instead she gave her talents for free, sharing herself for cultural development".

SISTER CLAIRE: Without censure or moralising, but with sympathy and understanding, she is an uncompromising believer in the sanctity of marriage and the family, especially devoted to the welfare of young and vulnerable schoolgirls.

Ferry service at Marigot Marina to Marigot Beach Resort

45

Aerial view of Castries

Villages stride ridge tops for coolness and safety from floods

VERONICA MARGARET ADLEY -Veronica Margaret Adley joined the Royal St. Lucia Police Force in 1958, the first woman police constable in St. Lucia. Educated at the Methodist Infant and Primary School, Veronica Adley qualified as a teacher Four years later, she made history by joining the Royal St. Lucia Police Force after a course at the Police Training Centre in Barbados.

Mrs Adley was promoted Sergeant, Inspector, and Assistant Superintendent in 1981. She served for 31 years of service in her beloved force, receiving the Meritorious Medal (1974), and the Long Service Medal (1980).

ADELINA AUGUSTE: Mrs. Adelina Auguste, was widowed early. She has three children, an accountant, a pilot and a teacher. She was educated at the Dennery Primary School and was secretary to the general manager of WINBAN, the banana growers' cooperative for sixteen years. She advanced to Secretary/Director of the First National Insurance Company, a post she held for seventeen years. She has been a councillor for ten years.

SUZIE AGNES-IDA D'AUVERGNE
Suzie Agnes-Ida d'Auvergne was the first St. Lucian woman Puisne Judge, appointed 1990. Justice Suzie d'Auvergne started her legal career in 1974, graduating from London University.

LAWRENCE MARTHA PRISCILLIA LAURENT: Ms Lawrence Martha Priscillia Laurent is the first St. Lucian woman Parliamentary Commissioner, appointed on December 29 1995. A graduate of St. Joseph's Convent, Ms Laurent holds a Masters Degree in Educational Administration. She started as a teacher at St. Joseph's Convent. She was an ardent feminist who fought for equal access to education and equal pay for male and female teachers.

From 1979-1984, Ms Laurent was the Principal of the Castries Comprehensive Secondary School, the first St. Lucian woman in charge of a Co-ed Secondary School. In 1984, Ms Laurent was appointed Secretary General to the St. Lucia National Commission for UNESCO, a position which she held until 1995. Ms. Laurent is an MBE.

MARIE GRACE AUGUSTIN: Marie Grace Augustin was born on June 2 1897, the seventh of eleven children of Mr & Mrs Marie Augustin. She spent her childhood on Aubayan, the family estate in Micoud. After school in Antigua - her mother's home country - she

Memorial to the Dead of the Second World War

returned to St. Lucia and qualified as a nurse. However, because of her brother's success as a lawyer. Grace took an unusual step. In 1923 she joined her brother's practice as a clerk and prepared for the Bar examination. However, sexist discrimination worked against Grace.

Marie Grace Augustin was an excellent horse-woman and thought of becoming a jockey, but her father dissuaded her. She also had cricketing ambitions, and overcame sexist discrimination, to enter a cricket club of the day. She met the requirement conditions by demonstrating her cricketing skills on the field.

Grace was one of the first planters to grow coconuts on a large scale and to tap into the copra industry. She also experimented on a variety of foreign crops and became a large-scale banana planter. She was founder and director of a number of agricultural associations, including the St. Lucia Banana Growers Association and the St. Lucia Agriculturists Association. She was the first and only woman director of the St. Lucia Coconut Growers Association and the St. Lucia Copra Manufacturers Association.

In 1954, the Government of St. Lucia nominated her to its Legislative Council. She was awarded the Order of the British Empire (OBE).

VERONICA MARGARET ADLEY: Veronica Adley, a qualified teacher, joined the Royal Saint Lucia Police Force in 1958 and was the first woman police constable in Saint Lucia

Mrs Adley was promoted Sergeant, Inspector, and Assistant Superintendent in 1981. She served for 31 years of service in her beloved force, receiving the Meritorious Medal (1974), and the Long Service Medal (1980).

IVES HERALDINE ROCK: Ives Heraldine Rock, St Lucia's first woman MP, started her career as a schoolteacher at the Methodist Primary School. In 1963 she became Public Relations Officer in the St. Lucia Banana Growers Association.

In 1964 she was elected first vice-president of the United Workers' Party - a post she held until 1979. In June 1964, Mrs Rock contested the general election, but was unsuccessful. Ten years later on May 3 1974, Mrs Rock was successful in the general elections, the first St. Lucian woman to be elected to parliament. She was appointed Minister of Government with responsibility for Community Development, Housing, Water, Sports, Youth, Social Affairs, Cooperatives and Ecclesiastical Affairs.

She was appointed a senator on the government benches.(1982–1987). Mrs Rock was awarded the MBE in 1983. In 1996, she was voted unanimously into the supreme accolade, the St. Lucian *Hall of Achievement*.

HELEN OF THE CARIBBEAN

St. Lucians have long felt a passionate attachment to their island. To witness the scenes of families at Hewanorra Airport awaiting relatives traveling on the British Airways flights from London before Christmas is an unforgettable experience.

Like most St. Lucians, the island has many names. The first inhabitants, the **Kalinago**, called it, **Joannalao**, usually spelt **Iouanala** in the history books. The name now commonly cited as the Amerindian name is **Hewanorra**. This is a corruption of **Joannalao**, which was in use as late as the 17th century. **Joanna** was the Kalinago word for iguana, and **Joannalao** has been rendered as Land of the Iguana, a creature which still survives in some remote parts of the island.

The first European name for the island seems to have been **El Falcon**. It first appears in a 1500 map of the Spanish cartographer, Juan de la Cosa.

De la Cosa traveled with the explorer Hojeda in his 1499-1500 voyage. They may have been the first Spaniards to visit the island, but the El Falcon name did not survive.

The common Spanish name was Santa Lucia. It first appeared in the Spanish Royal Cedula of 1511, giving marauding Spaniards permission to capture and enslave those who resisted them, and who were not Christian, from specified islands. The name is believed to have come from Santa Luzia, one of the Cape Verde Islands, long a Portuguese colony, off the coast of West Africa.

There are various Spanish and French versions but it is the English spelling of the name, Saint Lucia, that has survived. St. Lucy of Syracuse, martyred for her virtue and character, has been chosen as the island's patron saint by its Roman Catholic community.

In romance, if not in legend, the island has been named the Helen of the **Caribbean**, after Helen of Troy, the legendary beauty, over whom the Trojan Wars were fought. Like Helen, the island is beautiful. St Lucia has a fascinating history. Regarded as a pawn by the 18th century superpowers, the people have always, been enterprising and have a rich heritage- Amerindian, African, French, English, and so on.

KALINAGO - PEOPLE OF THE SUNRISE

The story of the first St Lucians remains shrouded in mystery. It is generally held that they travelled up the island chain from the South America mainland in open canoes. They are known variously as **Ciboney, Guatanabey**, or **Arawaks**. The **Kalinago** were those whom Columbus found in today's Caribbean region. Archaeologists have dated their earliest presence to around 5,000 BC. They have also traced the coming of others to two thousand years ago. The **Arawak** people's presence is believed to have a history of some 2,000 years.

Bridge Street, Castries 1901

The Caribs and Arawaks have long been held to be two distinct peoples, but recent multi-disciplinary studies have done much to refute certain pernicious myths spread from the time of the first European colonisers, for example that which claimed that Caribs killed and ate the Arawak men and took their women as captive wives. This tenacious myth can now be clearly seen as an ideological creation aimed at justifying colonial oppression and enslavement.

The people who the first Europeans encountered called themselves *Kalinago*, (from *Kalli*, bitter cassava, and from Kalina, "the valiant one"). They have been more widely and derogatorily known as **Caribs**.

The Kalinago were a valiant and proud people. To them, slavery was the greatest indignity imaginable. They fought the longest against the Europeans, and their three hundred year resistance remains among the most courageous stories of the native peoples of the Americas. They were never successfully enslaved. Although some were captured by the Spanish, they always sought to escape. Their nearest survivors, the Black Caribs of Central America, are still a proud and independent people.

Kalinago culture was full of ceremony and ritual. There was a deep respect and concern for the environment. According to their tradition, one was not born a Kalina, it was an honour earned. After a long, trying and painful initiation, one became a man, a true Kalina.

A great debt is owed to the native people of these islands. They taught those who came after them the art of survival. Their armed struggle kept the Spanish away and their resistance retarded French and British settlements, as well as the introduction of the plantation system to the Windward Islands of Dominica, St. Vincent and Grenada. It also reduced the extent to which slave regimes were established in these small islands, as compared to Barbados or Martinique.

The escaped slave communities, known as maroons, acquired the means of survival, knowledge of food and technology from these people, creating a strategy of resistance that was to sustain many a rebellion. The Kalinago-African alliance has had a lasting impact on the cultural development of the oppressed.

The Spanish did not settle in these small islands. The fact that there was no gold to be mined or extorted out of the natives is only part of the story. The overriding reason was that the Kalinago fighters discouraged and prevented any Spanish settlement. Throughout the sixteenth century, a protracted war ensued between the Kalinago and the Spaniards, although this is hardly mentioned in history books. The other European powers, contending for wealth and power with the Spanish, befriended the Kalinago, who formed alliances with them to their later regret. The Kalinago lived in small villages on the different islands, but considered themselves one people. Warriors from one island answered calls for assistance when others were threatened. Their simple spartan life spared them the ravages of the diseases that decimated other native peoples of the Americas.

Kalinago ceramic remains have been found all over the island. These are comparable with fine ceramics from anywhere in the world. Together with their petroglyphs, these ceramics have become part of St Lucia's cultural heritage.

Descendants of the Kalinago survive on the east coast of the island of Dominica, where they call themselves Karifuna. Another, much larger group of over 50,000 has spread out across the Central American countries of Belize, Honduras, Guatemala and El Salvador. They now call themselves Garifuna, the former Black Caribs, who were exiled by the British from St. Vincent in 1796. In St Lucia itself, the remnants of the Kalinago warriors, scattered and decimated, retired to Louvet and La Pointe Caraibe. Their crops and technologies still provide basic sustenance for a large number of people, especially in the countryís marginal lands.

THE COMING OF THE FRENCH

The French first attempted to settle St Lucia in 1650. Their contention with the British for control of the island was to largely dominate its history over the next period. The first French Governor, Rousselan, married the daughter of a Kalinago chief to cement the relationship. The small French community therefore lived in tranquillity until the death of the Governor. Following this, relations soured between the two peoples and a period of conflict followed. The British tried unsuccessfully to acquire the island between 1659-1664. Except for the short periods of British military occupation between 1664-6, 1762-3, 1778-84, 1794-95 and 1796-1802, the island was occupied by the French.

Basic family home

There were more than 14 disputes of one kind or another over the fate of St. Lucia. The island featured in five wars during the eighteenth and early nineteenth century, in 1744, 1756, 1778, 1793 and 1803. St. Lucia's involvement in so many battles was due to her geographical location.

When peace was restored, Britain always returned St. Lucia to France. The owners of the sugar plantations in Barbados were influential in the British Parliament and so were able to persuade the government to return the captured island, much to the dismay of the military. They did not wish to see a new colony producing sugar cane to compete with their own.

The French began a more systematic colonisation of St. Lucia in 1763, after the Treaty of Paris ended the Seven Years War. The cultivation of cotton, cocoa and coffee was extended and sugar was introduced. The first sugar works were built in Vieux Fort in 1765 and two years later in Praslin.

Around 1774, a plague of ants ravaged the sugar crops in all the French islands, including St. Lucia. This caused the failure of several estates and an exodus of planters to Trinidad. The British captured the colony in December 1778 and kept it until 1783. The following years, were another period of economic growth. Turmoil followed with the French Revolution, which started in 1789. In 1803, France lost control of St Lucia for the last time, but their heritage remains, to the extent that the island is regarded as a Franco-phone country.

WAR, REBELLION AND REVOLUTION

American Revolution

At the end of 1778, British naval forces captured St Lucia from the French in a new war after France had backed George Washington's rebels in the US War of Independence. They used the island as their military garrison and naval headquarters until 1783. In October 1780, a disastrous hurricane levelled every building in St. Lucia and destroyed the sugar works. The British military garrison was badly affected and, under the Treaty of Versailles, the island returned to French rule in 1783.

French Revolution

The French Revolution unleashed a wave of expectation on the island. Its principles and motto, *Liberte, Egalite, Fraternite*, held out the promise of freedom for all, both black and white. In St. Lucia, the planters wished to be free from the control of Martinique, the petits-blancs from the large planters, the 'free people of colour' from the whites, and the slaves, who were watching and waiting, earnestly longed for freedom from everyone.

St. Lucia sided with the revolutionary forces from the earliest days. Visits by emissaries from the new revolutionary government were well received. Jacobin Clubs were formed and Independence trees planted. After Royalist elements had fled, Governor Ricard renamed the island Ste. Lucia La Fidele (the Faithful), and changed the names of all towns and villages to revolutionary ones. Gros Islet became Ville de la Revolution; Vieux Fort, Ville de la Loi; Choiseul, Ville du Tricolor; and so on. The printer of the revolutionary newspaper *La Gazette de Ste Lucie*, M. Thounens, was elected as the island's delegate to the Republican Convention in Paris.

With war between revolutionary France and Britain, Ricard's requests to France for war material and troops proved fruitless. In 1794, British forces captured Martinique, St. Lucia and Guadeloupe, leaving France without a secure base in the Antilles. The French armed slaves, volunteers and conscripts, to join the revolutionary forces. On February 24, 1794, all slaves in French possessions were declared free.

The French appointed a St. Lucian mulatto, Lambert, as Republican Commander on the island, and sent a force of 450 under Gaspard Goyrand to recapture it. The Batallion des Antilles, defeated the British in Soufriere in April and in Gros Islet and Vigie in early June. On the night of June 1795, while the Republicans were preparing for the final assault on the British, the Redcoats fled the island, leaving stores, ships, the sick, women and children behind. For a year, the island was under a revolutionary government, with military commanders, mainly black, in each district.

Tribute to the French Resistance

Botanical gardens

In 1796, the British launched a determined bid to retake St Lucia, mobilising 35,000 troops, their largest expedition to the Caribbean. After a valiant defense, from April 26 to May 24, the defenders finally gave way. Such had been their valour, they were allowed the honours of war, marching out of the fort with their drums beating and flags flying. It was the first time that such an honour was given to a force of black soldiers by the forces of white European imperialism.

No other period changed the character of St. Lucian society as much as the ten year period of the French Revolution. From the maroons and the 'free people of colour' came the sense of being St. Lucian. They chose to fight as a unit with the revolutionaries from Guadeloupe. They fought with valour and honour to establish their freedom, defending their island against a numerically superior British force. Refusing to submit to British slavery, they fought on in a guerrilla war for eighteen months, costing the British some 4,000 troops. In a military sense they were never defeated.

Their resistance made a real contribution to struggles elsewhere in the region, not least to the mighty Haitian Revolution of Toussaint l'Ouverture. This was St Lucia's golden page in the history of anti-colonial freedom struggle.

St Lucia Volunteer Force

Africans, Bondsmen and Free People

Although brought to the island in chains, St Lucia's black people have always retained the cultural and linguistic influences of West Africa. Moreover, they soon developed a rich culture of their own.

Major uprisings occurred in 1794 and 1795. Slaves freed as a result of the French Revolution joined with maroons in the interior and revolutionary French forces to expel the British, who were supporting the slave regimes. Defeated a year later by a greatly superior British force, but unsubdued, they waged a 'take no prisoner' guerrilla war against the British for eighteen months, from 1796 to 1797. On both occasions, the British commanders offered amnesty to the freed slaves to return to the plantations. Only eight of them took up the offer. General Moore hanged over 100 of them found under arms. Following their defeat in 1797, erstwhile slaves were organised into an Africa-based regiment of the British Army.

Following the reassertion of British hegemony, slavery was to continue for another 35 years until 1838, but no new slaves were legally introduced into the colony for fear of fresh uprisings.

Abolition in 1834 was followed by an 'apprenticeship' of four years. Freedom came in 1838 with the removal of all bondage.
The freed slaves built churches and schools, maintained the roads under the corvee system and supplied food to the population. They continued to constitute the main labour force in the sugar industry.

Migrant workers from India, who came as indentured labourers, soon integrated into the economic life of the island.

St. Lucia and the Empire

St Lucia entered the 20th century in a state of deep recession. Since 1884, subsidies paid to European beet sugar producers had resulted in the dumping of German beet on the British market. This had ruined the Caribbean sugar producers. Moreover, the Panama Canal project went bankrupt in 1888, and workers returned home. A Royal Commission in 1896 did little to alleviate the distress of planters or workers. To compound the disaster, the naval garrison, which had provided employment and a market for local produce, closed in 1904. Local carriers went on strike in 1907. When they were joined by the sugar workers, the British sent in a warship.

Global economic depression and the rise of a modern working class led to strikes and other protests, and the formation of trade unions, in the 1930s. Following the outbreak of World War ll, British, French and US military forces all strengthened their presence on the island and an inexorable modernisation followed in their wake. While St Lucian soldiers were sent to fight in Egypt, with France's Caribbean colonies in the hands of collaborationist Vichy elements, the island welcomed those who flocked to join the Free French forces of Charles de Gaulle, perhaps repaying the emancipatory legacy of the French Revolution.

Local forces were waiting when a German submarine entered Castries Harbour on the night of March 9, 1942 and torpedoed two ships, the Bullard- King Line's "SS Umtata" and the Canadian ship the "C.N.S. Lady Nelson". There were 20 deaths from both ships, mainly St. Lucians. The survivors were taken in as refugees into people's homes. Particularly with the enhanced military presence of relatively affluent US personnel, the war brought changes to people's thinking and attitudes. Responsible positions, once the preserve of a few, were now filled by anyone capable of performing.

The first government school was built at Vide Bouteille in 1947, and health services were provided to rural communities.

In the 1960s, bananas replaced sugar after 200 years dominance by King Cane. This brought the biggest social and economic changes in the island's history. Tourism followed, and today has grown into another vibrant industry. The first Governor Dr. (later Sir) Frederick Clarke, took over its internal affairs, while Britain retained control of finance and foreign affairs. On aquiring Statehood the first Premier was Mr. John Compton, and the first Governor Dr. (later Sir) Frederick Clarke.

The 1970s saw the rise of strong nationalist movements initiated by students who had been at universities in the Caribbean, Britain and North America. Their ideas were fueled by the Cuban revolution, struggles elsewhere in Latin America and the Black Power movement in the United States.

St. Lucia finally gained its independence from Britain on February 22, 1979. Princess Alexandra represented the Queen. St Lucia chose to remain a monarchy, with a government similar to Canada's comprising

Bridge Street. St. Lucia

First street lights appear in Castries in1903

an upper and a lower house, with a Governor General representing the Monarch. The executive head of the country is a Prime Minister who heads a Cabinet of Ministers. Mr John Compton was the first Prime Minister. His party, the United Workers' Party (UWP), was voted out of office in the general election held later the same year. The new government, headed by the St Lucia Labour Party (SLP), remained in power for only two-and-a-half years, before being forced from office by right-wing vested interests. The UWP returned to power, and remained for fifteen more years, until it was conclusively defeated in the 1997 general election.

Hopefully, in the 21st century, new leaders will emerge, with a fresh vision of themselves and of development, to make the country worthy of what the people have shown themselves to be capable of.

FOR 'KING AND COUNTRY'.

Today, few St. Lucian, let alone visitors to the island, will likely recall or know that policewomen were not the first regimented and uniformed women of the country.

In fact, when the call to arms rang out from Britain at the beginning of World War II, instant response came from the far-flung outposts of the Empire, and soon it was found essential that women to be recruited to 'man' the home front, while their men were sent to face the enemy overseas.

St. Lucians were already familiar with the sight of US Armed Forces, British Officers and Warrant Officers – the former to guard the Caribbean's submarine infested waters; the latter to train recruits for overseas front.

There seemed to be an endless ring out of an old Army tune: "BOOTS, BOOTS, BOOTS, MOVING UP AND DOWN AGAIN! MEN, MEN, MEN".

Two uniformed women from Britain arrived in Saint Lucia towards the end of 1943. Senior Commander Grierson of the Women's Armed Forces and Junior Commander Theo Massey, along with Sergeant Wilson from Trinidad's ATS were to recruit young St. Lucian women into the British Army's Auxiliary Territorial Service (ATS). The response was instantaneous! Following the initial interviews, there was assembled a nucleus of excited and eager recruits with noble thoughts of serving 'King and Country' anywhere in the world. Of this group, more than one member came from the same family home. They included two St. Helenes, Ione and Pearl; followed a couple of years later by a third, Paula, who by then had reached the minimum age required. Two Sutherland sisters Joan and Beatrice; and a St. Prix, Florence, whose younger sister, Theresa, also followed 10 months later; two Barnards, Marie and Barbara. Others were one each from the Richmond, (Ursula) Deterville, (Marcelline) Eugene, Marquis, (Claudina) Wilson, Rose Aguste (Elsie), Osbourne, (Camilla) Cadlt, Burton, (Eileen) Theobalds, (Daphne) Andrew, (Antilla) Todd, (Mary) and MS Hinds. Dorothy Drayton joined just prior to the first overseas transfer. For those who had previously been members of the Girl Guides and Rangers groups, the introduction to the parade ground was not too difficult, but the young women had to appear indifferent to the stares and remarks of the macho male oglers, who thought there was no room for "dolls" on a man's territory.

However, the women proudly made it to their "passing out" parade in January 1944 at the Vigie Barracks grounds. First stripes were handed out then and adorned the neat khaki uniforms of Lance Corporals Helene and Ursula Richmond. Commanders returned overseas and assignments followed, under the supervision of Sgt. Dalison Wilson, wife of Army Captain Tony Wilson.

Special War Memorial section in Choc graveyard

Some months later, when the call for overseas transfer arrived, many were disappointed on being told that service in St. Lucia was just as important as overseas. Florence St. Prix, Camila Cadet, and Elsie Osbourne left for the United Kingdom to join the ATS Forces there.

Later that year, the Windward Islands Battalion HQ was moved to Grenada, and most of the ATS Detachment with it. The Sergeant in charge then was Sybil Comma from the Trinidad and Tobago Detachment.

Fresh recruitment in Grenada brought in sisters Eileen (Chiki) and Elaine Moore, along with Sheila Mahy Doreen Lagrenade, Muriel de Riggs, Cynthia Salhab and Alice (Alby) Fletcher. They were first billeted at the St. James Hotel, then moved to private homes. The hospitality of "Auntie" Belle de Coteau, whose wit and humor made the young ladies feel right at home, can never be forgotten. But Tanteen Camp was not to be the HQ for very long. Battalion HQ was back in St. Lucia for the Victory Parade in 1945. In that proud march through downtown Castries, the ATS Detachment was led by NCO in charge, lone St. Helene.

The Grenadian members, too, had returned and shared in the exhileration of having, contributed to victory and the peace of the world.

By February 1946, the Detachment was moved once more on transfer to Barbados and the process of disbandment of the Islands' Battalion began. The ATS Detachment was disbanded in June 1947.

In saluting the men of the Windward Islands Battalion in the celebration of their 50th Anniversary, one must look back on the ways in which life in the army also affected the young women of the island.

They had to live and work under strict conditions of discipline, obedience to authority, unfailing neatness of dress and appearance, toned down make up, jewellery and accessories, punctuality at all times, as well as knowing how to associate with men of all ranks and walks of life. Working hours were a mimimum of eight hours daily, pay packets were good, and, except in exceptional circumstances, there was no work on weekends nor a requirement to live in barracks.

Somehow everyone acquired a feeling of independence, not to mention of superiority over 'mere civilians'. No doubt, none of these courageous women would have shirked transfer to any of the active theatres of war. It was, of course, inevitable that some romantic attachments would ensue. Indeed, there were a number of marriages: Sgt. Comma to Lieutenant Jackman; Cpl Drayton to Lt. Pilgrim; Pte Barnard to Cpl Rudolfo; among others. Finally, in this memento of such memorable years, we should not forget a silent prayer for those members of this ATS St. Lucia Detachment, British Army, who have now passed away:

A.T.S. MARCHING SONG

Do you know of a little Island
Where the sea is so blue
And the girls of this Island
They have turned to something anew;
They had shed their pretty pretties
And donned the Uniform
Because their King and Country called them
to help weather the storm

It's only a little Island
But it's heart is full of gold
It's only a little Island
But the girls they have been told
So they came and joined the Army
And drilled upon the square
And now they're every bit the Soldier
But for their skirts and hair

But what does all this matter
When all is said and done
For they work without chatter
And their work is just begun
They will serve without flinching
to the very bitter end
for they know that you are returning
To wife and child and friend

AMERINDIANS

Amerindian remains or artefacts have been found all over Saint Lucia, especially around the coast. By studying the site and the artefacts, archaeologists can usually tell whether the settlement was occupied by Arawaks or Caribs or people from an even earlier period. Modern dating methods have shown some of the artefacts from these sites to be 1,500 years old.

The Ciboney from the South American continent, were probably the first to come to the island of Saint Lucia arriving by canoe around 400 years AD. They were a fairly primitive tribe who moved from place to place and made their homes in temporary shelters. They made no pottery and used only very simple tools. It is not known how many of the Caribbean islands they eventually occupied but the early Spanish explorers, when they arrived at the end of the fifteenth century, found parts of Cuba and Haiti already occupied by the Ciboney.

After the Ciboney came the Arawaks a peaceful tribe from Guyana who hunted birds and small animals with bows and arrows. If the Ciboney were still around when they arrived they probably drove them out or used them as slaves. The Arawaks cultivated crops like beans, yams, cassava or manioc and sweet potatoes. They also caught shellfish, lobster and lambi and many different kinds of fish, some so colourful that the rainbow itself could not have been brighter.

The Arawaks made pottery for both functional and ritual purposes and often decorated their bowls by stamping designs or painting patterns on them. They also carved figures or emblems on rocks. These rock carvings or petroglyphs are found at Dauphin, Choiseul, Balembouche and Soufriere. One of their earliest settlements in Saint Lucia was just behind the long beach at Grand Anse. On this site one of the finest specimens of a three-pointer stone found in the Caribbean was found.

After the Arawaks came the Caribs from the region of the Orinoco River. This river runs for hundreds of miles from the east coast of Venezuela deep into the dense rainforest of the interior. The Caribs fished and hunted but they cultivated no crops. They were fierce fighters and it is rumoured that they ate the bodies of enemies killed in battle. They would celebrate their victory with feasting. The women would lay out beautifully woven baskets of soursop, guavas, and custard apples and fill calabashes with a drink made of fruit juices and honey. There would be clay bowls of stewed iguana and turtle meat and oysters gathered from the roots of the mangroves. Freshly caught fish and the sweet flesh of little doves would be baked in the ashes of the fire, and for seasoning, small dishes of hot pepper mixed with lime juice called coui.

The men were a fearsome sight, their bodies smeared with a bright red paste over which they painted broad black stripes. Round their necks hung ornaments of bone and teeth and pieces of shell were stuck through holes in their noses, lips and ears. The Caribs systematically raided and destroyed the Arawak settlements, killing the men and taking

Reminders of the island's Amerindian inheritance are to be found throughout Saint Lucia.

the women into their own camps. Finally there were no more Arawak villages left to destroy. The Caribs ruled the tiny island. They called it Iouanalao, the land of the iguana.

In 1603, a ship that had been blown off its course stopped at the island for supplies. The Indians seemed friendly, willingly exchanging fruit and tobacco for some of the ship's cargo. Two years later another British ship, the Olive Branch or 'Oliph Blossome' as it is sometimes called, was also forced to anchor there. At first the Indians came every day to trade but they soon returned to their old ways. They ambushed the camp and killed many of the sailors. Only a few, who set out to sea in a small, open boat, escaped to tell the tale.

Other boats came and the Indians would paddle out in their canoes to trade with them. Then, in 1639, three or four hundred Englishmen came to settle permanently on the island. For over a year they lived in peace with the Caribs. Then, news came from Dominica that an English ship had captured several Caribs and taken them on board as slaves. In revenge, Caribs from Dominica, Martinique and St. Vincent joined forces with those in Saint Lucia to attack the small colony. The few Englishmen who escaped fled to Montserrat to start a new life.

Soon after this, the first party of French settlers came to the island. They built a fort which they protected with cannons. But within a few years they had lost three Governors to the clubs and arrows of the Caribs. In 1663, a group of Caribs went to Barbados to negotiate the sale of their island. The next year 600 Caribs together with an army of 1,000 Barbadians came to claim Saint Lucia for England. They forced French Governor, Bonnard, to surrender.

Sickness and wars with the Caribs eventually drove the British away. But not for long. Soon, the English and the French began to battle in earnest for possession of the island. The Indians with their primitive weapons were no match for the guns and cannons of the invaders. The Caribs who had earlier destroyed the peaceful Arawaks were now

Military Barracks converted to French Embas.

Cannon

SUNDIAL

G rand Anse Valley is located on the east coast of St. Lucia, behind the largest beach on the island. It is now fairly well established that one of the largest Amerindian villages in St. Lucia once existed in this valley.

The site has been investigated by several archaeologists. Professor Rouse in 1953, Professor Haag in 1960 and the Bullens in 1968, have obtained a carbon 14 date of approximately 600 AD for the site and a ceramic style from Grande Anse is now used by archaeologists in the early typology of the region, which occured around the height of Arawak cultural dominance in the Lesser Antilles.

ndial

In 1965, an airstrip was being constructed at Grand Anse by utilising sand from the beach berm. The tractor, while levelling the berms, exposed an American midden, which revealed considerable quantities of artefacts. The estate manager collected some of the finer pieces from those strewn about the ground. Among the salvaged pieces was a delicately carved stone with three points, much bigger than any yet found in the island, being the same size as the largest yet found in the region, in Guadeloupe.

Three-pointed-stones are thought to personify *Yokaha*, the sun god and giver of food. This particular "three pointer" is beautifully carved, highly polished and decorated with incised lines and grooves. The stone is delicately balanced on its concave base, conchoidal in shape, culminating at the apex with a 14° bias or tilt to one side. The stone measures 120mm wide, 150mm high and 300mm long, a unit ratio of 4 to 5 to 10, indicating that the creator of this artefact had both the knowledge and the ability to execute precise measurements. It is carved from light grey basaltic rock and polished to a very smooth finish.

If the stone is placed on a hard smooth surface, it can be rocked quite easily from side to side and will continue to rock on its own for approximately fifty occilations after being released, always returning to a vertical position when at rest. It seems that the stone could be tilted to either side in order to allow a person to see down the lines made by the chevrons, perhaps to follow the apparent movement of the rising and setting sun between the solstices.

It is generally accepted among regional archaeologists that the three-pointed-stones represent *Yokahu*, who gave the Arawaks manioc, their staple food. The Arawak practice of "planting" a small carved three-pointed-stone in the manioc patch, in the belief that it would assist crop fertility, lends credence to this view.

Most archaeologists subscribe to the view that Yokahu is male and the three-pointed-stone is phallic, while the fertility goddess is personified by a female called Atabeyra giving birth. However, this particular three-pointed-stone seems to also represent "fertility", as there is fairly clear evidence of female genitals carved into the base of the stone.

Brigands

The black freedom fighters of the Lesser Antilles became known as Brigands during the French Revolution. In 1792, the new Republic was expounding the ideals of *Liberté, Egalité et Fratenité*. This culminated in the Emancipation Decree issued by the National Convention in Paris on February 4 1794. The slaves in St Lucia and Martinique were denied freedom as these islands were captured by the British before the Decree took effect.

With the encouragement and support of Republican Victor Hugues in Guadeloupe, the slaves in the British controlled islands rebelled.

The British considered this an insurrection and endeavoured to restore "order" and slavery by force. Those who resisted were termed Brigands, a label that only had the effect of strengthening the slaves' resolve to defend their tenuous freedom at all costs. Encouraged by the French Republicans, the Brigands developed guerrilla war tactics, which they conducted from the interior, as a group called *l'Armee Francais dans les bois*, or Army of the woods.

The Brigand War in St Lucia lasted almost four years, before a cessation of hostilities in late November 1797. During that tense period, the Brigands developed an amazingly efficient series of strategic sites in the interior and along much of the coast of the island. Survival in the forest required good communication and reliable intelligence gathering, regular supplies of food and arms, and rapid mobility. Their camps and supply depots had to be well hidden and properly defended.

Over 100 Brigand sites have been located in isolated pockets throughout the island. Rock shelters, caves, tunnels, holes and mountain tops were used with considerable military skill and effect. The now famous General John Moore developed his Light Infantry strategies (which he later used to such advantage in the Napoleonic war), while charged with the unpleasant task of subduing the Brigands in St Lucia. This task proved almost fatal and he was sent back exhausted and ill to England. His successor, Colonel Drummond continued to use Moore's strategies and finally negotiated a conditional ceasefire. The Brigands, or freedom fighters, of St Lucia were placed in the First West India Regiment and sent to the West Coast of Africa to protect the British interests in Sierra Leone. Those black freedom fighters would now stand side by side with white British solders, an undeclared admission of their bravery and skill.

AN OVERDUE TRIBUTE

On May 24 1796, Republican-held St Lucia surrendered to the British. As the French soldiers laid down their arms, 2,000 black ex-slaves and former Brigands, who had fought the British under the French flag, marched out of Morne Fortune and were made prisoners-of-war. They were placed into the hold of several ships, commandeered as prisons. Some were sent to England, others escaped to continue the Brigand War in St Lucia. One of the ships that sailed back to England was the *London*, which was trans-

---

The Battle of Rabot

In April 1795, St. Lucia was technically in the hands of the British, who held the fortified posts of Morne Fortune, Pigeon Island and Vigie. In reality, the island was controlled by those known as 'Brigands', ex-slaves and runaways, a few French Republican artillerymen and engineers, who were being supported from Guadeloupe and supplied with arms by Victor Hugues.

Major General Stewart launched a major offensive against the 'Brigands' stronghold in Soufriere. Stewart's force consisted of 1,000 soldiers, made up of Malcolm's Rangers, the ninth and thirty-fourth Regiments of Foot and the sixty-first and sixty-eighth Light Infantry. The 'Brigands' set up an ambush near Rabot Lake, where they managed to halt the British advance and engage them in a prolonged battle on April 22, which resulted in the retreat of the British after seven hours of bitter fighting. Each side had lost about 200 men. This defeat set the British back so severely that they were obliged to withdraw to the safety of Morne Fortune, where they waited for reinforcements that never came.

The Battle of Rabot turned the tide of events in favour of the 'Brigands', who seized the offensive, drove the British off the island in June, and retained control of St. Lucia for almost a year. The British invaded the island in April 1796, capturing it in a month later. They then spent many months engaged in a guerrilla war trying to subdue and suppress the 'Brigands', who finally surrendered on agreed terms in late November, 1797.

Saint Lucia - in the process of honouring its heroes the Brigands

porting about 80 black ex-slaves shackled in her hold when she encountered a storm and was wrecked off Rapparee Cove near Ilfracombe, north Devon. At least six bodies recovered from that wreck were hurriedly buried near the cove.

In February 1997, some bones became exposed near the 1796 shipwreck site of the *London*. It is believed they may be the remains of some of the captured ex-Brigands from St Lucia. This story caught the public's attention. Bernie Grant, the Guyana - born British Labour MP, and St Lucian - born Ben Bousquet British Labour Councillor, have both campaigned for the martyred Brigands to be given the dignified burial that befits heroes. A formal request, for the bodies to be returned to St Lucia for burial, has been forwarded to the British Government.

Coincidentally, when this news first broke, St Lucia was already in the process of honouring its heroes - those ex-slaves or Brigands, the freedom fighters of 200 years ago - with another monument to be placed next to the existing Enniskillen Monument on the Morne, which honours the Regiment that captured the fort in 1796. Such a monument will at least balance the equation and give recognition to both sides in this conflict.

The staff of the North Devon Museums Service are sympathetic to St Lucia's request to have the bones returned to the island for their heroes' burial.

Historical Stamps

HISTORIC STAMPS RECALL BRIGAND WAR

On April 28 1995 three stamps and a Souvenir Sheet were released to commemorate the 200th Anniversary of the Battle of Rabot, one of the key events of what the British called "The Brigands' War".

Two years later, in commemoration of the final events of the War, four additional stamps were released. These depict:-

20c *The Taking of Praslin*
On January 10 1797 the British post of Praslin, which was located on the promon tory overlooking the Bay and Village of Praslin and the estates of Mamiku, was attacked and taken by the Brigands.

55c *The Battle of Dennery*
In February, the 8-hours, Battle of Dennery took place between opposing forces of British soldiers and Brigand fighters, when the latter assailed the outlying British post on the promontory overlooking Anse Canot and Fond d'Or Bay.

70c *Peace*
In November 1797, the "Brigands War" came to an end. The Brigands agreed to emerge from their hideouts in the centre of the island and laydown their arms on condition that they would not be re-enslaved but repatriated to Africa. The Lieutenant Colonel in charge of the cessation of hostilities on the British side was then promoted to become Governor General.

$3 *The West India Regiment*
At the end of the war, the "Brigands" were recruited into the 1st West India Regiment, which at that time was stationed in Sierra Leone. Their subsequent service added to the proud record of the Regiment.

STORMY HISTORY OF THE TURBULENT SEAS

Over the years, the seas around Saint Lucia have been the scene of several disasters; four of which have been commemorated with an issue of postage stamps.

20c On *February 24 1935*, the local motor vessel *St. George* was returning to Choiseul from an enjoyable Sunday outing to Laborie when, being unstable due to overloading, she capsized in the swells off Balembouche, resulting in the deaths of no less than 42 young persons.

55c On *June 18 1897*, the *SS Belle* of Bath foundered and sank off the north east coast of St. Lucia while carrying a cargo of oil in 5-gallon containers. Many of these broke loose and drift ed ashore where they burst upon the rocks and contaminated the hitherto pristine coastline. It was Saint Lucia's first oil slick.

$1 Fourteen days earlier, on *June 4*, the *SS Ethelgonda* had become stranded in rough seas on the rocks off of Anse Ger. In an effort to lighten the ship and refloat her, her cargo of wool was unloaded and laid out along the valley of Mabouya to dry.

$2.5 *October 21 1817* saw one of the worst hurricans ever to strike St. Lucia. The devastation caused deaths of many people; the most prominent being Governor Seymour, who was mortal ly injured when Government House was destroyed. Shipping was seriously affected, with no less than ten merchant vessels and scores of local craft wrecked on the shore, accounting for the majority of deaths.

A MAN NAMED BIDEAU

In the centre of Castries, a monument has been erected to a St. Lucian who has only recently gained recognition. In a square that has been christened Place Bideau, bronze busts of the Venezuelan liberator, Simon Bolivar, and St. Lucian, Jean Baptiste Bideau, stand a few yards apart in honour of two great men from different backgrounds whose association over a century-and-a-half ago was to shape the destiny of large parts of South America.

Although St. Lucia is rich in history, it is a history that has been dominated by foreign figures - mainly soldiers and adventurers - from present-day metropolitan countries that were once colonial powers. Ovedr the last few decades, St. Lucia's historians have unearthed the names of their own national heroes. For instance, history now records the feats of the Brigands who fought courageously against the British in St. Lucia.

Recently, a French mulatto named Jean Baptiste Bideau has joined the ranks of those St. Lucians whose heroic feats have been demanding official recognition, although it is only quite recently that Bideau's exploits in the Venezuelan war of independence in the early nineteenth century have come to light. It is the story of a man who became embroiled in one of the most bitter conflicts in this hemisphere - in the cause of a country that was not his own.

Bideau was born in 1770, in the eastern St. Lucian settlement of Desruisseaux. A sailor by profession, he made his home in Trinidad where he owned a boat-making workshop. By the time he was thirty, Bideau had already started to mix actively in Venezuelan affairs after distinguished service as a sea captain in the ranks of Victor Hugues in Guadeloupe in the service of the French Republic.

By 1811, with the Venezuelan war of independence already brewing, Bideau put his brigantine, *Boton de Rosa*, at the disposal of the Venezuelan patriots. Thus began his six-year involvement in a war that was to take him from lucrative business in Trinidad to his courageous death on Venezuelan soil.

The first battles of the war brought mixed results for the patriots. In 1813, Bideau was in the famous expedition from Chacachacare and was later appointed Chief of the Government of Guiria, from where he was forced to flee for his life in 1815. Later, Bideau arrived in Los Cayos, Haiti, where he met Bolivar. After a series of military defeats, Bideau suggested to Bolivar the details of a plan for the invasion of Venezuela and accompanied Bolivar in his attempt to land at Ocumare de la Costa. But disaster befell the patriots, for in the attack their forces were scattered. Bolivar suddenly found himself alone on a deserted beach surrounded by the enemy and it was then that Bideau enacted the most heroic deed of his life when he managed to seize a boat and rescue Bolivar. Fourteen years later, Bolivar, in a letter to a friend, was to recall the details of that incident. He wrote:

'I had been deceived at the time by an aide-de-camp and by the

Part of Town and M
Part of Town and harbour,

72

foreign seamen who had committed the most vile act in the world. They abandoned me among my enemies on a deserted beach. I was going to shoot myself when one of them, Monsieur Bideau, returned from the sea in a boat and saved me.'

In April 1817, the patriots launched their final assault and at Casa Fuerte de Barcelona, in one of the bloodiest battles of the conflict, Bideau was among the thousand men who were killed on both sides. But his efforts were not in vain. Bolivar lived on and went on to liberate several countries in South America, including his native Venezuela.

Bideau's exploits have been uncovered by the Venezuelan historian Paul Verna. It was this discovery that has now resulted in St. Lucians paying tribute to one of their own more than one hundred and fifty years later. Several important dignitaries were on hand in July 1983, when Place Bideau was officially named and a monument dedicated to the man whom history almost forgot.

Labour

The seeds of the Caribbean labour movement were sown following the emancipation of the slaves in 1838, when an emerging working class identified the need to safeguard its own interests.

Two significant events were instrumental in this development in St. Lucia - the Castries and Gros Islet riots, and the Cul de Sac protest.

In 1849, wage labourers and peasants, opposed to a forthcoming land tax, petitioned the country's governor. His rejection led to a confrontation in Castries. The governor's attempts to quell the disturbance with force left eight people dead and many sugar plantations in Gros Islet burned to the ground.

The second event occurred in 1893 when the mostly indentured labourers of the Cul de Sac plantation, protesting over working conditions, marched into Castries demanding an audience with the governor. The subsequent meeting failed to produce a satisfactory outcome, and a protest march to the plantation followed. Colonial police and troops were called in to break up the demonstration and several arrests were made.

Early campaigns by workers in the Caribbean, trying to improve their poor economic and social conditions, were sporadic and poorly organised. Coupled with the British Combination Act, which outlawed the organisation of workers to defend their collective interests, the future looked bleak.

However, by the late nineteenth and into the twentieth century, and despite many setbacks, workers in the region steadily gained valuable experience and knowledge.

In 1898, the first working class organisation in the English-speaking Caribbean was formed. The Trinidad Working Men's Association played a crucial role, and helped to create the island's first trade unions.

In the early 1900s, Castries was developing as an important coaling station. With one of the best natural harbours in the region and its central location in the Eastern Caribbean, St. Lucia became the hub of the coal trade.

Castries experienced a growth in employment but long working hours and low pay led to frequent agitation.

The sugar plantations of Roseau and Cul de Sac were booming, but pay and conditions were as bad as they were in Castries.

In 1907, with no change in their own degrading situation while the country experienced growth and prosperity, the workers in the coal industry and on the sugar estates rose up against the system. Once again, the working classes suffered the wrath of the colonial state as troops moved in, killing and wounding, until the rebellion was crushed.

In the thirty years following 1897, continued activity in some of the larger territories secured legislation legalising trade unions. But the colonial government acceded only to the demands it felt would placate the colonised peoples in an attempt to preserve the status quo.

The Caribbean working classes were engaged in a bitter struggle against the colonial regime and had to fight for every inch of ground.

*Inside the fruit & veg market,
Castries*

This created an explosive situation, made worse by the global economic depression of the 1930's.

Wage cuts and increased unemployment took their toll on the work force, and as a result there were strikes and riots were witnessed throughout the Caribbean.

The first strike action in 1930s St. Lucia was in Castries and, as in 1907, it began with the coal carriers.

History repeated itself once again, as the governor responded with aggression by enlisting a 'volunteer force', summoning a British warship and ordering marines to patrol the streets of Castries.

This reaction angered the citizens who saw no justification for such a show of strength.

Two years later, in 1937, the agricultural workers of the Roseau and Cul de Sac sugar estates went on strike, and again the governor responded with military might.

However, on this occasion the governor's actions were fiercely criticised by members of his own legislature who realised that the continuing labour unrest, combined with the deepening crisis in the colonial state, required a more sensitive approach.

This led to the formation of the Moyne Commission, which was given the responsibility of investigating the 'troubles', and to then make recommendations for the entire British West Indies.

The most notable recommendation of the new commission was that trade unions should be allowed throughout the English-speaking Caribbean.

Friendly staff at the Great House Restaurant, Cap Estate

This opportunity was immediately seized in St. Lucia and the first 'legal' trade union was formed in 1939. The St. Lucia Workers' Co-operative Union (later renamed St. Lucia Workers' Union) was initiated by a young Castries proprietor, Charles Augustin. Registered in 1940, it was joined in 1945 by the St. Lucia Seamen and Waterfront Workers' Union. The St. Lucia Workers' Union raised the hopes of the working people and, soon, had a membership in excess of 6,000, which represented 25 per cent of the labour force and ten per cent of the total population.

A victim of its own success, the fledgling union was unable to keep the support of its members. Most workers left when it failed to secure collective representation, and by 1945, union membership had slumped to a little over 300.

It was at this time that a young worker on the Vigie Airport Extension Project, George F. L. Charles, and a handful of his co-workers, joined the St. Lucia Workers' Union.

The airport project was suffering from the effects of sporadic strike action by workers demanding better pay and conditions, and Charles and his associates realised that by joining the union, their campaign for the workers would result in a decisive outcome.

The involvement of George Charles and his "camarades" soon generated new interest among the membership and the union decided to set up an Organising Committee to recruit new members.

By early 1946, union membership had increased to more than 5,000 - a resuscitation which led to the first wage agreement in the sugar industry.

The union's first official strike came when the bakers in Castries requested a pay increase and improved working conditions. The five-day stoppage ended in a satisfactory settlement, and was the first of many campaigns which gained respect for the union.

In 1951, the St. Lucia Workers Union announced the formation of the St. Lucia Labour Party. The leadership realised that in order to make social and economic advances, the working classes needed a political voice.

The political parties which emerged represented two distinct groups - the St. Lucia Labour Party represented the working classes, and the People's Progressive Party represented the employer, or merchant/planter, classes.

The first election, held in 1951, resulted in an easy victory for the St. Lucia Labour Party and George Frederick Lawrence Charles became St. Lucia's first Chief Minister.

In a climate of colonial rule, the party was still able to initiate programmes of social development and legislation to benefit the working classes. Schools, health centres and roads were built, electricity was brought to the villages, and the discrimination preventing working class children from attending the best secondary schools was ended. Laws for industrial compensation, the protection of wages, child labour and trade unions, were also introduced.

But despite further election victories in 1957 and 1961, the employer classes managed to gain office.

In 1964, the National Labour Movement - a breakaway group formed by members of the St.Lucia Labour Party - led by John Compton, merged with members of the People's Progressive Party to form the United Workers' Party (UWP).

Reeling from many defections "in the name of progress and development", the St. Lucia Labour Party lost political office to the UWP.

John Compton became Chief Minister, and his party initiated a programme of "industrialisation by invitation", which saw the relocation to St. Lucia of overseas companies - mainly North American - that were taking advantage of cheap labour and the offer of up to twenty years of tax concessions.

Tourism was developed as an economic activity and became one of the legs of an economic tripod of agriculture, light industry and tourism. In agriculture, banana cultivation, which had been introduced by the Labour Government, witnessed a substantial growth.

This period of economic boom saw an increase in light manufacture and commerce. Employment in the tourism sector was increasing, and a class of small and medium banana farmers was developing alongside the agricultural wage workers.

But, not everyone was benefiting from this time of prosperity and development.

In 1970, wage workers on the large banana estates were earning anything between $2.40 and $3.20 per day - considerably below the living wage - and there was a significant presence of child labour, paid at a substantially lower rate. It appeared as if nothing had changed in the last fifty years and, still, the planter class was prospering.
In 1974, workers of the Roseau and Cul de Sac valleys went on strike under the leadership of George Odlum and what was to become the Farm and Farmworkers' Union.

Union membership among urban workers also began to rise as new unions were formed. A new militancy was sweeping through the labour movement.

The National Worker's Union was created under the leadership of a former St. Lucia Workers' Union member, Tyrone Maynard.

George Charles formed the Agricultural and General Workers' Union after his unsuccessful attempt at a comeback in the St. Lucia Workers' Union.

The Teachers' Union and the Civil Service Association emerged in the mid-seventies.

The period from 1973 to 1979 saw a series of industrial actions in both the private and public sectors. With comprehensive union demands coupled with the government's insensitive approach to the working classes, the Labour Party triumphed over Compton's UWP leadership in 1979.

The demise of the 1979-1982 Labour Government, saw the return to power of the 'new look' UWP, which appeared to seek a partnership with the labour movement.

With this development, the Committee of Trade Unions was formed, and was later to develop into the Industrial Solidarity Pact, an organisation which was to secure a degree of unity among the main trade unions on the major industrial relations issues.

In May 1997, an new era for the country's Labour movement dawned, when the *Saint Lucia Labour Party*, under the leadership of Dr Kenny Anthony, swept into office, winning 16 out of 17 seats in the national elections

The Media

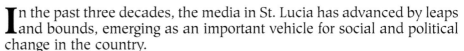

In the past three decades, the media in St. Lucia has advanced by leaps and bounds, emerging as an important vehicle for social and political change in the country.

This progress has occurred on many fronts. Just imagine that up to the mid-1960s St. Lucians received all their televison programming from nearby Barbados. Today, St. Lucia not only produces programmes of its own and receives dozens of satellite-transmitted stations from the United States and Europe, it also has five television systems, one of which has the capability of beaming 'live' programmes throughout the region and the rest of the world via satellite.

Three radio stations broadcast programmes nationwide, compared to one point in the 1960s, when a substation of the Grenada-based Windward Islands Broadcasting Service (WIBS), now defunct, constituted the entirety of St. Lucia's electronic media. Radio stations are a vital tool in the dissemination of information, especially among the rural folk through their use of programmes entirely in Kweyol or Patois, still widely spoken in the countryside.

But the most dramatic and significant changes have occurred in the newspapers, which have been in existence for more than two centuries. Newspapers are considered the leaders in St. Lucia's media system, fearlessly analysing, debating and commenting on the issues of the day, educating, and informing the public and keeping politicians on their toes.

The first record of a news medium in St. Lucia dates back to 1780, when **The Saint Lucia Gazette** appeared on the scene. This was 50 years after Barbados got its first newspaper.

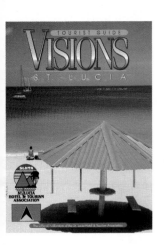

During the following 100 years, no less than 15 other publications appeared, most of which went out of business within months. Indeed, in the years 1817 and 1861, St. Lucia was without a single newspaper. **The News** (1836) has the distinction of being referred to as the first independent newspaper on the island, even though it was published by the Government Printer.

During that period too, St. Lucia boasted newspapers that were published in English and in French, like **La Courier des Antilles** (1820) and **L'Impartial Journal Politque Commercial et Litteraire de SteLucie** (1823), reflecting the island's dual heritage that survives to the present.

The longest-running newspaper of that era was **The Paladium and Free Press** (1838), whose launch coincided with the abolition of slavery. **The Paladium** stayed around for 18-years, and was published weekly by one Charles Wells, who appears to have started a career in journalism two years earlier, when he launched **The News**.

Another newspaper which remained in business for a while was appropriately named **The St Lucian**, and went into print in 1863 under the editorship of Ingmac Antoine. Also a weekly, it lasted for 10 years.

The year 1885, however, saw the launch of **The Voice of St Lucia**, a newspaper that is still in publication. In fact, it is the oldest newspaper in the Eastern Caribbean, older even than the prestigious **Barbados**

Advocate. Robert George McHugh, an Irishman who had taken early retirement from the civil service for the express purpose of venturing into journalism, began publishing **The Voice** in January 1885, as a four-page broadsheet, four columns to a page with advertising dominating the front and back pages, and editorial matter on the inside pages.

With Milton's "Give the liberty to know, to utter and to argue freely, according to conscience, above all liberties" as its watchword, **The Voice's** appearance was not coincidental. It was launched for the purpose of advancing the cause of a Federation, comprising St. Lucia, St. Vincent, Grenada and Tobago. McHugh made the point quite clear in his inaugural editorial: "We wish to state most emphatically and once and for all that this newspaper has been started in the interest of no class or clique; nor to advocate any set of opinions, but to give an opportunity for every man and woman in St. Lucia, of having their say in public matters generally, and especially to express their opinion with respect to the proposed confederation of St. Lucia, St. Vincent, Grenada and Tobago under one government who, as well as the chief officials, is to reside in Grenada."

McHugh himself served as Editor until 1910 during which the paper changed its motto to **Statio Haud Malifida Carinis** ("A safe anchorage for ships") in tribute to the growing importance of the capital Castries as a major seaport in the western hemisphere.

After 112 years, **The Voice** has now become a veritable institution in St. Lucia, a training ground for most of the journalists who have emerged in the profession locally over many decades. The paper has switched between local and foreign ownership countless times, and it has been twice razed to the ground in the great Castries fires of 1927 and 1948.

Today, it operates a modern, well-equipped plant just on the outskirts of the city with its main operations computerised. It is the most regular of all the island's newspapers, being published thrice weekly, on Tuesdays, Thursdays and Saturdays.

After **The Voice**, the only other newspaper of long-standing in the country is **The Crusader**, which started in 1934 as **The West Indian Crusader**. A weekly, it functions as the political organ of its owner and publisher, who has been actively involved in the political life of the country for nearly three decades. Fulfilling similar roles are THE STAR (1987) and **One Caribbean** (1980), also weeklies. The youngest 'kid on the newspaper block' is **The St Lucia Mirror** (1994), which became the first to publish its policy, one that included a well-defined social and moral agenda, for example its refusal to accept advertising promoting alcohol or tobacco.

Freedom of the press does not appear as a fundamental right in the Constitution of Saint Lucia. The best that the supreme law of the land does for the media is to guarantee them freedom "to receive and communicate ideas and information without interference".

Past administrations have been accused of violating or threatening freedom of the press, either through their closure of media houses (two

radio stations were closed down by the Government in 1979 and in 1996) or as a result of scathing criticism by politicians in power regarding the manner in which the media play its role. Be that as it may, politicians now recognise that the media is indeed quite a powerful tool, and it is quite likely that in the years ahead there will be fewer and fewer attempts to criticise or intimidate it. St. Lucians have a new admiration for its work and would certainly rally behind it should danger signs appear.

Soufriere jetty

La Toc Battery

Caribbean architecture, Soufriere

Helicopter Tours: *See St Lucia in an unusual and thrilling way. A unique opportunity to see what the country has to offer and a great way to take some superb photographs.*

COMMUNICATIONS

The year is 1871, and the West India and Panama Telegraph Company lands a submarine cable at Yellow Sands (Sandals La Toc beach), connecting St Lucia to Martinique, Dominica, Guadeloupe, Antigua, St Kitts, St Thomas and Puerto Rico. By March 1872, the US and UK had been linked, and St Lucia was now connected to the 'Mother Country'!

In 1938, the company changed its name to Cable & Wireless (West Indies) Ltd.

In the period up to 1966 Cable & Wireless operated the international communications to St Lucia, with the Government providing local telephony. During that period, external communications continued to be enhanced, with ship to shore radio added in 1924, High Frequency (HF) radio in 1928 and an inter-island tropospheric radio system in 1965. St Lucia was also the home base of a series of cableships used to maintain the submarine cable in the region and beyond. A submarine cable storage depot was located at what is now the vendors' arcade on Jeremie Street. To make an international call required a visit to the company's office on Bridge Street, giving the caller's name and phone number to the attendant, and waiting to be invited to a public booth when the call was eventually established, perhaps hours later.

In 1966, the Government signed a 20-year agreement with C&W to provide for the installation and maintenance of an islandwide automatic telephone system. The first automatic exchanged was opened in December 1966, in what is now the ground floor of the Ministry of Education building, with a capacity of 800 lines. During the next few years, the towns and villages were progressively connected to the automatic network, until a total of eleven exchanges, ranging in capacity from 20 lines in places like Canaries to the 1,200 in Castries. In contrast, the smallest exchange is now 256 lines in Desbarra, and the largest in Castries is 9,000, making a grand total of 33,000 lines, network-wide.

During the ensuing years, emphasis was placed on expanding capacity fast enough to cater for rapidly growing demand.
Direct international dialing by the operator was introduced in 1971. The result was to drastically reduce the waiting time for completion of international calls. In 1977, what was then the longest island hopping analogue microwave system in the world was commissioned, spanning the 800 miles between Tortola and Trinidad, including the French controlled islands. Where there was a scarcity of telephone lines, the company ensured that public payphones were installed so that communities were not left isolated. Both payphones and prepaid cardphones have now been installed islandwide.

The telephone system's current phase began in 1982, when St Lucia moved straight into digital, bypassing the intermediate stage of crossbar switching altogether. Not many countries in the world could boast using digital technology at that time, including the UK and most of Europe. This technology ushered in international direct dialing (IDD), and itemised billing for IDD calls.

In 1982 Saint Lucia moved straight into digital

In 1987 C&W obtained a separate, non-exclusive license, to operate a Cable TV system to relay satellite delivered programming available on US domestic satellites. From a modest start with six channels, CableVision now offers thirty-five channels in the Castries basin area, with construction underway to Vieux Fort.

C&W continues to upgrade its systems. Underground fibre-optic cables now straddle both east and west coasts, and the Eastern Caribbean Fibre-Optic System (ECFS) links the island to the Global Digital Highway, giving an alternative to the satellite based links with the outside world.

The cellular service offered by Cable & Wireless Caribbean Cellular - formerly Boatphone - has been upgraded to provide better coverage.

Cable & Wireless' contribution to developmental infrastructure in St Lucia has been substantial - over EC$250 million in five years in addition to an annual corporation tax bill of more that $10 million. This is supplemented by corporate donations in excess of EC$500,000 annually to the arts, sports, and other worthy causes.

Cable & Wireless donate in excess of EC $500,000 to the arts, sports and other worthy causes

Saint Lucia is in touch with the world

Anse Chastanet

Anse Chastanet, prounced as "ants-shas-tan-ay," was named after one of the French aristocratic families who settled on the island during the French occupation in the 18th century, the Chastanet family who originated in the Bordeaux region, "Anse" is old French for "Bay."

The Anse Chastanet estate was owned by a variety of French, then British families until it was purchased by the developers of Anse Chastanet Hotel.

Anse Chastanet Hotel was built in 1968 by a group of Canadians. Imagination and determination was needed to carry through the construction project: at that point, there was no road leading to Anse Chastanet, so all the construction materials had to be brought from Soufriere by canoe and then carried to the hill top by manual labour, mostly on the heads of strong women.

Anse Chastanet was sold to the present owners in 1974. Mr Troubetzkoy, the Chairman and Managing Director of Anse Chastanet and an architect by profession, immediately saw the potential of Anse Chastanet and started a thorough reconstruction programme by tearing down walls blocking the views and by redesigning and opening the accommodations and public areas to the spectacular scenery. Ten more rooms were added, including one - and two bedroom suites.

In 1985, 12 beachside deluxe rooms were designed and built by Mr Troubetzkoy. It was his intention to use island materials only, in particular for the furniture which was designed by him and then handmade in Soufriere with the exclusive use of island woods such as teak, mahogany, wild breadfruit, greenheart and purpleheart.

In 1990, the same concept was applied for the addition of 11 hillside deluxe rooms which also display locally made furniture and other craftworks.

All rooms are decorated with a colorful fabric called Madras. It originates in India and is the material which the national costumes in St Lucia and other Caribbean islands are made.

Part of Anse Chastanet's 500 acres of land is the old French colonial plantation of Anse Mamin, just north of Anse Chastanet beach. One can get there either by boat or by walking - just follow the coastline at the north end of Anse Chastanet beach and walk along the water's edge. After about 10 minutes, a beautifully deserted beach and a sleepy plantation are awaiting the explorer.

Anse Mamin has a very colorful history: it is one of the earliest estates established on St. Lucia and the first owner was French, the Baron Marie Antoine Y'Volley, and his wife Henrietta. The original Anse Mamin estate included 723 acres of land and a sugar cane works. The ruins of the house and the sugar works, including the remains of a huge waterwheel, a viaduct water system and a 1 1/2 million gallon water reservoir can be seen to this date.

It is alleged that, in the old days, some of the slaves of Anse Mamin ran away and established a settlement at Bouton to the north east. Bouton eventually became the first "free" village in St. Lucia, where cer

*At Anse Chastanet, - less than
50 feet from the shore, are some
of the best reefs in St Lucia*

tain slaves, who had legally obtained their freedom, joined with their
brothers and obtained their "supplies" from the neighboring Anse
Mamim estate.

There are records of a mortgage for Anse Mamin estate, drawn up
in 1834, designed presumably to resuscitate the estate after the hurricane of 1831. The plan seemed to have failed.

In 1852, the estate is listed as being in the possession of the heirs
D'Y'Volley. One Stephen Williams was appointed administrator of the
estate on July 29, 1839 and it appears to have been sold to a member of
the DuBoulay family in 1859. It changed hands one more time before
the entire estate was purchased by Anse Chastanet in 1984.

Besides the historical ruins, a great variety of tropical fruits, plants
and vegetables and flowers can be found at Anse Mamin.

Property

Those wanting to own a home on this enchanting island will find the following information useful:

LAND ON WHICH TO BUILD: Many people favour the areas in the north of the island - Rodney Bay, Cap Estate, Bonne Terre or Marigot Bay just south of Castries. Plot prices vary with size and location - from US$40,000 to US$160,000. You must start your development/building within 2 years.

BUYING AN EXISTING PROPERTY:

A house/villa. Many are in excellent locations with fine views. US$250,000 is a reasonable starting price with a few over US$500,00. Most have 3 bedrooms, 2/3 baths and a swimming pool. You can let them out profitably.

Community developments - condominiums. Smaller in size, 1 to 2 bedrooms with security and management services. Prices well below US$100,000. Marina front town houses in Rodney Bay are in the US$200,000 to US$300,000.

TIME SHARE/INTERNATIONAL OWNERSHIP

These have not caught on in St. Lucia, but are available in Windjammer Landing, Marlin Quay and Oasis in Marigot Bay. Prices for one week from US$12,000 -15,000.

Prestige property sales are on the increase

Purchasers must allow for 13-14% "closing costs" which includes license from Government, stamp duty and legal fees.

Developers have their own sales force, but you may find it better to start with a local estate agents who is likely to be more dispassionate in his assessments.

Tropical Villas (Fax.no.758-450-8089) can provide information on villa accommodation while you are still finding your way.

odney Quay town houses are truly the bastion of luxury living

*Interior shot of
town house*

Top: Pigeon Island. Above: Petroglyph, Jalousie Estate, Soufriere

*Saint Lucia is more than **Simply Beautiful**, it is incredibly diverse*

'ON TIME EVERY TIME'

St. Lucia National Car Rental is owned by John Orlandre Elliott, who started with one car back in 1972, and built his company up to a fleet of 75 vehicles by 1990, during the boom years of development for the St. Lucia economy. As the economy leveled off, he was forced to reduce his fleet to 45 vehicles, which includes 4x4 Jeeps, small economy vehicles like the Daihatsu Curoes and Charades, as well as manual and automatic air conditioned vehicles, like the Daihatsu Applause, Nissan Sentra, and so on.

St. Lucia National Car Rental now operates locations at Hewanorra International Airport, George Charles Airport (formally Vigie Airport), Club Acquarius Hotel, Le Sport Hotel, Islander Hotel and Pointe Seraphine Duty Free Shopping Centre at the Dock.

In 1994 and 1996, the St. Lucia Ministry of Tourism National Service Annual Award for Best Car Rental Company was awarded to St. Lucia National Car Rental.

The company's motto is:

(a) *Provide defect free vehicles and services to our customers.*

(b) *To fully understand the requirements of our jobs and support one another.*

(c) *To fulfil these requirements on time and every time.*

NATIONAL Car Rental provide a service determined to meet business and tourist needs

THE SPIRIT OF THE ST. LUCIAN

The people of St. Lucia are the product of their history. They are a people composed of many races. The first inhabitants were Amerindian. According to Bishop Charles Gachet, in his *History of the Catholic Church in St. Lucia:* "The Caribs who inhabited the island at the time of its discovery continued to live in it, at least periodically, up to 1660, when, by a treaty of peace with the French and the English, they renounced all claims to the ownership of most of the Lesser Antilles, on condition that they be left in peaceful possession of St Vincent and Dominica." It seems that only a few Caribs remained in the island after this period.

The first settlers came to St. Lucia about 1651, when the French in Martinique decided to occupy it. But the settlement was very small, being made up of a few Europeans and African slaves. The British based in Barbados could not tolerate the French occupation because of the excellent harbour which could be used in times of war.

This rivalry, which lasted until 1814 when St. Lucia was finally ceded to British by the Treaty of Paris, prevented the island from developing into a prosperous colony, and the population only increased very slowly.

Sugar cane was not introduced until around 1764, and by 1775 the population had increased to 851 whites, 233 'free coloured' and 6,381 African slaves. By 1790, this had increased to about 22,000, with whites accounting for 2,170 and "free coloureds" 1,636. This was followed by a decline, registered in the census of 1810, to a population of 17,485, with whites amounting to 1,200 and 'free coloured', 1,874. Not included in the census were a few Ameridian families living in the Choiseul area, traces of whom are still exiant.

The uniqueness of the St. Lucian character can be traced to a number of factors. The island was never a successful plantation colony, only enjoying two brief periods of relative prosperity around 1764 to 1771 and between 1790 and 1834. The first black people seemed to have arrived with the first French settlers from Martinique, who whenever possible brought their priest with them to administer to the spiritual welfare of both the French and the slaves. Because of this arrangement, slavery in St. Lucia was comparatively less severe than that of the other British colonies, the relationship between the master and slave being partially influenced by their common religion. From the beginning, there was a significant proportion of "free coloureds", which soon equalled that of the whites, and later surpassed them. Whereas the whites were chiefly plantation owners, the "free coloureds" engaged in trade and commerce.

Whenever the island changed hands between the British and the French, the slaves took the opportunity to escape into the impenetrable forest from where they were reluctant to emerge. Therefore, there was always a spirit of freedom among them which was intensified by the French Revolution of 1789.

The Revolution was hailed in St. Lucia by all the people, except the administration and officers of the army, and at a Legislative Assembley in March 1792, "all free men of whatever colour" were allowed to vote in the Parochial Assemblies, and were elegible for all posts, provided they possessed the necessary qualifications. That year, the Republic was proclaimed in France and an emissary of the government was sent to the French Antilles. He was not allowed to land in Martinique, but was welcomed in St. Lucia. It is reported that the emissary succeeded in getting the whites "free coloureds" and blacks to eat and dance together, while deploring the prejudices of the whites, when already two "coloureds" were members of the municipal Council of Castries and another two members of the Colonial Assembly. On February 4 1794 the abolition of slavery was proclaimed by the French in St. Lucia.

From then on, it became almost impossible to get people to accept the status of slavery, so that when the British recaptured the island later in 1794, their attempts to re-establish it were very unsuccessful, with many of the slaves taking to the forests. By June 1795, the St. Lucian freedom fighters, consisting of both slaves and French revolutionaries, defeated the British and forced them to evacuate the island. From that time onwards, the white population of St. Lucia has remained very small.

In 1796, the British again invaded St. Lucia and, in the greatest battle yet fought in the island, the St. Lucians were defeated at Mount Fortune. But it was not until the following year, after a number of military campaigns, that the 'Brigands', as they were called, were persuaded to enter into negotiations. Although slavery had been reintroduced by the British, this was a time when the call for emancipation was gaining force both in Europe and in the colonies. Large numbers had been granted their freedom before the final British occupation; and events developed into an inevitable march to emancipation and, ultimately independence.

The relative freedom which always existed under the French, the social and economic insecurity that characterised the island until the middle of the last century, the topography and tropical vegetation which allowed the runaway slaves to live clandestinely, the early introduction of French revolutionary philosophy, and the near absence of clergy, made the people spiritually independent, so that by 1973 they were able to introduce the concept of the Black Christ into the Roman Catholic Church in the island and elsewhere in the Caribbean.

This spirit of freedom has spared Saint Lucians the sense of inferiority that has accompanied the history of slavery, so that all the people have combined harmoniously into the modern St. Lucian, a social and cultural mix of African, European, Indian and Amerindian.

The language is an African-French dialect which is rich with expressions more reminiscent of Africa than France and clearly reflects the thinking of the slaves in their struggle to survive in the unequal world they lived in, for example "Ou pas cas suenir chuval pour officer", mean-

Above & opposite:
Wall murals at the Rainbow Hotel by St Omer

ing 'One does dont groom a horse for someone else to ride'.

The music seems to have been adopted from the French planters, with such names as Begin, Polka and Codrille. However, Conte seems to be African. Correspondingly, the national musical instruments are the drum, the quarto, the chac chac and the baha, although the lead instrument has always been the violin, which until recently was made of wild breadfruit wood.

The most enduring of local festivals, the La Rose Fete, and its corresponding rival, La Marguerite, may be considered as the root of local culture. These festivals are represented by two friendly societies, one with its emblem the Rose, and the other with its emblem the Marguerite. Some people attribute the names St. Rose and St. Marguerite, with the festivals, but it was only recently that the Church officially nominated St. Rose of Lima as the patron of the Rose festival.

The La Rose, which is the more popular, may be described as an attempt by the slaves to compensate for their lack of status by imitating the court of the masters with its own royal court of king, queen, princes, and princesses, and other court attendants, including the magistrate, nurse and policemen. It is a form of folk drama which is perfomed by many different groups in all parts of the island.

While the modern invasion into St. Lucian music, with the development of the electronic media, has seen considerable inroads in the culture of the people, the old culture is already beginning to reassert itself, with Reggae being composed in Patois.

The Roman Catholic Church, which came with the French settlers, has dominated the life of the people and has been adopted by the people of African descent to become part of their own culture. Even before most of the people had become literate, they were celebrating their masses in French, Latin and English, and with the new self-confidence arising from independence, Patois has been included in the litergy. A Creole mass was written by a celebrated St. Lucian musician. Recently Spanish was added. At Christmas, the traditional Midnight Mass becomes a great opera, in which the whole congregation joins in a chorus of some of the finest European and St. Lucian music.

All these factors have made the St. Lucian an independent person, famous for his or her natural courtesy and generosity, and whose philosophy is deeply rooted in Christianity, so that, since 1846, a visiting bishop stated that, "nowhere in the world was there a Catholic population more pious, not even in Ireland."

This fusion of races and cultures has created a people with a natural universal perspective that exemplifies the equality of people. St. Lucia has produced the only Nobel Laureates of the Westindies, Sir Arthur Lewis, in Economics, and Derek Walcott, in Literature. Complementing their achievements are the paintings of Dunstan St. Omer of the Black Christ, and a host of artists, musicians, dancers, poets and writers, of whom Garth St. Omer, the novelist, is considered one of the finest prose writers in the English language.

Religion

The St. Lucians are known as a deeply religious people and they practice and uphold a complex system of beliefs. These range from African ancestral religions, such as kele, to Christianity, best illustrated by the predominant Roman Catholic congregations, as well as by modern day Protestant religious denominations and other branches, of Christianity, including Jehovah's Witnesses, Redemption Ministries, and Seventh Day Adventists. For most of the population of the Christian faith, the day of worship is on Sunday, which has taken on a specific character, and is a major influence on individual and public life.

In almost every community, the church building is a notable landmark, so central to the lives of the community that it serves as a school, community meeting place, and a shelter in times of natural disasters. Some of the larger Roman Catholic Churches have for the past decade become home to the murals of St. Lucia's leading artist, Dunstan St. Omer.

Just over seventy per cent of the St. Lucian population are Roman Catholic, the religion which introduced Christianity to the island following the colonisation by Europeans in 1667. The Roman Catholic Church in Soufriere was the first to be built on the island, in about 1746, when priests from neighbouring Martinique visited regularly to minister to the colonists and their slaves. There are now 22 Roman Catholic parishes in St. Lucia, all with churches and resident priests. The cathedral in the capital city, which was built in 1897, has become a tourist attraction, mainly due to the local artisitic impressions of God, images which symbolise the coexistence of Christianity and local culture. There are over 25 religious festivals on the calendar of the followers of established Christian denominations, in addition to Roman Catholic, principally Anglican and Methodist. Among these, the feasts of St. Rose de Lima (August 30) St. Marguerite Alacoque (October 17), St. Cecelia (November 22) are actually national cultural festivals. And it is not surprising that many national public holidays, including Good Friday, Easter Monday, and Harvest Thanksgiving, Christmas and Boxing Day are all "religious" holidays.

The Anglican and Methodist churches, according to the 1990 census, account for 2.5 per cent and 0.5 per cent of the population respectively. There are Anglican churches strategically located in Soufriere and Riviere Doree (west coast), Vieux Fort (south), La Caye (east) and in the capital, Castries, in the north of the island. Of particularly historical significance is the Anglican Church and cemetery in Riviere Doree on the south west coast, built about 1790, where it is reported that a descendant of African nobility is buried.

Other denominations which have grown in following over the past thirty years include Baptists, Pentecostalists, Salvation Army, Jehovah's Witnesses, Evangelical Church of the West Indies, and Seventh Day Adventists. Perhaps the denomination which has grown the most over the past thirty years is the Seventh Day Adventist - from 1.8 per cent in 1960 to 6.5 per cent of the total poplation in 1990. In 1997, there were

Church of the Nativity of the Blessed Virgin Mary

e highest graveyard in St lucia
located at Morne Fortune

35 Seventh Day Adventist churches in all communities on the island, and an additional five congregations which are yet to build their own churches. This denomination is also well known for its introduction of religious crusades held under large tents, which in some cases were later replaced by permanent places of worship. There is still a growing number of "new" religious denominations and organisations, some of them with, as yet, no fixed place of worship. They use schools, community centres and other public buildings for meetings on any day of the week. In 1997, a total of 32 religious denominations and organisations were registered in St. Lucia, among them the Pentecostal Assemblies of the West Indies, National Spiriitual Assembly of the Bahai's, Wesleyan Holiness, Born Again Revival Tabernacle, The Native Full Gospel, Streams of Power, The Islamic Missionairies Guild, Christian Brethren, and Assemblies of Yaweh.

After 1970, the Rastafari faith spread across the island. The followers of this faith believe in the divinity of Emperor Haile Selassie of Ethiopia, that the black people are the chosen people referred to in the Bible who have been taken into captivity and scattered abroad, and that marijuana is a sacred herb to be used in communal worship and "the healing of the nation".

Ancestral religions of both African and Indian descent survive and are practiced to a declining extent in selected communities in the island. The most controversial of the African religious ceremonies is the kele.

The role of religion is evident in St Lucian society

This involves the sacrifice of an unblemished sheep, honouring of the gods of Ogun and Shango, thanksgiving and supplication.

Religious practice and belief in St. Lucia is popular and pervasive and affects every area of people's lives, often in complex and seemingly contradictory ways. Many citizens who are devout Christians or members of formal denominations are known to make daily decisions relating to medical care, nutrition, travel and finance based on their belief in traditional ancestral Gods. The average St. Lucian would have gone through his or her rights of passage from being christened in a church at birth, as a teenager receiving first communion in a church, being married in a religious ceremony and being interred at death at a ceremony involving a religious spiritual leader.

Religious organisations and denominations have played a very significant role in the development of education. Ever since colonial days the Anglican, Methodist and Roman Catholic denominations have operated schools. At present, the Roman Catholic Church manages jointly with the government of St. Lucia, 52 infant and primary schools. Two of the leading secondary schools in the island, St. Joseph's Convent (girls) and St. Mary's College (boys), are managed by the Roman Catholic Archdiocese of Castries. The Seventh Day Adventist (St Lucia) Ltd operates three elementary and one secondary school.

Notwithstanding the complexity of beliefs and practices, the current trend is for people in general to worship together in a physical location, irrespective of the denomination in which the individual was socialised. While television and radio evangelists are increasing in popularity, they have not made any significant impact on the social and cultural lives of the people, which involve going to Church on a Sunday, and, to a lesser extent, a Saturday.

The Black Madonna

In this highly personal and moving account, leading St. Lucian artist Dunstan St Omer, recalls how his painting of the black Christ exorcised the restless ghosts of slavery and ushered in an era of spiritual liberation to complement the advent of political independence.

I was brought up in a typical working class family. My father was a customs officer, my mother took care of all of us, and my maternal grandmother loved me. From them, I learnt of the absolute love of God, as a parent. I am a St. Lucian Roman Catholic.

I discovered art before I entered school, because it was what I could do best, and at school I was singled out for the best in that subject. In those days, it was called drawing. I was invited to the studio of the first accomplished artist in the island and painting became my career.

The artist inspired and never taught and so I started on my own odyssey which led me to the art of Europe and the world. I was self-taught.

While exploring European art, I encountered the cultural exclusion of my race. African art had not yet become universally popular, and modern art, that is starting from the Impressionists, was just beginning to replace the classical masters.

The icons in the churches and in all homes were European and my first vision of Christ, at five years, was the Sacred Heart on the wall coming alive.

It was sacrilege to think of God or Christ as black, and although I loved God all my life, somehow, we never got very close. He was too remote and powerful and as the absolute judge he was much closer to the French priests, who were white, the English Administrator, the Chief Justice, the Chief of Police, the rich planter or bank managers. One could not dare to mess around with him. The grains of sand on all the beaches in the world could not amount to one day in eternity and to court hell was idiotic.

I followed all the rules and the Church set the rules; the Church was the Christ. God dominated my life. We had nowhere else to go, no other one to appeal to, for slavery was still with us and our colonial masters were our masters because God had ordained it so. We fell into our allocated places. It was God's Will. Life went on; but the world was changing.

The imperialists got into a struggle with the facists. Haile Selassie had evoked the judgement of God and History, and the Pope had blessed the Italian army on their way to Ethiopia. But the black man always had a secret God, he was ignorant and so that God did not conform to theology. He was the ultimate father, protector and benefactor. He was the only one to call on to judge against the enemy and that was not the devil.

The war ended, the enemy was either scattered or in confusion and dogmas and certainties became casualties. The God of the slaves was alive.

When I was approached in 1973 to do a painting on the main altar of a new church, in a rural district, as the priest did not have enough

The Black Madonna in the Church of the Holy Family

money to import the appropriate statue, at last I realised the opportunity to accomplish my greatest dream, to create an altarpiece that would reflect the new faith.

All the priest could afford was EC $300, the equivalent of US $100, but the more than 800 sq. ft. of the wall would override every mortal consideration.

It was a new church, a rural church. Easter was approaching and the priest wanted to dedicate the church on Easter Sunday. I had only one week to do it. I took a week's leave and finished it in time.

It 's the Church of the Holy Family, and Vatican II had given me the freedom to express my religion according to my conscience, and so I took the opportunity to do the crowning achievement of my life. If I am black, and if the people of St. Lucia are black, and if God is their father, then in all decency, God must be black, and since his Son conveniently left no evidence of his race, then Christ could be black.

Christ had to be black for a people just emerging from slavery and taking the first steps towards independence. Their God, the highest ideal of their race, must be black. To perpetuate the white God would negate the act of independence and establish a state of perpetual slavery to the Spirit of the former masters. Already, independence was moving the minds of the people in search of other Gods, in search of new Saviours, so I had to restore to them their former dignity.

As a Christian, I believe that the only way that my people could earn their freedom, being poor, downtrodden and not technically advanced, would be to be spiritually dominant. It is their spirit from Africa and Roman Catholicism that has sustained them through the dark years, never allowing them to be completely subjugated. It is the accommodation of their God with Christianity that has given them access to the two worlds of their own and that of the former masters; and it is through that spirit that they will survive and triumph.

The mural attempts to achieve their liberation, first by translating the Old World Christianity, identifiable with the former masters, into the new religion of life. It attempts to dispel the dark shadows of hell and replace them with the light of the sun dominated by prismatic colours with the darkest shadows a blue green that contrasts with the fertile lemon greens and veridian.

The atmosphere is one of joy, thanking God for the gift of life, with

The Black Madonna in the Church of the Holy Family. **Artist D St. Omer**

Church mural:
Artist D St Omer

no time to contemplate the horrors of Hell, but experiencing the joy of love that is life itself. The old European images give way to that of the local people, easily recognisable to everyone. It is the first time that black people earned citizenship of heaven. On the altar one will find fishermen, farmers, dancers, musicians, tradesman, a priest and an artist.

The painting has stepped down from heaven and is now occupying the earth. It is a painting of incarnation - God visible in man in his black children. And they rejoice at the union. The central figures are the Holy Family, from the heart of which emanates the church, along with the valley and the surrounding country.

The figures of Mary, the Christ child, and Joseph are prismatic and semi-abstract, as if to take the mortal and elevate it to the divine. The traditional white rays emanating from the Blessed Sacrament are subtly substituted for black in a complete reversal of the psychology of white being good and black bad, and the glowing black cape of St. Joseph has removed forever the use of black as a shadow, establishing it as a primary colour.

Instead of harps and trumpets, the herald is a fisherman blowing his conch shell, a musician with his chac-chac, and the inevitable African drum beating the rhythm - the heart beat of the children of Africa.

The landscape has altered from the landscape of Tuscany, giving place to the jungle greens of the tropics which enroach even to the surface of the painting, making it all encompassing, the shallow perspective of modern painting combines with the remote distance of the classics, which aspire to merge with heaven.

The mural is modern renaissance. Renaissance because of the contemporariness of the subjects, 16th century Italian, 20th century St. Lucian. The donor is represented by the priest holding up the model of the church, the builder assisting the priest, and the artist recording his presence. He is a subject in his work, and his work is his subject.

The Black Madonna:
Artist D St Omer

This church mural was the first of the new Covenant, and many more of the Black Christ followed, at Fond St. Jacques, Monchy, Desruisseaux, the seminary in Trinidad, the Church of St Michael in Martinque, the Cathedral of the Immaculate Conception, and even ventured into the realm of the antiquity, with Christ as Prometheus on the wall of the University Centre.

Appropriately, the church was dedicated on Easter Sunday 1973, and the congregation sang, "This is the day the Lord hath made; Let us rejoice and be glad." The Easter miracle was achieved; the people had been rescued from the bondage of history and entered into the new life of freedom with Indpendence in 1979; followed by the achievement of two of its sons, Sir Arthur Lewis gaining the Nobel Prize for Economics, and Derek Walcott, the Nobel Prize for Literature. The people had arrived.

Carnival

Carnival has, it seems, from time immemorial, been celebrated in February/March to coincide with the beginning of the Catholic Lenten season.

What is Carnival, how did it come about and from where? Although there are many schools of thought on these questions, it is widely accepted that Carnival is a cultural tradition with roots in Europe and Africa.

The origins of the St. Lucia Carnival date to the period when the French planters established their settlements and Shrovetide celebrations were the order of the day. By the beginning of the 19th century the celebrations took the form of friends getting together dressed as skeletons or devils, dancing and parading in the streets, sugar cane cutters dressed in rags and covered with black paint singing and dancing their own songs came to the main town centres, along with parading groups of costumed children. Meanwhile, masked private parties were held by the elite with entertainment provided by singers and dancers from the poorer sections of society.

As in Trinidad and other islands, Carnival is said to have become organised after World War II. The St. Lucia Red Cross seem to have been the first to organise a float and costume competition in George V Park, with prizes donated by local merchants. However in 1947, fifteen persons, dressed in rags produced a small Trinidad-style Carnival when they paraded the streets to the rhythms of bottles and pieces of steel on Shrove Monday night. The following day, Shrove Tuesday, others hurriedly put costumes together to parade the streets. By the following year, these days were declared holidays, and steelbands, calypso competitions and costume bands all featured in the 1947 Carnival celebrations.

European religious connotations explain why Carnival has always been associated with the pre-Lenten season. Carnival also expresses African belief systems, centred around the worship of nature in a symbolic form.

Carnival, is, therefore, more than just a masked celebration which has come down to us through the ages. As a festive gathering, according to one writer, "it provides the only occasion during the year when all members of the society, no matter what their class affiliation or social position, come together and interact as a whole community."

Carnival, besides being a historic tradition is also an economic enterprise, an arts festival and a celebration of social equality. According to Father Patrick Anthony: "Carnival cuts right across the social stratification of the society, breaking down barriers of race, class, and, in some cases, even religion. In carnival, people freely unite in a national surge of abandoned joy and apocryphal celebration. Here life is art, and art is history."

Other cultural traditions are also associated with Carnival. These include the Terre Bois Bois, which was found in Choiseul, with the disposal of an effigy representing the symbol of carnival. The origins of this tradition seem to have been in the 1940s.

Carnival - a unique expression of national life

St. Lucian Carnival has been no stranger to controversy over the years. In 1948, for example, there was a row in the press after the then Principal of St. Mary's College chastised some of the students for participating in carnival.

In 1954, categories for bands were established. This was followed by controversy in 1955, with two queen shows held by rival committees, one of whom, the Miss Ebony Queen Show Committee, felt that black women were not included in the choice for Carnival Queen contestants.

In 1967, there were new competition categories, including the King and Queen of the Bands Show.

In 1970 the Carnival Development Committee was established and in 1973 it took control of all areas of Carnival. However, controversy erupted again in the 1970s when the poor economic situation did not allow for much investment in Carnival and costuming, and there were complaints that the organisation was too last minute.

From the 1970s the organised activities for Carnival have been the King and Queen of the Bands show, costumed bands parade, Jour Ouvert competition, steelband competition and the calypso show. The organisation, disorganisation and reorganisation of Carnival have continued through the years.

Carnival is also a means of documenting popular history. In St. Lucia there are more calypsos than books, more costumes than paintings, more calypsonians than writers.

Festivals

FLOWER FESTIVALS

The virulent red of the rose, still speaks to many a St. Lucian. So does the marguerite flower. Between them they spin a tale of more than two centuries. Despite imperialism of all shades, domination and cultural invasion, the twin flower festivals of La Rose and Marguerite persist, a testament to a people's resilience.

The precise origins of the La Rose, and the La Marguerite flower festivals are unknown. As one writer has asserted: "The history of the Antilles is involved in such total obscurity in all that concerns the black population that it would be impossible at the present time to trace the origins of the Roses and Marguerites." However, another writer adds that "La Rose and its rival society, La Marguerite, were born in St. Lucia during slavery." The first known references date from 1769.

The Roses and the Marguerites are really floral societies into which some members of the St. Lucian community divide themselves. Although they are now primarily singing associations, there was a time when they formed "important segments of the island's social structure" and most persons in the community were somehow affiliated to one or other of the groups.

The structure of these two societies would seem to indicate something of their function within colonial society. Both are hierarchically organised, with a king and a queen as head of each society and other dignitaries patterned upon the socio-economic structure of colonial society. Thus, after the king and queen come princes and princesses, and "a number of other pseudo-legal, military and professional personnel including judges, policemen, soldiers and nurses". The element of role performance or masquerading is evident from this internal structure. All of the roles performed during the festival, kings, queens, doctors, lawyers, etc. are roles far beyond the real aspirations of the mass of people in earlier times. This relates to the carnival ethos that is so much a part of Caribbean society. At carnival time whole sections of the population will put on 'masks' and for two days will assume roles they would never be able to play in real life.

rchard La Rose group - King deste receives trophy

Although the role performance in the flower society becomes most evident during the festival period, they are more permanent than the 'mass' played at carnival time. If one plays a king or a queen in a band for carnival, then one assumes the role only during the days of revelry. Not so with La Rose and La Marguerite. One can be a king or a queen for several years, with influence from these roles extending beyond the contours of the festivals into actual life.

La Marguerite Flower Festival Kings and Queens

THE FESTIVALS

Preparations for the respective La Rose and La Marguerite festivals begin several months before the actual feast days, August for the "Roses" and October for the "Marguerites". Each group would rent a hall (if it does not own one) and on weekends hold 'seances'. These consist of all night singing and dancing sessions where drinks are sold and various games played. Most of the groups' funds are raised in this manner.

The central figure at the seance is the "shatwel", or leadsinger, who sustains the spirit and tenor of the evening's entertainment. Most groups have one outstanding or leading "shatwel", although there may be two or three others in a group. The shatwels are usually female, but there are sometimes a number of male ones.

On the actual day of the festival, all members of the society, dressed in costumes of their respective roles, march to church for the service which preceeds their parade through the streets, before returning to the hall for the "Grande Fete".

MUSIC

There are many songs and dances associated with La Rose and La Marguerite. There is more variation and spontaneity at 'Seances' than at the Grande Fete, when the significance of the occasion demands more discipline.

The shatwel is the central figure in the musical tradition of the twin festivals. She (or he) leads the song, with the other members of the group acting as chorus in a call-and-response pattern. Instrumentation includes any combination of violin, banjo, quatro, guitar, shak-shak, baha and drums.

The song of the shatwell is called Belair. Some Belairs are vibrant and boisterous, galvanising shatwel and chorus into vigorous dancing, while others are of a plaintive and melancholy character, the quavering, piercing tones, and the careful enunciation suggesting the singing style of French 'chanteuses', while the chorus is sung in the manner of Sankey' hymns. Most are sung in Patois, St. Lucian French Creole, although there are many new compositions in English..

La Rose and La Marguerite Belairs may be divided into four types: those which laud the beauty and power of the rose, the society and its members, particularly the king and queen; those which sing likewise of the marguerite; those which poke fun at the Roses; and those which poke fun at the Marguerites. The art of outwitting, abusing or teasing (mepwi) members of the rival society is the favourite subject of the Belairs. Thanks to the musical creativity of Charles Cadet, who prepared the music for Roderick Walcott's two plays on the flower festivals, **The Banjo Man** and **Chanson Marianne**; as well as to the work of *Joyce Auguste and Hewanorra Voices,* a number of La Rose and La Marguerite songs are well known and quite popular in the wider St. Lucian society. However, the gruelling task of preservation and popularisation of the La Rose and La Marguerite songs, against all odds, has fallen on the backs of the myriad shatwels of extraordinary talent all over the island. Without their passionate love and dogged commitment, these traditions would have perished.

The La Rose mural by the artist Dunstan St. Omer, at the Church of St. Rose de Lima, Monchy, is graphic evidence of how radically attitudes have changed towards the flower festivals. Here, in the 1970s being depicted in a Catholic Church, with the full authority and support of the local Bishop, a tradition which had once been condemned by the same Church. At the Church, which is dedicated to St. Rose de Lima, the patron saint of the La Rose flower society, St. Omer paints a mural on the La Rose festival.

Against the background of infinite petals the artist portrays all the traditional roles associated with the Grande Fete: king, princes, princesses, soldiers, nurses, shatwel, musicians, etc. The mural is divided into two sections, one portraying the 'ascetic spirit'; the saint, the first communion child, the nurse, the policeman and other social workers, and the other portraying the Dionysian ethos of the celebrations, the revellers and merrymakers. The infant Jesus gives a crown of roses to either side, indicating, according to the artist, the validity of both lifestyles.

Creole Mother

Mothers, mothers, mothers!
Young as you might have been
When you conceived in that Moment Serene-
This Infant, this Child, now a Teen
To listen, love,
To embrace, cuddle, to touch-
When growing pains confuse
And distressing signals conflict
This inward searching:
O what is right?
What must I do?
Her dating on impulse
That wild enjoyment
The fun turned sorrow
When pregnancy surfaces
On the morrow!
Her pain increased by your anger.
Your contempt and disdain,
Her lover's abandonment
Sharpened by your refrain
"GET OUT", you shout,
"You've made me so ashamed
I've spent so much on you
But you took a lout!"
Doors shut in her face, so
Belly inflated
Self esteem deflated
Tearfully on the road-
Can she bear her new load
Alone, no love, no care?
Choices narrowed by fear
As in desperation she seeks
The Meek solace that masquerades as peace
In the beckoning vision
Of an overdose
Those throbes to still
or shall it be
Another lout whose hypocrisy
Offers a love that can never be
Aught but another misery.

Tammy Wynette

Saint Lucia Jazz Festival

Neal McCoy

St. Lucia's lively annual Jazz Festival attracts many famous names from home and abroad. Luther Francois and Gregory Emmanuel are two of the best known local names with an international reputation.

The Festival has been a huge success since in inception in 1992, with visitors to the 1996 event reaching an all-time high of 20,000.

At the launch of the 1997 Festival, Desmond Skeete, Chairman of the St. Lucia Tourist Board said: "For this year's line-up we have tried to broaden the variety of jazz offered at the festival, ranging from traditional jazz bands to acid jazz. The festival attracts a wide range of visitors from true jazz afficionados to holidaymakers who come to enjoy the party atmosphere of the festival, and our aim is to cater for all tastes." The main sponsors of the Festival include Cable & Wireless, BET, American Airlines/Eagle, the St. Lucia Tourist Board and the St. Lucia Hotel & Tourism Association.

The Festival is a four-day event, not only acclaimed for the splendour of its music, but also for the grandeur of the settings of some of the jazz concerts. One of them is the picturesque Pigeon Island, where the artists perform among the ruins of an ancient fort, against an ocean backdrop. Smaller, more intimate performances are held in the evenings at selected club venues and hotels.

Saint Lucia Country Festival

Don Williams

An exciting new festival will take place on Pigeon Island for the first time in December 1997 - the Saint Lucia Country Festival. The two-day event attracted international Country and Western superstars Tammy Wynette and Don Williams, to top the bill with the Charlie Daniels Band and a host of top entertainers and singer/songwriters.

Judging from the immense success of running the Saint Lucia Jazz Festival - which attracts huge audiences - the organizers, the Saint Lucia Tourist Board, are confident that the Country Festival will grow in popularity year by year. Country music is very popular in the Caribbean and many radio stations feature Country and Western shows. A recent development in the Caribbean scene has been the merging of reggae and country music. Check out this exciting musical extravaganza.

The sponsors of the Saint Lucia Country Festival are American Airlines, AA, Saint Lucia Tourist Board, SLTB and the Saint Lucia Hotel and Tourist Authority, SLHTA. For details contact the Tel: (758) 452 4094. Fax: (758) 453 1121

St Lucia Jazz Festival: *The festival has been an overwhelming success since its inception in 1992, with visitors to the event reaching 20,000.*

Artists

VINCENT JOSEPH EUDOVIC

WOOD CARVER

Born at Babonneau on April 15 1942, Vincent Joseph Eudovic started sculpturing at a very young age and competed in his first exhibition, when he was 12 years of age. His piece of sculpture, named 'ALIBARA' won first prize at this exhibition. The prize was fifteen dollars.

From then on Eudovic was set in his vocation and at the end of his schooling, he migrated to Trinidad. There he became a protégé of Ricardo Vincenté and continued his studies in sculpturing for a period of ten years.

During this time he competed at various exhibitions and won a number of prizes.

After returning to St. Lucia, Eudovic was employed by the Government to teach his art to others, but he felt he still had more to learn himself so he applied for a UN scholarship, hoping to travel to some country where he could perfect his skills. The United Nations proposed Nigeria. The seven months he spent there were the greatest experience in his life.

In Nigeria, Eudovic discovered many extraordinary artists who taught and influenced him a great deal. He first studied monumental sculpture with artists who worked on gigantic pieces almost twenty feet high. After he was initiated into the traditional art of the Yoruba people, he studied the artistic symbols and their highly elaborate tradition of sculpturing. He also studied modern art.

When Eudovic returned to St. Lucia, he continued to work with the government, teaching many young men the art of sculpturing. He also held workshops around the Caribbean. He gradually moved on to form his own Gallery and workshop, which is to be found at Goodlands, Castries.

Eudovic uses local woods for his abstract carvings, and, since no two roots are the same, every single sculpture is unique.

The main wood he uses is Laurier Canelle, which is now extinct. However, the old stumps and uncovered roots can usually be found deep in the forest. Laurier Canelle has a remarkable beauty which one can see after a sculpture has been completed. It is also highly durable. Other woods he uses are Mahogany, Teak, Laurier Mabouey and red and white Cedar.

Eudovic has participated in many exhibitions over the years, including the Caribbean first wood carving exhibition held in Guadeloupe in 1975, where he won the Golden Medal Award for Best Caribbean Wood Sculptor.

Life size sculptures at Anse Chastanet Resort by Vincent Joseph Eudovic

CEDRIC GEORGE

ARTIST

Cedric George, one of St. Lucia's leading artists, was born in the capital, Castries. He studied Art at the Edna Manley School of Art in Jamaica between 1985-1988.

Cedric George's theme and subjects are quite broad but he is inspired, primarily, by the beauty and sensitivity of his country's landscapes, capturing the spirituality and character of his subjects with light, colour mode and depth. One is struck, too, by the religious commitment in his paintings, but he is not shy of innovative ideas, and is at times controversial. Some of his innovative forms of painting involve the creation of parallel lines, which add texture and space to illustrate nature's surfaces and surroundings which he calls 'line painting'.

Cedric George has exhibited his works both at home and abroad and he features in many permanent collections.

LLEWELLYN XAVIER

Environmentally conscious Artist

Life size sculptures at Anse Chastanet Resort by Vincent Joseph Eudovic

Llewellyn Xavier is St. Lucia's most innovative and internationally respected artist. He was born in 1945 in the coastal village of Choiseul and came from a large family of humble means. An agricultural apprentice, he left for Barbados in 1961 for further training. That was the end of his nine to five life. A Barbadian friend forgot a box of watercolours at his house one day and Xavier "started fooling around with a brush and things just seemed to appear." His hidden genius was revealed, and after the sell-out success of his first exhibition, it was impossible to talk about art in Barbados without including his name.

He moved to England in 1968 where he created Mail Art, a new and original concept of modern art. Its immense popularity and critical acclaim made him instantly famous. In this new form, Xavier spoke out against racial injustice. He wrapped a piece of art on the outside of a cardboard tube and sent it to George Jackson, the imprisoned African-American revolutionary. The piece accumulated prison visas and postmarks as well as Jackson's comments. In a similar fashion, the work acquired contributions from John Lennon, Yoko Ono, Jean Genet and James Baldwin. The George Jackson (Soledad Brothers) series was first shown in London at the D.M. Gallery.

Since 1971, Xavier's work has been exhibited in such prestigious galleries as the Museum of Modern Art, the Saratoga Gallery in New York, the Art Gallery of Ontario, Nova Scotia College of Art and Design, and Spedale Degli Innocenti in Italy. Among others, his one man shows have graced Oxford University, Sussex University, Whitechapel Art Gallery, Mazelow Gallery in Toronto, the Afro/American Historical Museum, Howard University, Gallery III in Montreal, and the Barbados Museum. His work is in permanent collections at the Museum of Modern Art, the Art Gallery of Ontario, Oxford University, Nova Scotia College of Art and Design, the Archdiocese of Halifax, the Barbados Museum, and the Metropolitan Museum of Art.

His position in the art world was well established, but at the age of 34, Xavier began to doubt his ability. He entered the School of the Museum of Fine Art in Boston, Massachusetts as a student. During this time he became aware of a growing spiritual awakening, and he spent periods in monasteries in the United States and Israel. In 1985 he sold all his possessions and became a monk at a Benedictine monastery in Montreal. But the spiritual satisfaction he was seeking never materialised and he left to return to his art.

He married Christina in 1987 and returned to St. Lucia. He was horrified at the amount of environmental damage he saw at home and he became a founding member of the St. Lucia Environmental Development and Awareness Council (SLEDAC). "Other than the souls of men, I think the environment is unquestionably the most important problem facing mankind today. If we permit our unique environment to be destroyed, then we invite our own destruction," says Xavier. He wanted to express his concern in art. He took Mail Art one step further and created a masterwork, Global Council for Restoration of the Earth's Environment. The work is made from recycled materials, incorporating 18th and 19th century prints of birds, fish, animals, and plants.

St Lucian National Costumes

Southcoast: *a view from the Moule-a-Chique lighthouse.*

Cape Moule-a-Chique Lighthouse *at Vieux Fort. The second highest Lighthouse in the world.*

Castries Harbour

Sulphur Springs: *Drive in volcano, Soufriere*

Reduit Beach

Anse la Raye

Anse-la Raye

Anse la Raye has always been a fishing village and if you examine its name it is easy to see why. When the early French settlers arrived in Saint Lucia, Anse la Raye was one of the first areas they visited. As they sailed into the bay they may have stopped to admire the beautiful, forested hills behind it. They would have seen the two large rivers that flowed from them down to the sea. Perhaps they looked over the side of the boat and saw the shoals of fish swimming in the clear water.

There were many different kinds of fish. Among them were some strange flat fish that flapped around on the sandy bottom. They too were sandy in colour, with strong whip-like tails. Their two eyes were set close together in the top of their flat heads. In English, they were called 'skates' but to the Frenchmen, they were known as 'raie'. This may be why the place was called Anse de la Raie - the Bay of Skates. The two rivers got their names from the bay. They were called Petit Riviere de Anse de la Raie and Grand Riviere de Anse de la Raie. The spelling of these names changed depending on who was doing the writing! On the map drawn by Bellin in 1758 the village is called Ance de la Raye.

The church records show there were 107 estates in the Anse la Raye district in 1775. That is more than in any other part of the island. It sounds a lot but in those days Saint Lucia was divided into only nine districts or quarters. The quarter of Anse la Raye stretched from the Roseau River all the way to Canaries and far back into the rainforest.

During the years of the French Revolution, Anse la Raye, like all the other places in Saint Lucia, was given a new name. It was Egalite. In 1795, there were fierce fights between the French and the English for possession of the island. The slaves had been told they were free. Many of them refused to go back to the plantations. They plundered the estates, killed the planters and their families and set fire to the buildings. Like Dennery, Micoud, Laborie and Choiseul, Anse la Raye was ransacked and burned. Most of the village records and documents went up in flames. Only the walls of the church were left standing.

FISHING AND FARMING

Eventually the wars came to an end and slavery was abolished. People still worked on the land but now they could choose where they worked and for whom. The seas around Saint Lucia were full of fish and some men left the land to become fishermen. They made canoes from the trunks of the gommier trees that grew in the forest. They used the tough vines that hung from their branches to make fishpots.

Today, fishermen have engines instead of sails and their fishpots are often made of wire mesh. But, their boats still come back loaded with jackfish, flying fish, kingfish, bonito, barracuda, tuna, snapper and sometimes even a shark.

Fresh local fish for tourist mer

In deep water, fishermen use nets and lines armed with strong hooks baited with small fish. Closer to shore they use fishpots or a net called a seine. Some fishermen stay on the beach holding fast to one end of the seine while others, in the boat, move slowly away from shore. Gradually, the rest of the net is let out. When the boat reaches the middle of the bay they will turn in a circle and head back.

The net hangs down in the water like an enormous curtain. It is held upright by floats that bob in a wide curve on top of the waves. As the canoe returns to shore, the men leap out still holding the other end of the net. Now everyone helps to pull in the net with the fish trapped inside it. As the circle made by the net gets smaller the water starts to

130

splash and heave as if it is boiling. Fish leap all about as they struggle to escape. When the catch is finally brought ashore everyone who has helped will get a share.

There are many estates around Anse la Raye. Some of the largest are Venus, Invergoil, Chapine and Anse Galet. In the old days they produced sugar, cotton, copra, cocoa and coffee for export. Now very little is grown. At Invergoil, the old mill is being rebuilt to give tourists a glimpse of what life on the plantation was like. There were no buses or pickups then and the estate roads were not much more than muddy tracks. Produce was loaded onto wooden carts pulled by two strong bulls, then trundled down to the jetty. Here it was put aboard a large canoe called a mail boat with a captain and three men to pull on the oars. These large canoes carried passengers and goods regularly from the villages on the coast to the town of Castries.

About a hundred years ago, a Soufriere family called Charlery went to live in Anse la Raye with their little daughter, Veronica who grew up in the village. She worked as a labourer on the land and married a man called Joseph. They had two children.

THE LEAN YEARS

Because jobs were becoming more and more scarce, many men left the village to look for work. In 1948, they went to Curacao to work in the oil industry. From 1956 to 1960 some took off by boat for England. Others went to the Virgin Islands or to the US - anywhere where they could find work. Sometimes they sent money back to the families they had left behind. Veronica's only son had gone away long before this. Like many other Saint Lucians, he went to Cayenne to look for a better life. He never returned.

The road to Castries was narrow and winding and the journey by bus was hot and uncomfortable. For a while there were boats, like the 'Bernadine', the 'George' and the 'Jewel'. They left town soon after midday, like the buses, to make their trip back down the coast. Men who found work in the city had to stay there. Sometimes they went back to the village at weekends or for holidays. The villagers were depressed. People driving through would see them sitting outside their houses. They had nothing better to do than watch the tourists as they drove by on their way to Soufriere. The buses and cars seldom stopped. They missed the beach with its flamboyant trees and the fishing nets drying in the sun. No-one had bothered to tell them it was worth a visit.

They didn't know either that just behind the village was some of the most beautiful scenery on the island. Everyone knew about the Pitons and the Sulphur Springs and that's where they were going!

In time, bananas became the island's biggest export crop. Demand for other crops fell and so many estates cleared away everything else to

ditional truck transportation

131

plant bananas instead. The bananas though were not so easy to handle. They needed good roads or they very quickly got damaged and were not fit to sell. The roads leading to the estates around Anse la Raye were still poor. It didn't make sense even to gather what little fruit the estates were still producing. Dishonest people took advantage of this. They stole the produce to sell for their own profit. They went into the forest with chainsaws and devastated the land. They even cut valuable cedar and laurier trees just to turn them into charcoal.

There were other things to worry about as well. Very few houses in the village had proper toilets. The people managed as best they could, but their children were often sick. Many of them died. When doctors conducted a survey to see what was wrong they found the children were suffering from worms and other parasites. This was because of the poor sanitation. Something had to be done, but what?

SPOTLIGHT ON ANSE LA RAYE

The first thing that happened was that Save The Children Foundation picked Anse la Raye as the site for a day care centre for children. They provided the money. Government helped with land and materials and the people of the village donated their labour. The centre was officially opened in 1982. Next to it is the Anthonian Home for the Poor, where the old and homeless people of the village live. A committee was formed to co-ordinate all these activities and raise funds. This attracted even more attention to Anse la Raye.

Then, in 1982, the village was chosen as the location for a large workshop in appropriate technology. Appropriate technology means using the tool or method that is most appropriate for what you want to do. Perhaps you live in a place close to a river but far away from the water mains. Then it is more appropriate for you to use river water for your garden than to pay the high price of bringing in piped water. If you find a cheap and easy way to bring water from the river to your garden, then you are using appropriate technology.

The workshop was attended by people from all over the Caribbean. They demonstrated different ways of using the sun, wind and water for energy. They built clay stoves in peoples' back yards. They made water tanks using bamboo and cement. A large solar panel was put on the roof of the Multi-Purpose Centre to provide hot water. At Au Tabor, on the road just before the last steep hill into the village, a windmill was put up. It gave enough electricity to power lights and a television in the house beside it.

For a whole week the village bustled with activity. All sorts of projects were going on. People came from all over the island to watch and learn. There was even a film made of the workshop that was shown on local television.

In 1983, Anse la Raye took part in the Plus Belle Village annual competition and came first. But in spite of all that was happening, jobs

Family house in Anse la Raye

Anse la Raye fishing village

were still hard to find. A small factory opened that packed spices and curry powder. Some of the women found work there, but the men still had to look outside of the village. The tourists were still driving to Soufriere, straight on through the village. They seldom stopped.

Veronica Joseph heard about it all from other people. She no longer left her small wooden house behind the main street. She was now 102, and was cared for by her daughter who was herself growing old.

LOOKING AHEAD

Anse la Raye Waterfall

The villagers of Anse la Raye have worked hard as a community to improve their surroundings, but sanitation is still a problem. The village is low-lying with water on all sides. In most places the ground is too marshy to dig deep enough to put in a septic tank. After heavy rains, or when the sea is higher than usual, the rivers overflow. Then the drains fill up and the playing field becomes a sheet of water. During the ATECH '82 workshop, sanitation engineers from Jamaica, Antigua and Mexico wrote a report describing a sewage system they thought would work. Other engineers later came from Canada to do a more complete survey and to design the system. As with most things, the problem is money.

Not all the buses and taxis clatter straight on over the red, iron bridge to Soufriere. Every now and again, one will stop and the passengers will get out and stroll around. Some even go through the village, past the new Hess School with its large playground into the countryside beyond. The estates are neglected, and the cocoa and citrus trees are covered with weeds, but it is still beautiful. A thick carpet of sweet-smelling ginger lilies covers the ground. Where the river splashes down over the flat rocks sandpipers wade on stilt legs looking for food. Further down, among the reeds are families of waterfowl. Their feathers are black and glossy and the red patches on their beaks bob up and down as they feed.

Portrait by Cedric George

Now, behind the Multi-Purpose Centre there are two factories: one packaging spices, the other making bleach for the local market. During National Day celebrations in 1985, Veronica Joseph, dressed in her best clothes, was brought from her house to sit in the place of honour. She was 103 years old. When the cornerstone for the new church was blessed in 1907, she was already 25 years of age, married, with children.

There are motor cars now that were not there when she was young and many new buildings, but there is a lot that has not changed. The village had been her home for a hundred years. If it is to be a good home for the children growing up there today, change must come. Better sanitation, better health, more jobs, not in the next hundred years, but now.

Babonneau

*Flower festival scene.
by D St Omer*

THE PLACE

Our tour of Saint Lucia has taken us right around the island, from Gros Islet in the North to Vieux Fort in the South. The places we have visited all have one thing in common, they are on the coast. Now, for a change, we are going to travel inland to visit the district of Babonneau.

On the map, Babonneau is roughly three miles from Castries. That, of course, is as the crow flies. If you travel by road, it is much further. The Atlantic is four miles to the East. The Caribbean is just over four miles to the West. Seven and a half miles to the North is the channel that separates Saint Lucia from Martinique. If you draw a line across the map of Saint Lucia from Coubaril Point to the old air strip on Grande Anse, it will pass through the centre of Babonneau.

What does the name Babonneau mean? Some people believe the place was named after a family who lived in the area and were called Babonneau. Others think that the name tells us something about the place. They say that it comes from the French words, barre-bonne-eau. In English this would mean 'the ridge where there is good water'. Look carefully at the map and you will see why this might be true. Many rivers begin in this area. Some of them join the Marquis River which comes from the rainforest above Forestiere. Others flow into the Union and Grande Riviere Rivers.

Further south is the towering cloud covered mountain, la Sorciere. The rainfall here is very high. It is one of the island's most important water catchment areas. From the pumping station at Talvern, water is piped to Hill 20 just south of Cabiche. Most of the water for Castries and Babonneau is collected and treated here to make it safe to use.

In the past, Babonneau had a good water supply from its many deep, clear rivers. These rivers, like all the other rivers in the island, are fed by the rain that falls on the rainforest. The rainforest above Babonneau is disappearing fast. More and more land is still being cleared for cultivation. Unless the forest is protected, the rivers will dry up.

St Lucia's mountains ensure adequate annual rainfall

THE HISTORY

The people of Babonneau are of African, Indian and European descent. Some of their ancestors were slaves, brought here against their will. Others were indentured labourers from India who had to work on the estates to pay back their passage money. In the days of the early French settlers, Joseph Gaspard Tascher de la Pagerie had a small estate at Morne Paix Bouche in the area of Babonneau. In 1763, his wife gave birth to a daughter, Marie Joseph Rose, whose birth was later registered in Martinique. Yeyette, as she was called, married Napoleon Bonaparte, the great French General. He changed her name to Josephine and made her Empress of France.

Many of the old houses and estate buildings of this period were destroyed at the time of the French Revolution. Others were burned afterwards during the Brigands War which followed. On Marquis Estate you can still see the ruins of a church, a sugar mill and the home of one of the former Governors of Saint Lucia.

In more recent times, men like Simeon Joseph and Peter Joseph MBE have made their mark. Both have become well known for the work they have done in the Babonneau district. Mr Simeon Joseph, was a

Cable & Wireless provide 'state-of-the-art' service technology

farmer and a carpenter. He helped to organise the Friendly Societies and to get the people of Babonneau their own church. The cornerstone of the Catholic Church at Babonneau was finally laid down in 1947. It is used by people from the entire Babonneau area. Mr. Joseph kept alive some of the ceremonies like the *kele* that were brought over with the slaves from Africa. Now that he is dead some of the links with the people's African ancestors may be lost forever.

The other Mr. Joseph came to live in Babonneau in 1940, when he became Principal of the Babonneau Combined School. He held that post for over twenty years. Much of the credit for Babonneau's many voluntary organisations goes to him. Mr Peter Joseph MBE helped to organise a farmers' cooperative. He encouraged the young people of Babonneau to become Scouts and Guides. When he retired his place was taken by Mr. Barthelmy Gaspard, one of his own pupils, born and raised in Babonneau. Dr. Michael Louis, Saint Lucia's Chief Education Officer, is another past pupil of the Babonneau School.

In 1962, Cable and Wireless built a station on the hill at Monier. It receives and sends out signals and is Saint Lucia's telephone and telex link with the rest of the world. Radio St. Lucia also has a transmitting station at Babonneau.

THE COMMUNITIES

The people of Babonneau live in many small communities scattered over a wide area. Babonneau proper, Boguis, Laguerre, Chassin, Fond Assor, Paix Bouche, Marquis, Balata, Garrand, Cabiche, Cacao, Plateau, Ti Morne and Desbarras, are all Babonneau communities.

The small Catholic school that was built at Marquis in 1895, was the first in the Babonneau district. Later, schools were built at Paix Bouche and at Fond Babonneau. These two schools were moved to Babonneau proper in 1932. One of these old wooden buildings is still in use as the Infants School. Because it was no longer big enough, a new building was added. The other wooden building was replaced in 1952 when the Primary School was built.

La Gare, Bogius, Fond Assor, Balata and Desbarras all have their own schools. Only Babonneau proper has a separate Principal for the Infants and Primary schools.

At one time, many people from the Babonneau district worked on the Marquis Estate. This estate was once one of the largest and best in Saint Lucia. Today, under new ownership, some of the land has been sold. Other parts have been divided up for development. Certain areas were set aside for housing, others for agriculture.

Special arrangements were made for people who worked on the estate, so many of them were able to buy a small piece of land for themselves.

The land is fertile and the crops grow well. Although most of the

Empress Josephine was born in Saint Lucia

farmers grow bananas, a few have also tried raising chickens and pigs. In 1962 the Babonneau chicken farmers started their own cooperative. This closed down after Hurricane Allen damaged their building in 1980. Now the chicken farmers and the pig farmers of the district market their produce through cooperatives that serve the whole island.

The Babonneau Social and Cultural Club has been involved in many community projects. One of these was building the bus shelter at Choc where many of the Babonneau people wait for transport. They were also responsible for getting Babonneau a Multi-Purpose Centre. This is where the Babonneau Queen Show is held. There is a library in the building and a day nursery for young children. Now the Club wants Babonneau to have a home where its old people can be properly cared for.

Mr. Alan Bousquet has been the representative for Babonneau for over twenty years. Many improvements in the area have been the result of his work for his constituency.

St Lucia is blessed with rich, fertile soil

THE CULTURE

The people of Babonneau work very hard to keep the local culture alive. Their twenty two Mothers and Fathers Groups are the best organised in the island. They represent all the different communities in the district. The Social and Cultural Club, started in 1978, is also very active. They organise the Babonneau Carnival Queen Show that takes place each year in the Multi-Purpose Centre. In May, there is Mothers Day. In June, Fathers Day is celebrated. Then, of course, there are the fetes for the Rose and the Marguerite. Fete la Rose is on the 30th August and Fete la Marguerite is October 17th.

Around December there is Belair and Kont but before that, in October there is Babonneau Day. Babonneau Day was celebrated for the first time in 1981. Now, people from all over the north of the island go to Babonneau for their special day.

Some groups, like the Fedor Dancers and the Babonneau Steel Band, have become well-known throughout the island. They perform at many large events. In 1986, members of the Fedor Dancers went to England to represent Saint Lucia at a Festival of Caribbean Culture.

The *kele*, another traditional ceremony, came to Saint Lucia with the slaves who were brought from Africa. It was only performed on very special occasions. Simeon Joseph was one of the few men who knew how this should be done. A sheep was sacrificed to the sacred stones or *shango*. Its head was cut off with one swift blow. If its feet moved afterwards, as if it was dancing to the drums, this was supposed to be a good sign. Like Mr. Joseph, most of the men and women who took part in these rituals are now dead. Perhaps the need for the rituals has also become part of the past.

Religion plays an important part in the community. As well as

After the decline of sugar bananas became Saint Lucia's main crop

*Lucia is rich in
[l]xuriant plant life*

Catholics, Anglicans and Methodists, there are Baptists, Seventh Day Adventists, Jehovah's Witnesses, Bahai's and members of the Pentecostal Church and the Church of God.

One tradition is certainly not dying out in Babonneau or the rest of the island. That is the quadrille. Although the young people may not be as good as some of the old folk, they are learning and enjoying the dances. There is now an island-wide Schools Quadrille Competition. The children practice the steps to the la Comette, the Italian Polka and the 'figures' of the quadrille, hoping their school will come first.

THE FUTURE

Babonneau's future lies in doing what it has always done well, farming. The busier Saint Lucia becomes, the more people there are to be fed, the more important the role of the farmer will become. Instead of being labourers on a large estate, many men now look after their own small piece of land. With better roads and better farming methods they are doing well.

An important part of any development in this area must always be the protection and conservation of Babonneau's forests. This is where the water for all the northern part of the island is collected. When the water supply begins to dry up, the farmer is always the first to suffer.

St Lucia's rainforest is one of th[e] most stunning features of the country's natural wealth

The owner of a large estate can afford to leave some of his land covered with trees. In this way everyone benefits. In some places, these trees act as a windbreak. In others, especially on the high slopes and ridges, they prevent erosion. In every case they help to increase the amount of water stored by the land after rain. It is impossible for a man who has only a few acres of land do this. It is far better if the forested areas are not sold for development at all. Government has already bought some parts of Marquis Estate to protect them for future watershed areas.

The fast growing population also affects the farmer. More people means more houses. Many houses are being built on flat, fertile land that was once used for agriculture. This forces the farmer to clear new land. Often the land that he clears is on the hillsides where it would be wiser to leave the forest undisturbed.

Babonneau has an important part to play in the future of Saint Lucia. Without a good water supply there is no real progress. The people of Babonneau must use their land wisely to protect the valuable watershed areas remaining in that part of the island.

Canaries

Canaries

Piton under a cloudy cap

The village of Canaries lies halfway down the west coast of Saint Lucia. Behind it, deep ravines and jagged mountain ridges run back to the central rainforest. To the north and south are high headlands that enclose the village. To the west is the Caribbean Sea. If you draw a straight line across the island from Canaries, the line will touch Dennery on the other side. They are both fishing villages, but, unlike Dennery, Canaries had to depend on the sea for much more than fish.

The road from Castries only reached Canaries about thirty years ago. Until then the villagers had to travel by canoe to Soufriere or Anse la Raye where they could get transport up to Castries.

The village is not even shown on many of the old maps of Saint Lucia. Bellin's map of 1758, shows a place called 'les Canaris' on that part of the coast. On other maps this same place was marked Anse des Canaries, or just Canaries. Many early settlements were given the names of people who were important at the time, like Micoud, Dennery, Laborie and Choiseul. Others had names like Vieux Fort, Soufriere and Anse la Raye that described something about the place. No-one knows for sure how Canaries got its name. Some people believe it comes from the Amerindian word for the clay cooking pots.

Amerindian sites have been discovered all around the coast of Saint Lucia, from Vieux Fort right up to Cap Estate. However, there are no signs to show there was ever an Amerindian settlement at this spot.

Amerindians travelled by canoe. They were usually happy to settle anywhere where there was a good supply of fresh water. This part of the coast has plenty of rivers so maybe it was the snakes that kept them away!

The sailors who called this place 'Canaris', may have done so for quite another reason. Off the north coast of Africa there is a group of islands called the Canary Islands. Many of the ships that came to the Caribbean from Europe would have stopped there. It was the last place they could take on food and water before setting out across the Atlantic Ocean. The Canary Islands are mountainous and volcanic. Perhaps this part of Saint Lucia's coastline reminded the sailors of the places they had left behind - places they might never see again.

THE BEAUTIFUL VALLEY

Behind Canaries, the distant hills are still covered with thick forest. From them flows the Canaries River, winding its way through deep valleys to the sea. In some parts there are waterfalls cascading over rocky ledges or tumbling down between huge boulders. Below the waterfalls are pools of cold water. At the edges, where the water is frothy with bubbles, the damp rocks are covered with bright green moss. Sometimes the water is clear enough to see the quick, transparent crayfish that dart about in the shallows. Ferns grow here as do orchids that get their nourishment from the air. Everything is lush and green. The bush is full of plants that are not seen lower down where it is hot and dry.

Before the island began to attract the farmers and speculators who would develop it, this valley was a wild and beautiful place. Virgin forest covered the slopes and many different birds could be seen. The Red-necked Pigeon made its home in the tall trees. Flycatchers would swoop down to catch insects hovering over the water. A Saint Lucia Oriole with its black and orange feathers might perch on a branch with his mate. Even the Saint Lucia Parrot could sometimes be heard. Its loud, harsh voice would echo off the hills in the early morning as it flew out to its feeding place.

When sugar became a major crop in Saint Lucia, even Canaries was affected. The main Canaries Estate covered hundreds of acres. It enclosed the little village and stretched way back up the valley. There was very little good land left for the villagers to farm. They needed to grow vegetables and root crops for their families and for sale. Many of them trudged miles into the bush to find a place to do this. Trees were cut down and made into charcoal. Undergrowth was cleared and burned.

Soon the hillsides were covered with patches of bare earth or scrub. The farmers had their gardens but the price was high. The rainforest that was so important to the whole island was being destroyed. When the gardens were abandoned, only scrub grew back. The sound of the parrots were no longer heard.

THE FORGOTTEN VILLAGE

Records show there was already a small community at Canaries in 1763, but no-one knows how long it had been there. The first settlers were probably Frenchmen. In 1725, the French Government had offered grants of land to any of their countrymen who wanted to settle in Saint Lucia. Some people came from France, others came from the island of Martinique. Martinique was just a few miles north of Saint Lucia. It had quite a large population and most of the good agricultural land was already taken. Sugar was beginning to be an important crop. There was money to be made. People were glad of the chance to move to Saint Lucia and set up new estates. The valley of the Canaries River would have been a good place for them to do this.

What did those early settlers find when they landed on that lonely beach? Had there been people living there before? Were they perhaps still watching the newcomers from the bush? We will never know. The settlers probably made a rough camp right there on the shore where they had pulled up their boats. It would be safer if, for any reason, they needed to make get away in a hurry.

At first they might have built simple houses, just enough to shelter themselves and the goods they had brought with them. Later they probably built estate houses further inland. More labour was brought in to work the land, and the little community by the shore grew bigger. Beside

Traditional Carib house

looking northwards to Canaries village from the road to Mahaut

the houses a large water wheel was set up, to work the mill that crushed the sugarcane. From the sugar factory, barrels of molasses were rolled right down to the waiting ships. Still, in many ways, Canaries was the forgotten village.

The first schools in Saint Lucia were established by the Mico Trust in 1838, but there was no Mico School in Canaries. Nearly forty years passed before the children of the village had a school to go to. In 1876, a Catholic school was built for boys and girls. It started with more than a hundred students. By 1880 there were 109, 50 girls and 59 boys. Until 1929, it was the only school in the village. Then, the Presbytery, where there had been no resident priest for some time, was turned into a school. Now, there are 281 children attending the Primary School and another 146 at the Canaries Infant School.

SEARCH FOR WORK

The road from Castries to Soufriere did not reach Canaries until 1959. By this time the price of sugar had dropped way down and the large estates were no longer growing sugarcane. All over the island, mills were lying idle. The valleys of Roseau and Cul-de-Sac were the only large areas still under cane. Even here it was on its way out.

By the early 1960s, it was clear that bananas were the crop of the future. This was a crop for the small farmer as well as the large estate. The Geest boats called at the island every week to load fruit for the British market. A Banana Growers' Association was started, to collect and market the bananas. Now anyone with a couple of acres of land could make a regular income from it.

1909 - Sugar Press

The road that now passed through the village made communications with the rest of the island much easier. Canaries was still too far away from Castries to get any real benefits. For the people of Canaries the new developments had come too late. The estates had not been fully worked for some time and so there was a shortage of jobs. Not having proper roads inland made it difficult for small farmers to get their produce out. Instead of working on their own land, many of them left and went to work elsewhere. Some even left the island. They went to England where they hoped to find jobs that would pay well enough for them to send some money home. When they got work and were settled they sent for their wives. The wives also found work and so the children were often left behind with their grandparents.

Suddenly, it seemed that Canaries had become a village of the very old and the very young.

Some of the people who left never came back except to visit. For others, Canaries would always be their home. They sent back whatever they could afford to support their families and have a house built. One day they would return for good. When that day finally came, Canaries would be waiting and ready for them. It was the overseas money coming into the village that helped keep Canaries going.

THE ROAD TO CHANGE

Anglican Church

Roads play an important part in the development of any community. A village on the coast can move goods in and out by sea, but road transport is easier. For many years Canaries was like an island, cut off from the rest of Saint Lucia. The villagers even had to take a boat to go to church in Anse la Raye. If they had a case to be heard in court, they had to go by boat to Soufriere. In 1878, when a priest came to hold a service in the village chapel, he asked the people why they didn't go to Mass in Anse la Raye more often. He was told that sometimes the sea was rough and men who had been fishing all week didn't want to go out again on Sunday. The women complained that even when the men did go, they wouldn't take them along.

...naries fishermen ...ich their boats

Finally, in 1903, Canaries got a church of its own. A few years later, a presbytery was built on the hill overlooking the villag. During the time of Father Barreau, who lived there from 1906 to 1913, the belfry was added to the front of the church. In those days, cement was not often used. Father Barreau made blocks himself to show the villagers how to do it. When he was transferred to Dominica in 1913, no-one came to replace him. For nearly fifty years there was hardly ever a priest living in the village. Mass was said by the priest from Anse la Raye, who came, like everyone else, by boat.

In 1960, Canaries became a Parish with its own priest, but the village had grown, so the old church was no longer big enough. In most villages, new stone churches had been built to replace the old wooden ones. In Canaries the wooden church was left to be used as a Parish Hall and a new church was built where the sugar factory had once stood. Now Canaries can boast of having two churches in the centre of the village.

The drive from Castries to Canaries takes nearly an hour. The road winds up and down from one valley to the next and is full of twists and bends. If there were some magic way to straighten it out, it would only be about half as long in time and in distance. A better road already runs from Soufriere to Vieux Fort. From there, using the East Coast Road, a good driver can get to Castries in about an hour. Many people prefer to drive south to Vieux Fort and up again to Soufriere rather than creep and bump their way through Canaries.

Now, at last, a new West Coast Road is being built. It has already passed Anse la Raye. When it finally gets to Canaries perhaps it will bring development to a village that has struggled alone for so long.

147

Castries

LE CARENAGE

Some old maps of Saint Lucia show Vigie, where the airport is now, to be the site of an old fort. Nearby, in a small creek or inlet, boats were pulled up to have their bottoms cleaned or repaired. A place where this is done is usually called the CARENAGE. After a while, the inlet and the settlement that grew up around both became known by this name.

The fort had been built by a group of Frenchmen who came to Saint Lucia in 1651 hoping to make the island their home. They knew the Caribs had wiped out a colony of several hundred Englishmen just eleven years before. They did not want to end up the same way. They brought cannons to arm the fort and dug a moat all around to make it more secure. Their leader, de Rousselan, had married a Carib woman so at first the Indians did not trouble them. But, after his death in 1654, the Caribs killed three French Governors, one after the other.

Then the quarrels began between the French and the English over ownership of Saint Lucia. For 100 years or more they fought over it. Finally, in 1763, the 'Treaty of Paris' gave the island to the French. They immediately began to build roads and establish their plantations. They shipped the sugar, cocoa, coffee, spices and other crops they grew to markets in Europe.

It was decided to move the little town of Carenage to a more protected place. The townspeople chose a site on the banks of the river that flowed into the Petit Cul de Sac Bay. Warehouses and other buildings were put up and a wharf was built for canoes and long-boats to tie up alongside. In 1767, the people of le Carnage began to move into their new home.

By 1778, the English and French were at war again and England once more took over the island. Then, in 1780, a terrible hurricane struck. It flattened crops, destroyed buildings and killed thousands of people. Only two houses in the old town were left standing

The Marquis de Castries advised King Louis XVI to get Saint Lucia back at all costs. In 1783 a new treaty was drawn up, the Treaty of Versailles. This forced the English to hand the island back which made the French colonists very happy. They wrote to the King asking him to reward the Marquis. In 1785, the capital was renamed Castries in his honour but on some old maps it is still shown as le Carenage, or le Petit Cul de Sac.

CASTRIES IN THE 19TH CENTURY

Now came the period of the French revolution. In France, the King and many of his followers were beheaded. The revolutionaries even travelled overseas to continue their fight. In Saint Lucia, many churches, estate houses and other buildings were destroyed. Plantations were abandoned and the slaves ran away. Their masters were forced to do the same, or be killed by the soldiers of the New Republic. Castries

Castries

Cruise ships in the port at Castries

*...ne of Castries' most colourful
...od and drink stalls*

was now given a new name, Felicite Ville. Some say the guillotine was set up in the Town Square which, in those days, was called the Place d'Armes. There was confusion and disorder everywhere.

However, the French hold on the island was coming to an end. In 1803 the British returned. They started to repair some of the damage done during the Brigand's War after the revolution. But the influence of the French occupation remained. There were 1,200 whites, 1,800 'coloured' people and 14,000 slaves in Saint Lucia at that time.

Most of the whites were French-speaking creoles and their slaves spoke a Patois based on that language. A few words of English crept into the Patois, but even when English became the official language of the colony, Patois remained the language of the people.

The new names given by the Republic did not last. Eventually, the towns, the villages and the estates, all went back to their old French names. Castries was once again Castries.

The town grew. By 1840 there were about 600 houses and 4,000 inhabitants. In 1847, a convent and schoolrooms were built by the 'Filles de Marie'. Later, this convent was taken over by the nuns of the order of St. Joseph of Cluny. It became St. Joseph's Convent. Castries now had a library, a museum, its own Fire Brigade and a new system for

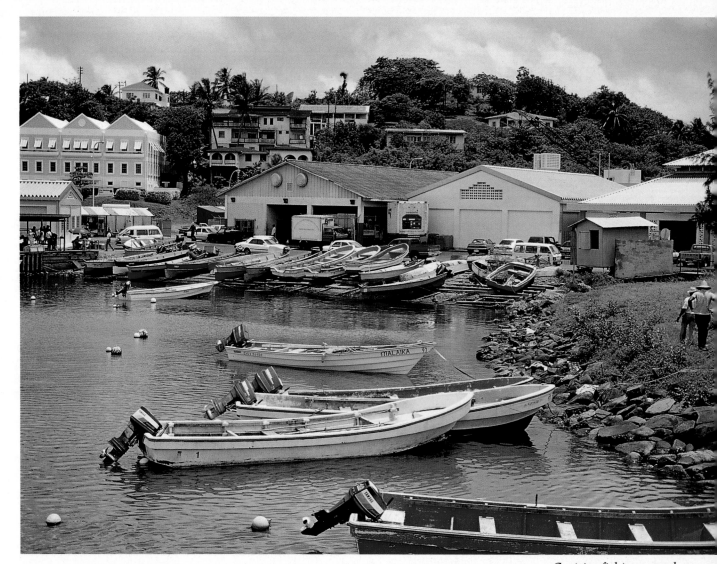

Castries fishing complex

bringing fresh water into the town. In 1885, the first copy of the *Voice of St. Lucia* was printed and in 1894, the first stones for the Cathedral of the Immaculate Conception and for Government House were laid. In September 1898, just before the end of the century, another violent storm hit the island. Many buildings in the town were damaged, but they soon went up again, stronger and better than before.

ORDEAL BY FIRE

Central Library, Castries

Most of the buildings in Castries were made of wood. Lumber was cheap and a wooden house could be put up very quickly. It was also easy to move! This was important because not many people owned the land on which their houses stood. Wooden houses however, had their faults. They could be blown down in a hurricane or catch fire and burn to the ground in minutes. Most cooking was done on an open fire and houses were lit by candles or oil lamps. There were often accidents. Fires would quickly blaze out of control, destroying the house where they started as well as others nearby. As the town grew, the houses became more numerous and more tightly packed. On May 14 1927, a

150

Coal heaps near to Castries Harbour - in the days when coal was King

Castries Harbour in the early 1900's

The container trans-shipment development in Castries Harbour

fire started at night in the business quarter of Castries. It soon spread from one building to the next until half of the town was a smoking black ruin. The Post Office, the government buildings and many private homes were all destroyed. So were most of the business houses. Very few people had insurance so a relief fund was started to help the victims to rebuild. Still more trouble lay ahead.

In 1948, an even bigger fire destroyed all but a small part of the town. It started in a tailor's shop, perhaps from a candle that had fallen over. The flames consumed the tailor's small wooden shack and quickly reached the buildings on either side. There was a strong wind. It fanned the fire and helped it to burn fiercer and faster. When the sun rose on the morning of June 20 it shone down on a black, smoking wasteland. Just the day before, these ruins had been the town of Castries.

The Post Office and the Courthouse were once again demolished as well as most other government buildings. The books in the Carnegie Library were nothing but ashes, just like the goods in the burnt-out stores. But the Cathedral was saved, so was St. Joseph's Convent and St. Mary's College. The College moved to one of the old military barracks at Vigie. The Convent burned to the ground just eleven years later.

The fire left more than two thousand people homeless. Columbus Square was piled high with furniture and other belongings that had been snatched from the blaze. It took much longer for the town to recover this time, but it did. Like the mythical phoenix rising up from the ashes of its funeral pyre, Castries was built up once again.

PORT CASTRIES

The harbour the French called le Petit Cul de Sac, or le Carenage, became one of the busiest ports in the Caribbean. For years the only activity it had seen was the shoals of fish that swept in and out. Then the Amerindians came to fish in the bay and search among the mangroves for oysters. During wars between the French and English, fleets of ships had sailed into the harbour. They anchored in the deeper water and put longboats over the side for the men to go ashore.

Castries was a trading centre. Merchant vessels brought passengers and goods to the island and loaded up with produce from the estates. They paid a tax of a penny a ton if they were 50 tons or more, four pence a ton if they were less. For water they paid two pence a trip. If they were under 50 tons or registered in Castries, they paid six pence for half a year. The taxes were collected by a Town Warden appointed by Government.

In 1851, a Town Council was elected and HH Breen became the first Mayor of Castries. This Council controlled the wharves until 1871. Then, it was decided that money collected for harbour taxes belonged to the whole colony, not just to Castries. By the end of that century steamships had replaced the old fashioned sailing ships. To produce the steam that powered them they heated their boilers by burning coal. Since most of their valuable space was needed for cargo, they had to take on extra coal whenever they could. Castries became a coaling station and the docks and wharves became busier than ever.

Gradually, the need for coal became less. Now boats were usually powered by diesel. Women still hurried to the wharf when certain boats appeared. Only they carried bananas on their heads instead of baskets of coal. Today the bananas are carried by machines.

As traffic increased, the harbour was enlarged and improved. The northern wharf was built in 1886 to allow large freighters and cruise ships to come alongside. Now it was no longer big enough. On the western wharf, where the Geest banana boats docked, there was no longer enough space for all the traffic on loading days. Even the Prince Albert Basin, where schooners and coastal boats tied up, had outlived its usefulness. The Basin was filled in. New warehouses and docks were built as well as a facility for cruise ships on the other side of the harbour. Port Castries was keeping up with the 20th century.

Anglican Church

THE CITY OF CASTRIES

On March 1st 1967, Saint Lucia became a State with internal self-government. The British Administrator was replaced by Sir Frederick Clarke. He was the first Saint Lucian Governor to reside in Government House. In December of that same year, Castries became a city. It no longer had a Town Council and a Chairman, but a City Council and a Mayor. There had been Mayors before, starting in 1851, with Mr Breen, but after twenty years or so the title had been dropped and 'Chairman' was used instead. The first Mayor of the City of Castries was Mr JH Desir.

Castries vegetable market

Le Carenage, with its 4,000 inhabitants and 600 houses, is buried in the pages of the history books. The old fort, with its small band of Frenchmen, is lost even further back in time. But they are not forgotten. Today, the City of Castries completely surrounds Petit Cul de Sac. In each of its many districts are hundreds of houses and thousands of people. One third of the total population of Saint Lucia lives within the city boundaries.

Cruise ships no longer unload passengers onto the wharf. Instead, on the far side of the harbour, Pointe Seraphine, with its docks and shops, waits for them. Vigie airport is just five minutes from the centre of the city. The planes that land there bring in many visitors. They also provide good business links for Saint Lucia with the rest of the Caribbean. Because Castries is the capital all the Government buildings are there. There are also churches and schools, too many to list. There are parks and playing fields where the people can play and relax. There are stores and supermarkets with goods from all over the world.

Kaycees, Castries - a fine example of Caribbean architecture

reet map of Castries

he impressive interior of astries' Cathedral of the maculate Conception

Yet still, all around are reminders of the past. There are military barracks on the Morne and at Vigie. The heavy buttresses that supported the railway up to Morne Fortune can still be seen half-hidden by bush. At La Toc Battery, are underground passages, ammunition stores and the remains of fortress walls. The battles are over but the buildings remain. Some are empty, covered with leafy green vines and pink coralita. Others are now classrooms, or offices, or homes. From the lookout opposite the entrance to Government House, you look down on Castries far below. The city with its busy streets encloses one of the most beautiful harbours in the Caribbean.

153

Choiseul

ANSE CITRON

Many old maps of Saint Lucia show a place called Anse Citron where you would expect to see Choiseul. In English that means 'Lime Bay'. Perhaps the sailors who went ashore for wood and water found limes growing there. This would have been an important discovery. Lime juice was a protection against scurvy, a disease caused by being too long at sea without fresh fruits or vegetables to eat.

Until 1763, the village near the river mouth was also called Anse Citron. In February of that year, the English and the French signed a pact called the Treaty of Paris. It made Saint Lucia a French possession. They celebrated by renaming the village Anse Choiseul in honour of the Duke of Choiseul, French Minister for Foreign Affairs. This was later shortened to 'Choiseul'.

During the French Revolution, the Republican General Ricard was sent to govern Saint Lucia. He gave all the towns and villages new names. Choiseul was now called 'le Tricolore', like the French flag with its bands of red, white and blue. In 1796, the British defeated the French and le Tricolore became Choiseul once again.

Choiseul is about halfway between Soufriere and Vieux Fort on the southwest coast of Saint Lucia. To the north is the Gros Piton, to the west the Caribbean Sea. This part of the island is not lush and green like the countryside behind the Pitons. It is more open and much drier. The rivers do not flow through wide valleys as they do in Dennery, Cul de Sac and Roseau. Instead they run swiftly between the steep banks of deep ravines.

In one place, the River Doree tumbles along at the bottom of a canyon 150 feet deep. A bridge, barely 20 feet wide, crosses it from side to side. If you stand on the bridge and drop a stone, several seconds go by before you hear the splash as it hits the water.

There is a story about this bridge. People say the man who built it made a pact with the devil. He promised that when it was finished the devil could take the first person who walked over it. When the bridge was completed, he was so excited he forgot his promise and ran across. Fortunately, his little dog ran ahead and reached the other side first. The devil must have been satisfied with his small prize. They say the dog vanished and was never seen again. Ever since then it has been called the Devil's Bridge.

LAST OF THE AMERINDIANS

Although the French gave Choiseul its name, they were not the first people to inhabit that part of the island. The Amerindians had settled there long before. First the peaceful Arawaks, then, later, the Caribs. When the early English and French settlers started to arrive, the Caribs were still in control of the island.

Choiseul

Choiseul Village

The first group of Englishmen came ashore near Vieux Fort. They lasted only five weeks before they were attacked and driven out. A second, larger colony, started by a Captain Judlee in the south of the island, survived for more than a year. Then, in 1640, they were also attacked and almost wiped out. Caribs from Saint Lucia, Dominica, Saint Vincent and Martinique banded together to get rid of them. Very few of the men managed to escape.

Several small colonies of Frenchmen who came after them suffered the same fate. The Caribs resented these new arrivals and did their best to drive them away. They were proud people who fought hard, but their time in Saint Lucia was coming to an end. By 1774, there were only three or four Carib families left. They lived at a place called La Pointe or Pointe Caribe, in the shadow of the Gros Piton.

All around Choiseul there are places where evidence of Amerindian settlements can be found. Close to the road running through the village is a rock with an Amerindian carving or petroglyph on it. Further inland, at Morne Lezard, stone axes and other stone tools have been found. On the banks of the Piaye and Balembouche rivers, and on Balembouche Estate, archaeologists have discovered more remains or artefacts left by these early settlers.

Perhaps more important than the rock carvings, axes and other tools are the skills that the Amerindians left behind. They used the local clay to make cooking pots. They gathered vines to be woven into baskets. They cut and dried grasses to be made into mats. There are no pure Caribs left in Choiseul today, but many people in the district make their living by making mats, baskets and clay pots. The methods they use are not so very different to those used by the Amerindians centuries ago.

CHURCHES, SCHOOLS AND SUGAR

Sugar was introduced into Saint Lucia in 1764. The first estates to plant this new crop were in the Vieux Fort area. Others very soon followed their example. Mills were built to crush the cane. Some were powered by water, some by animals, and just a few by wind. At Balembouche and River Doree, the sugar mills were powered by water from the nearby rivers. The water ran along canals or aquaducts, then fell onto the paddles of the wheels forcing them to turn round.

The wheels turned heavy iron rollers that crushed the cane and squeezed out the sweet juice. This was boiled to make sugar. On some estates it was not possible to use water, so animals walked round and round in circles turning the machinery. A third type of mill was also built with sails that were turned by the wind. Remains of three of these windmills can still be seen at le Riche, but they may not be there much longer. Their stones are being hauled away and used to build other things.

Petroglyph at Choiseul

*...arnival 'jump up' is a time
...o let your hair down*

When the Great Hurricane hit Saint Lucia in 1780, Choiseul suffered badly. Lives, crops and houses were lost in one of the worst storms ever recorded. Boats were thrown up on to the shore or blown out to sea. The wooden church in the village was destroyed. The only church left standing was the one at Dauphin and that was built of stone. There were about 50 sugar estates in Saint Lucia at this time, quite a few of them were in the Choiseul district. The hurricane flattened them all. Other crops like cocoa and coffee also suffered heavy losses.

After the hurricane, stone churches were built in all the parishes to replace those the storm had blown away. Choiseul's new church was completed about 1789. It stood for over a hundred years. The corner stones of the present church were laid in 1906.

In 1866, Choiseul got its first school. It was built by the Lady Mico Trust and had 75 pupils, boys and girls. By the time the two Catholic schools were built near the presbytery in 1879, it had already closed down. The new boys' school had 81 pupils, the girls' school had 38. By 1898, each had over a hundred students. In 1909, a separate building was put up for the infants. None of these three school buildings exists today.

Reunion has a Junior Secondary School for girls and boys with over 400 students and an Infants School with about 200. There are also schools at Delcer, Roblot, Monrouge, River Doree and Dugard.

LIVING OFF THE LAND

Today, a lot of good agricultural land at Choiseul is lying unused on large estates. Labour costs have risen and often it is no longer possible to produce crops economically. Rather than face a loss, the workers are paid off and the land is left idle. Small farmers often have to make the best use they can of steep slopes and dry, windblown places. Irrigation is always a problem. Farmers make terraces to safeguard the precious soil and keep the water from running off. This way they are able to grow a variety of crops.

Sweet potatoes, yam and dasheen all grow well in this part of the island. So do pigeon peas and peanuts. The peanuts are sold locally but some of the other crops, like sweet potato and yam, are shipped to Canada and England. They are mainly bought by the West Indian communities in those countries. Tomatoes, carrots and cabbages are also produced here, and inland, where it is not so dry, bananas and citrus fruits are grown. Copra is still important on some estates, but the harvest has dropped because of the mite that has attacked the coconut trees.

*Community scene from the **Black Madonna** by D St Omer*

Just south of Choiseul is a business that deals in plants of a different kind. It is called Windward Island Tropicals. This 30 acre estate is almost completely planted with ornamental palm trees and other exotic plants. Some of them grow in the open but many others are protected under frames covered with black plastic mesh. Every week thousands of small plants are flown from Hewanorra to England. Another two or three thousand palms and larger plants leave each week by sea. Before they are shipped, the soil around their roots is carefully washed off. This is to prevent them from carrying any insect pests or bacteria on their journey. In the chilly English climate these plants would not survive outside as they do here. They will be kept indoors, to brighten up peoples' homes and offices instead.

Not all the people in Choiseul live off the land. Fishing boats set out from this village as they do all around the coast of Saint Lucia. At nearby Anse L'Ivrogne, they still make their fishing canoes in the traditional manner. The fishermen of Choiseul now belong to a cooperative and use engines rather than sails. Even so, going to sea in a small boat can be a dangerous way to make a living.

CHOISEUL'S HANDICRAFTS

Choiseul Handicrafts in Castries Craft market

If you want to see some of the work that has made Choiseul famous, you should go to the Craft Centre at La Fargue. You could also visit the market in Castries. Many stalls there have baskets, table mats, mats, coalpots or flowerpots made in Choiseul. The women do a lot of the work. They shape the pots from local clay and leave them to dry. Then they are piled up in a heap, covered with bush and fired, just as the Amerindians did so long ago.

Education is Saint Lucia's ... priority for its younger ... generation

It is women too who cut the vertiver or khus-khus grass and spread it along the roadside to dry. They gather the dry leaves of the screw pine or pandanus. They split them lengthways and trim the edges to remove the sharp spines. They also collect the rushes that are used to cover the seats of the local chairs.

The men usually make the sturdy shopping and laundry baskets. The materials they use grow in the rainforest. They must have a licence from the Forestry Department before they can gather them. The lianas or vines are really the roots of creepers like the *awali* and the *ti kanot*. They are epiphytes, which means they grow on another plant but do not feed on it. They cling to the branches of the tall trees to get closer to the light. Then they send down masses of long thick roots to suck moisture from the damp air beneath the forest canopy. Sometimes their weight is enough to bring the tree down.

The men travel a long way on foot to reach the place where they can gather the vines. Often they stay in the forest overnight. After they are cut, the roots are boiled in a large drum for about an hour. The *awali* can be peeled ready to use but the *ti kanot* is left soaking in the river for another two weeks. Then it is pounded on a rock to remove the skin.

The Jacquot feeds on the fruits of the *awali* and nests in the trees on which it grows. To make sure these rare birds are not disturbed during the nesting season, no licences are issued at this time. Protection of the parrot and the forest means protection for Choiseul's basket makers. Without the forest their supply of material would disappear.

Foreign currency is important to the island. The people of Choiseul do their bit. Not many tourists actually visit Choiseul but hardly any of them leave Saint Lucia without taking something from Choiseul with them.

Diamond Falls

The Church of Saint Peter in Dennery Village

Dennery

HOW DENNERY GOT ITS NAME

Some of Saint Lucia's towns and villages have names that tell us something about them, Gros Islet, Soufriere and Vieux Fort, for example. Others, like Castries, Choiseul, Laborie, Praslin, Micoud and Dauphin were named after Frenchmen who were important at the time. Dennery was named after the Count d'Ennery, Governor General of the French Windward Islands from 1766 to 1770.

Before that it had been called Anse Canot. Canoes, carved from the trunks of large trees like the gommier, were brought down the river to the coast to be launched. There is still a place at Dennery called Anse Canot.

Behind the village, the wide valley that stretches back to the forest was known as the Grand Mabouya. Mabouya is the local name for the harmless little gecko. It hides during the day and comes out at night to hunt insects. Mabouya also means evil spirit. In the old days, most people believed in spirits, both good and bad. Perhaps they thought the thickly forested valley of the Grand Mabouya River was a good place for them to hide. Today, with its open fields, brightly painted houses and busy roads it hardly seems a place where evil spirits would hang out! Maybe they all went back to Ravine tous les Diables, way up the Dennery River.

The French Revolution gave d'Ennery a new name, le Republicain. But as soon as the island became British once more the village went back to using its old name again. This time though it was spelt Dennery.

In 1850 about 1,000 people lived in the district of Dennery. By 1900 there were 3,000. The village was a busy place with markets where meat, fish and vegetables were sold. On dark nights the streets were lit by Coleman lamps and at Christmas almost every house had a lantern lit by candles in the window. The water in the Dennery River was so clear you could see the crabs walking on the bottom. Children bathed in it and women did their washing on its banks.

On Sundays and holidays people came from all around to attend Mass at the Church of Saint Peter. And on Good Friday, all the housewives fried accras to give to their neighbours. Today, there are more than 10,000 people living in the Dennery district. Many of them go to church at La Resource.

Dennery

Main Street, Dennery on a Good Friday

SUGAR AND SLAVERY

When the French took over Saint Lucia, they divided it into districts called *quartiers*. At first, Dennery was part of the district or *quartier* called Trois Islets or Praslin. Later it became a separate district. Dennery was one of the eleven parishes that were listed in the records of the Catholic Church for 1775. The first village church was a simple, wooden building on the seashore. It was dedicated to Saint Theresa of

Dennery village

Avila. In it was a fine silver chalice given to the Dennery church by the Count d'Ennery.

The French already had large sugar estates on the neighbouring island of Martinique. They saw the chance to start many more in Saint Lucia. They offered free grants of land to anyone who would come to settle. By 1760, there were already about 1,000 settlers spread all over the island. Most of them were French, but there were a few English and also some Irish among them. There were also some 4,000 African slaves.

The climate of the West Indies did not suit the European settlers who suffered from both heat and disease. They were also ravaged by malaria and yellow fever.

Behind the small settlement of Dennery was a large mangrove swamp where mosquitoes bred freely. Their bite spread these diseases and caused many deaths. The African slaves who were forced to work on the estates also fell prey to disease, many of them being claimed by cholera epidemics.

By 1775, the Dennery district had 61 estates with more than 1,000 people living and working on them. Although sugar was the main crop, cotton, tobacco and spices were also grown. The estates did well. Most of the wooden estate houses were large and airy with high ceilings and shady verandas. The slaves were not nearly so fortunate. After a long, tiring day on the land they would return to a small hut made of woven twigs, with a dirt floor.

When the French Revolution reached the Caribbean the slaves were to be freed and paid for their labour. Some, fortunate enough, immediately seized the opportunity and fled into the forests and mountains.

WARS AND WHIRLWINDS

In 1780 Saint Lucia was hit by a hurricane. It ruined the sugar estates and destroyed every church on the island except the one at Dauphin.

Dennery's first church had not been much to speak of. The hurricane of 1780 blew it away. Soon, a much larger, stone church was built to replace it, but the new church did not survive the Brigand's War that followed the French Revolution and it's freeing of the slaves from bondage. In this period of struggle and upheaval estate houses were burned and often their owners were killed. Fearing for their lives, over half the white population left the island. Many of the freed slaves died in the bush, of hunger, disease or snakebite. By the time the war ended in 1797, Saint Lucia's population had dropped from 22,000 to 14,000.

The island was finally handed over to the British in 1815, and the wars between the English and the French ended. But the hurricanes did not. They kept coming. In 1831, a Dennery boat was lost and a fisherman drowned. In 1898, the sea smashed the houses along the shore as it crashed inland. In 1960, the villagers had to leave their homes because heavy seas threatened to carry them away. In 1980, Hurricane Allen struck the island. Dennery suffered again from high winds and the surging, pounding sea that roared up the beach and into the streets.

This time the whole waterfront was a disaster area. Houses were tossed upside down in the road, or left hanging on the hillsides where the wind had thrown them. Today, houses are built to be strong enough to withstand high winds, but the threat of the sea is always there. The fishermen of Dennery, like fishermen everywhere else, know this. That is why the church on the hill is dedicated to Saint Peter, the big fisherman.

RUM AND BANANAS

Fresh bananas and vegetables

Dennery, like Roseau and Cul de Sac, had a factory where the sugarcane was taken to be crushed. When the juice was crushed from the cane by the heavy metal rollers of the mill, it was collected in large vats. The juice was then boiled in big iron pans until the dark sugar crystals were formed. Treacly black, rich-smelling molasses were left behind. From these molasses the sugar factories made rum.

The fires that kept the cane juice boiling were fed by wood. In time, most of the forest on the hillsides close to the factory were cut down to provide fuel for the fires. Sugar was king and the planter's greed for more profit was all that mattered. The plantocracy cared little about ecology and most were ignorant about the disasterous impact of their land clearing policies. No one realised that without the forest, their precious water supply would soon dry up.

Cacti on Fregate Isla
Nature Reserve - a sh
boat trip from Denne

At La Caye, on pay day, people gathered in the shade of the big tamarind tree. Here, vendors sold food and drink to the labourers who had come to collect their wages. The rum shops too, did good business selling the strong liquor made at the factory, or the local pirate brand. Sugar kept the community alive.

In 1961, Saint Lucia's last field of sugar cane was cut. Dennery farmers, like all their compatriots, began to plant bananas in a big way. The Dennery factory was still making rum, but now the molasses that were used were shipped in from Guyana. Soon, bananas stretched out from both sides of the road for miles outside the village. They covered hundreds of acres. Dennery Estate alone produced 3,824 tons in 1975,

*Altar Boys attending Dennery
village church on Good Friday*

more than 10 per cent of the island's total production. This same year, the rum-making stopped and the factory finally closed completely.

In December 1979, the 2,700 acre Dennery Estate was sold to the government. It included lands at Perle, Montrose, La Caye and Fond Díor. The land was leased to the Dennery Farm Company, in which the government had shares. Bananas remained the main crop, but for a while, a lot of the land could not be used because of flooding caused by the silting up of the Mabouya River. A new drainage system was put in and eventually the flooded land was reclaimed. In 1984, the estate produced 2,898 tons of bananas. By 1990, production for the year had risen to 4,024 tons.

DENNERY TODAY

The Castries-Vieux Fort highway no longer runs through Dennery. Now it passes to the west of the village. At the entrance to the village is a sign that says 'Welcome to Dennery'. Unless people turn off here, they will just speed on past. They can see the big church and the hospital on the hill behind Bay Street. They can see the new school buildings and the playing field where the mangrove swamp used to be. They might even see the top of the radio tower by the Police Station, and the rocky island in the bay. But they will be too far away to see the fishermen hauling their boats up the beach.

Many of the boats are still carved from huge tree trunks. With modern tools, this is now an easier job. Although the design has not changed much, something has been added. On the back of each canoe is an engine that runs on diesel or gasoline. There is hardly a sail to be seen. True, this means the fishermen must charge more for their fish, but it also means they can go wherever they want. They no longer have to go only where the wind will take them. Even with no wind at all, they can still go out to sea.

Dennery village

Dennery has no sulphur springs, like Soufriere, to attract tourists. There is no International Airport like the one at Vieux Fort, no fine harbour for shipping like Castries. Visitors to Dennery come to see the large, fertile valley that still has some of the island's most beautiful waterfalls and unspoiled rainforest.

In the past, many small farmers in the Dennery district worked land to which they had no legal right. In 1985, the Land Titling and Registration Project helped some of them to get proper title. At La Perle, Roots Farming has shown that with hard work and the right methods, many different crops can be grown. Not only corn and cabbage, but soybeans, rice, sweet peppers and eggplant. Perhaps if more of Dennery's farmers were able to farm small plots of land in this way, Dennery could become a very important area for produce.

The village's fishing warehouse

Gros Islet

WAR FROM THE SEA

For hundreds of years, the Amerindians were Saint Lucia's only inhabitants. They lived in small groups, usually on the coast close to a river. They made canoes, carved from the trunks of gommier trees. In them, they paddled around the coast fishing and gathering shellfish. Broken pieces of their pottery have been found around the village of Gros Islet. This tells us that they must at one time have had a camp here. In those days the hills would have been covered with trees. The mangrove swamp would have been so large it would have taken up most of the flat land behind the bay. Ducks and waterfowl lived among its tangled roots and herons nested in the branches. Pelicans and boobys dived into the sea around the nearby island, catching fish.

The island had once been a Carib camp. Later it became a hideout for pirates. They would sail in and anchor in the sheltered waters close to shore. On old maps the place is marked 'le Gros Islet' which is French for the big island. When the English Admiral Rodney built his fort there the name was changed to Pigeon Island.

At first the Caribs tried to drive off the strangers who came to the island. They shot at them with poison-tipped arrows and with burning sticks but they could not win. The strangers came in tall ships with billowing sails. Their ships were armed with deadly cannons. For over a hundred years the invaders fought fiercely among themselves for possession of Saint Lucia. During that time the island was taken, first by one and then the other, as control passed between Britain and France no less than fourteen times.

The bay at Gros Islet was a good anchorage and both, French and English ships sailed in and out. In 1781, French troops, led by the Marquis de Bouille, captured Gros Islet. Rodney from his stronghold on Pigeon Island, forced them to retreat.

Then, in 1793, the French Republic claimed all the French territories in the Caribbean. They renamed all the towns and villages in the island. Gros Islet became 'la Revolution'. Not too long after this, the British took over once again and the village went back to its old name.

Today the Amerindians would no longer recognise the place. The flat land is covered with small thorny bushes and dry grass. It is grazed by cattle and goats. The swamp is gone. In its place is a marina full of yachts and power boats from all over the world, as well as hotels, apartments, restaurants and bars. Pleasure craft motor through the narrow channel loaded with holidaymakers.

WORK ON THE LAND

After the first French settlers arrived in 1651, Saint Lucia's landscape began to change. Large plantations took over most of the valleys, the plains around Vieux Fort, and all of the northern part of the island. In

Gros Islet

100 years more than three quarters of the island had been claimed by private owners. By 1775, there were 802 estates, 47 of them in the quarter of Gros Islet. Large estates included those of Monchy, Bonne Terre, Morne Giraud, Marquis and Esperance. They stretched north to Cap, south to Bois d'Orange and Corinth and eastward to the sea.

Gros Islet now had a population of about 2,000. The 'Chemin Royal' or Royal Road that circled the island ran through the village. It came up from le Carenage, which would later be called Castries. Leaving the village, it went out through Monchy and across the island to Marquis, Esperance and Dauphin.

Sugar was the main crop throughout this period, although cotton, tobacco and spices were also grown. These crops fetched high prices in England and elsewhere in Europe, so the French and the English continued to battle for control of the island. Almost every estate had its own mill. They were usually powered by large water wheels turned by water channelled from a nearby river. After the heavy rollers of the mill crushed the sweet juice out of the cane it was boiled in big iron pots, called *chaudieres*.

In 1817, a terrible hurricane hit the island and the big wooden church was completely demolished. The one that replaced it was said to be 'the poorest in the island.'

In 1838, the slaves who had been brought from Africa were finally set free. Some still tried to make a living from the land, others became fishermen. The village continued to grow. Rows of neat wooden houses with wooden shutters lined the narrow streets. Fishing boats set out from the beach each morning to fish in the open sea.

In 1871, a new parish priest came to the village, the Abbe Chassang. With the help of his parishioners and money from his estate at Monchy, he built a new church. It had three fine marble altars, but like the earlier churches it was still made of wood. It was wrecked completely by an earthquake in 1906. Only the bells were saved. Twenty years later, in 1926, the foundation was laid for the Church of St. Joseph the Worker, where people worship today.

WAR IN THE AIR

The sugar estates disappeared one by one. Sometimes the land was replanted with coconuts, citrus fruits or cocoa but often it was abandoned. Land left without the protection of trees or crops quickly became dry and useless.

World War Two broke out in 1939. When the United States entered the conflict, they decided to use Saint Lucia as a base for their aircraft. A runway was built at Vieux Fort for the planes to land. At Gros Islet, 221 acres was turned into an air base. In 1941, the marines moved in.

There was no runway at Gros Islet. The planes that arrived were flying boats and their landing strip was the sea. They were on the look-out for enemy submarines and they patrolled the Caribbean from Trinidad to

Archdiocesan Pastoral Centre, Gros Islet

170

Right: A fine example of
Caribbean architecture in
Gros Islet

Puerto Rico. They would fly in low over the water and land in a shower
of spray. Then, with engines roaring, they would move toward the concrete ramp that had been built on shore.

Certainly the most distinguished visitor to arrive in and leave the
island in this way was the US President and wartime leader Franklin
Delano Roosevelt. His presence had an electrifying effect throughout the
Caribbean, reinforcing the islanders' appreciation of their indispensable
contribution to the war effort.

When the war ended in 1945, the strange aircraft also disappeared.
The base was closed, the marines went back to the US and the buildings
were dismantled. Bush grew back over the land. After a while, the ugly
concrete ramp and the broken down jetties were all that remained.
Today, on a small, paved area, squeezed between the Yacht Club and a
hotel, young men gather to play games where the seaplanes once roared

The long sandy beach at Reduit was one of the best in the island.
On Sundays, people drove out from Castries in their small English
Austin and Ford motor cars. The road was narrow, twisting and bumpy.
After they left La Clery and Bisee behind they were really in the country,
with hardly a house to be seen. Before reaching Gros Islet the road
passed through a thick shady grove of coconut trees close to the beach.
Here they would turn off, to change their clothes in the wooden rest-
house under the palms. Then they would bring out their picnics and
their bottles of rum punch.

After swimming, they might stroll along the beach. They would walk
past the ramp and the cemetery to the shallow stream that marked the
edge of the village. A bridge of wooden planks crossed the sluggish drib-
ble of swampy water. It creaked and cracked every time anything drove
over it. On the other side was Gros Islet, with its straight, narrow streets

171

and neat wooden houses. Black and white ducks waddled along the beach and fishermen's nets hung in rows drying in the sun.

LAND AND SEA

After the Rodney Bay Development Project began, great changes took place in the district of Gros Islet. In 1970, the mangrove swamp that had spread from the 'Chemin Royal' to the hills at Bonne Terre, finally disappeared. The Americans had tried to fill it when they built their base there in 1941, but had failed miserably. As fast as they pumped sand into it from the bay it sifted away again. The stagnant edges of the swamp were full of mosquitoes, but it was also an important nursery for fish. Birds fed and nested there and each year flocks of migrating ducks rested there on their way south.

Now it was gone for good. In its place was not land but water. Since it had been impossible to drain the swamp it was dredged and filled with water instead. A channel was cut to connect the new marina with the open water of Rodney Bay. The channel was made deep enough for even large boats to go in and out. It passed right through the place where the rickety old bridge had crossed the muddy stream. Now there was no bridge and no road.

A new road was built. Not a narrow, twisting lane but a wide, well-paved highway from Castries to the gates of Cap Estate. It passed east of Gros Islet, crossing the road that led from the village to Massade and Cas-en-Bas. Just before it reached Cap there was a turning. It went toward the sea, cutting across the old village road that had wandered up to Cap, and going on across the bay to Pigeon Island!

The people of Gros Islet had watched for many months as this fantastic land bridge appeared. It grew, stretching and getting wider until it touched the island. Then the new road was built on it. All of a sudden the whole world seemed to be driving or sailing into Gros Islet.

But of course they weren't. The boats sailed on to their anchorages in the marina. The cars sped along the highway to Cap or to the new causeway. Hardly anyone turned off to go into the village. And that was not all! With the building of the causeway and the destruction of the mangroves, fishing was not as good or as easy as it had been. There were new jobs for the villagers, but it was not like before when the road had passed through the village. Regular bus services started up between Gros Islet and Castries but it still didn't bring people to the village. Something had to be done!

FROM SEA AND SKY

The new road, the causeway and the marina were not the only changes that had been made. All around Gros Islet, luxury hotels, private villas and neatly arranged housing estates were springing up. Tourists came by air and by sea to lie in the sun and enjoy the swimming and the scenery. It provided jobs for the village people and customers for the catch the fishermen were able to bring in. After the Air Base at Reduit had closed, ten years or more had passed before the first hotel was built. Jobs had been hard to find. Many men had left their families and gone away to look for work.

There was very little agriculture around the village so most of its income came from the sea. The nets were spread across the bay to come up bulging with shoals of blue and silver jackfish and sardines. When the boats went into deeper water the fishermen returned loaded with dolphinfish, kingfish and fine red snappers. At only 50 cents a pound, they still often had more fish than they could sell. Lobsters that they caught in fishpots sold for 40 cents a pound, but there was no-one to buy them! Now they are a luxury, costing $20 or more for one that weighs no more than two pounds.

Lambi has also become expensive. Because they fetch a good price, fishermen sometimes bring up the immature shells, something they would never have done before. The piles of queen conch shells with their brilliant pink lining, no longer litter the beaches. Even the small

Catholic Church,
Gros Islet

ones are too valuable to throw away. They are sold to tourists as souvenirs.

The fresh fish, lambi and lobster led to a new way of life for many people in the village. They opened restaurants to tempt tourists and islanders with these local delicacies. On a Friday evening now, when many other places are closing their shutters for the night, Gros Islet comes alive. Music blares out from dozens of bars and the smell of grilled lambi and fried fish is everywhere. There is a friendly, holiday atmosphere in the crowded streets. Even the roadside vendors with their coalpots and their barbecued chicken legs are busy.

Going to the village has become a regular weekend activity. Tourists mix and mingle with local people. They try a new drink, sample a new dish or dance in the street to the lively music. Gros Islet is now a town stretching from Bay Street to the busy highway, but under its thriving, busy surface the village atmosphere survives.

Laborie

ISLET A CARET

The village of Laborie lies on the coast in the south-west corner of Saint Lucia. It is some five miles north of Vieux Fort. Two large rivers mark the boundaries of the district of Laborie. The River Doree in the north and the Black Bay River to the south. The Balembouche River and the Piaye River also flow down to the coast just north of Laborie Bay. Amerindian artefacts have been found by all these rivers, even as far inland as Getrine, Banse and Fond Berange.

Laborie was probably first settled by the French in the 18th century. The village is not on a river but on a beautiful bay. A large reef runs from the southern end right up to Balembouche. It protects the beach and encourages large deep water fish to come in to feed. It also provides a sheltered anchorage for boats, once they can find their way through the reef to the calmer waters inside.

On Bellin's map of Saint Lucia, drawn in 1758, there is a small island lying offshore, close to where Laborie is today. On the map it is marked Islet-a-Caret, which is French for Turtle Island. *Caretta caret* is the proper name for the loggerhead turtle. Turtles need a sandy shore for nesting so the island may have got its name because turtles went there to lay their eggs. It was probably only a sandbank that built up on top of a reef.

In 1763, there were just about a dozen houses in the small community of Laborie. By 1770, more houses had been built along with a church. By 1775, there were 81 estates in the quarter of Islet-a-Caret. Their main crops were sugar, cotton, cocoa and coffee. Twelve years later, in 1787, Lefort de la Tour's map still showed the village as Rade et Anse de l'Ilet a Carret, meaning Turtle Island Anchorage and Beach.

Some time between 1787 and 1789 the village received a new name. The hurricane of 1780 had destroyed most of the houses and the church. The church was rebuilt by the Baron de Laborie, Governor of Saint Lucia from 1784 to 1789 and so the village was renamed Laborie in his honour. Father Louis Tapon laid the cornerstone of the present church in 1907.

The hurricane did more than blow down buildings. The little island in the bay also disappeared about this time. Perhaps it was swept away by the high winds and the rough seas during the storm. Anyway, after this the small island no longer appeared on any maps. Soon there was no one left alive who remembered seeing it.

THE CARIBS AND THE FRENCH

We do not know when the first Amerindians settled in Saint Lucia, or who they were. We do know that the Arawaks came here hundreds of years before the Caribs. However, in the early part of the 17th century, when the British became interested in Saint Lucia, there were only Caribs living on the island.

Laborie

They met the foreigners as they came ashore or rowed out in their canoes to where the boats lay at anchor. They carried turtle eggs with them along with dried turtle meat. They took freshly gathered fruit, vegetables and wild yams. They showed the strangers where to get fresh water. In exchange they were given knives, beads or other cheap trinkets. Sometimes they went on board and consumed the strong liquor they were offered.

Although the Caribs traded with the strangers, they did not like it when they saw them building homes and settling in. They began to feel threatened by their presence. They managed to drive away the first two colonies of Englishmen with bows and arrows and heavy war clubs. The French, who already had many fine estates in Martinique, were much more determined. They looked at Saint Lucia's good fertile soil and they wanted it. Their attitude was that if the Caribs didn't want to cooperate, they knew what to do. They built forts to protect their pioneer settlers and armed themselves with guns and cannons. The remains of one of these forts can still be seen at la Batterie.

Between 1651 and 1659, the French sent five Governors to Saint Lucia. The first one was smart. He married a Carib woman and so was left in peace, but died after only three years. However, the three Governors who followed him were all killed. The fifth died of a fever. The French still didn't give up, even though they were also encountering some serious opposition from the British. By the beginning of the 18th century, France was offering her citizens title to land in Saint Lucia if they would go there and settle.

Soon, all around Islet-a-Caret, large areas were claimed and cleared. The first of Laborie large estates were being born.

EXODUS

The French were the first to have large estates in Saint Lucia. They introduced sugar as a plantation crop. When the British took over the island in 1814, many of the French landowners remained on their estates. Sugar continued to be the main crop for many years and Laborie was still one of the island's most productive areas. Then, at the beginning of the 20th century, farmers in Europe started to cultivate sugar beet. Before long, this brought down the price of sugar on the world market. Other crops were now planted, coconuts, cotton and some bananas, but now labour was a problem. More and more of the land was being left idle.

During the Second World War, a US base opened at Vieux Fort. This tempted many men to leave the hard work on the land with its poor pay. They preferred the regular hours and the good money they could get working at the base. Some went even further. They left their homes and went away hoping to make their fortunes. They went to Cayenne and

Our Lady of Purification, Laborie

...fore and after the washing machine
...washing clothes in the river

Panama and to the Dutch islands of Curacao and Aruba. Some of them never returned. Those who did usually had enough money to build a house or start a small business. If they did go back to the land, they were able to buy their own land instead of working for somebody else.

In the 1950s there was another, strong movement of labour away from the island. Men were tired of being out of work, or working for less than two dollars a day. Hundreds of Saint Lucians from Laborie and the other villages, bought passages on ships going to England. They sailed three thousand miles to a country they had never seen, hoping for a chance at a better life.

They sent money back to the families they had left behind. Sometimes, after a while, they were also able to make the trip back.

The larger estates were finding it more and more difficult to make a profit. Labour was scarce, markets were uncertain, and ships did not call regularly. The fishermen still went to sea. They came back with catches of kingfish, dolphin, flying fish and tuna. But the young men, whose fathers had worked on the land, were drifting away. They went to Vieux Fort or even to Castries, looking for other work. In Laborie, if the land wasn't being worked, there was nothing else.

Saint Lucia's spectacular southea *coa*

MEN WHO MADE THEIR MARK

During this time, there was another sort of exodus from Laborie not people going off to find work and wealth, but young men and women searching for a better education than they could get at home. The first schools to be opened in Saint Lucia were started in 1838, by the Lady Mico Trust. Laborie was one of the first villages to benefit. In 1839, its small Mico School had 80 pupils, both boys and girls. It was on Main Street, in the same building where the Community Centre is today.

By 1880, the number of pupils in the Mico School had grown to 122. There were 87 boys and 35 girls. There was also a Catholic Girls School with 93 pupils, that had opened in 1873. This school later became the Laborie Infants School. All the Mico Schools in the island were closed down in 1891. By this time the Catholics had opened a second school for boys. By 1895, the two schools had a total of 227 students, 121 boys and 106 girls. The Boys School is still in the same spot today, but it has been made longer by about fifteen feet.

The population of the island at this time was about 42,000. There were schools in all the villages, but only St. Joseph's Convent and St. Mary's College offered higher education. Unless a child's parents could pay to send them overseas they had to fight for the few places that were available. Competition was fierce and government scholarships were few. The children had to be really good to succeed.

In spite of the drawbacks, Laborie produced brilliant scholars. Alan Louisy, retired judge and the Prime Minister of Saint Lucia from 1979 to 1981, was one. His family own an estate at Laborie called Sapphire. Keith St. Aimee is another Laborie man. He was Saint Lucia's Representative to the United Nations from 1982 to 1985. Sir Lennox O'Reilly, a famous West Indian lawyer and his two brothers, also lawyers, were born in Laborie. Another outstanding legal figure was Judge JEM Salmon.

Even now, in Laborie schools, there may be students who will one day bring fame and recognition to their village.

LETTING GO

In the past, large estates, like Balembouche, Parc, Londonderry, Mont Lezard, Perle and Sapphire, made Laborie an important agricultural area. Many still have the ruins of the mills that once crushed the sugarcane. Some still have large areas planted with coconuts, put in when the price of sugar started to fall. All now have many acres lying unproductive and useless. Some old people in the district remember when sea island cotton was grown here and there was a factory making bay rum. These things belong to the past. The days of the large estates are over.

Even with bananas, the island's most important crop, good results are quite possible on quite small plots of land. Finding a market for their produce is always a problem for the small farmer. Many farmers belong to cooperatives which enable them to market their produce collectively.

The island's bananas go by sea to England, but air freight has helped to open up markets for other produce. Saint Lucia now ships mangoes, soursops, golden apples, breadfruit, plantain, hot peppers, pumpkin and other vegetables to Britain, Canada and the United States. Some bananas are also shipped to other Caribbean islands, including Barbados and Antigua.

Many people would return to the land if they had some that they could call their own. It is not beneficial for a country to have good agricultural land used for building or left idle. Perhaps some of the large estate owners need to accept this and release some of the land they no longer use.

The road from Castries to Vieux Fort and on to Laborie has been improved. There are also better links from the International Airport at Hewanorra to Britain, North America and the rest of the Caribbean. Industrial development in Vieux Fort has created more jobs so that, in time, young people from Laborie may no longer have to leave home to find work.

Change is never easy. If Laborie is to keep pace, perhaps it is time to let go of the past and start looking to the future.

Micoud

THE FIRST SETTLERS

Of all the places you might visit on your tour of Saint Lucia, Micoud is probably richest in Amerindian history. Between Micoud and Canelles, archaeologists have found evidence of eight or nine settlements. Remains of cooking pits, tools, pots and ornaments have been discovered at Troumasse, Micoud Bay and Anse Capitaine. Artifacts have also been found on the banks of the River Ger and on the two headlands north of the Canelles River.

Why did the Amerindians come to this part of the island? Was it because the large rivers full of fish and crayfish? Was it for the sheltered bays where they could safely anchor their boats, or on account of the strong, fresh wind that blew from the sea? Perhaps they stayed because everything they needed was here in one place. Much of the land north of Micoud ends in high jagged cliffs. On the West Coast, the sea is calmer, but heavy forest and bush came right down to the shore.

The Amerindians came to Saint Lucia from the South American mainland. They came from the flat lands at the mouth of the Orinoco River and the coastal plains of Guyana and Surinam. Rivers were their roads and water was a natural part of their life.

The land behind Micoud slopes gently away to the distant mountains and the rainforest. They might have thought the forests were full of wild animals or evil spirits. They preferred the windy headlands or the river banks.

The women spent their days working in their vegetable patches, grating cassava or making clay pots. They often decorated the pots by painting them with dyes made from plants. They also gathered grasses which they dried and wove into mats and baskets. The men fished in the river with bows and arrows or collected crabs and oysters in the mangroves.

During the 17th century, Spanish, Dutch, French and English ships sailed the waters of the Caribbean. Saint Lucia with its rivers and forests, must have looked very inviting to them. Sailors went ashore to trade for wood, water and fresh meat. Some of them thought it would be a good place to settle and make a new life.

The Caribs did not want this. They attacked the new settlements. They even got Caribs from Saint Vincent and Dominica to help them. But their bows and arrows and axes were no match for the guns that were soon turned against them.

THE FRENCH LEAVE THEIR MARK

The French built forts to protect their early settlers, but the Caribs still attacked them. They had already had enough problems fighting with

Micoud

Religion lies at the heart of national life in Saint Lucia society

...icoud is the main centre for ...e Rose and Marguerite ...ower Festivals

the English so, after a while, they withdrew. But they didn't give up. They went back to Martinique and Guadeloupe where they were more secure. Then, in the early part of the 18th century, they returned.

Soon there were French settlements from one end of the island to the other. Most of them were on the west coast. In the north there was Gros Islet, Carenage and Anse la Raye. Further south came Soufriere, Anse Citron (Choiseul) and Islet-a-Carret (Laborie). By 1760, the Caribs were no longer able to mount a credible resistance. Only two small communities remained. One at Choiseul and the other at Anse Louvet.

After two thousand years or more, the Amerindian control of Saint Lucia was over. Micoud's first inhabitants had vanished leaving hardly a trace. Some of the places where they had lived were already buried under bush. They would remain there, hidden, until archaeologists started to uncover them in the 1950s.

A new settlement grew up by the mouth of the Troumassee River. The settlement had the same name, but it was spelled 'Troumassee'. In 1770, this small community moved away from the marshy river mouth to the windy headland overlooking Anse Ger. Below them, to the south, the Ger River flowed through the mangroves on its way to the sea. On some old maps these names are written 'Angere' and 'Angere Point'.

Around that time, the French decided to re-name these places in honour of Monsieur de Micoud, Governor of Saint Lucia from 1768 to 1771. The settlement became the bourg or village of Micoud. Then there was Micoud Point, Anse Micoud and the Micoud River. One name, however, did not change. The Amerindians who lived on the banks of the River Ger called that area Kajouka. Today, the people of Micoud still call it by that name.

In 1773, a church and a presbytery were built and Micoud got its first priest. Unfortunately, neither the priest nor the village lasted long. In 1780, a hurricane destroyed the church and the houses around it. The Priest died the same year. On an old plan of the site, a cross marks the place where the church once stood. On the headland traces of the building still remain.

Sugar, introduced by the French, quickly became a major crop. Slaves were brought from Africa to work the land. By 1775, one sixth of Saint Lucia was under cultivation. The district of Micoud had 84 estates. It was becoming one of the island's most important agricultural areas. Some of the descendants of those slaves now own and farm their own land.

MICOUD MOVES NORTH

After the hurricane of 1780, the village of Micoud moved once more. This time it went north. It moved beyond the earlier site at the mouth of the Troumassee River to a small bay. The place where the village had been before the hurricane was now called Vieux Bourg. That is French for Old Town, the same name the site has today.

Even though the village was now more than a mile away, the bay, the headland and the river were still called Micoud. The new village of Port Micoud grew. Transport overland was slow and difficult. Produce from the estates around the village was brought to Micoud to be loaded onto ships and taken to the capital. In the old days several boats would sail up together as protection against the pirates who prowled the seas. By the end of the 18th century that danger had almost disappeared.

After the start of the French Revolution in 1789, Republicans came to Saint Lucia and freed the slaves. They also gave all the towns and villages new names and so Micoud became Union. In 1794, the English took over the island. In 1795, the French took it back, but not for long. In 1796, Sir Ralph Abercrombie, with an army of 12,000 men, captured Morne Fortune. Sir John Moore, who was made Governor of the island, set out immediately, to do battle with the Brigands.

The Brigands' 'Armee dans les Bois' was made up of freed slaves and French revolutionary soldiers. Micoud, like many other places, was affected by their clashes with the English imperial army.

Finally, the French and the English put an end to their fighting. Slavery, which had been reintroduced by the English, was eventually

St Lucy's Catholic Church, Micoud

abolished, new buildings were built, and Micoud became the centre of a busy and important agricultural district once again. But one important problem remained. Along the coast, especially at the river mouths, where swamps swarming with mosquitoes. Their bite carried sickness and death.

To protect themselves, the Amerindians rubbed their skin with castor oil mixed with the seeds of the urucou tree. They also closed up their houses as soon as it began to get dark to keep the insects out. Europeans were not equipped with similar knowledge. Nearly all the priests sent to Micoud between 1838 and 1888 contracted malaria or yellow fever. Five of them died.

MICOUD ON THE MAP

Micoud, a tightly packed blend of old and new houses, lies close to the shore. At one time, the main road from Castries to the south ran through the village. Today the new highway, with its speeding traffic, swings by much further inland. Only the sign 'Welcome to Micoud' reminds you that the village is still there. Most Saint Lucians need no such reminder. Micoud was put on the map in 1964, when John Compton became Chief Minister.

John Compton was leader of the United Workers' Party and representative for the district of Micoud. His estate, Mahaut, was once owned by Elwin Augustin, whose sister Grace was the first Saint Lucian woman to study law. Grace owned Patience, an estate that is still known for its fine timber.

The estates around Micoud stretch from the coast to the very edges of the rainforest. Mahaut, Patience, Cannelles, Fond, Beauchamps, Troumassee, Volet - their names tell us they were all established in the time of the French. In those days, sugar was the island's main crop. On some estates, the ruins of old factories and water wheels can still be seen. They remind us that sugar was once as important to Micoud as it was to the rest of the island, as important as bananas are today.

Anyone familiar with the culture of Saint Lucia will know that the other thing that is important in Micoud is music. This is one of the main centres for the Rose and Marguerite festivals. The Societies of the Rose and the Marguerite were started soon after the abolition of slavery. They collected money to help keep the church buildings in good repair. Each year on their special feast day their kings and queens, with all their followers, would attend a solemn Mass.

There was competition between the two groups and also fierce quarrels. Their songs and dances were often high-spirited. The priests disapproved, especially of the dance called the 'Bel Air'. They tried to have it stopped and at one time Catholics were forbidden to join the Societies - now, people from all over Saint Lucia and overseas go to Micoud for these fetes.

Roman Catholic Infant School, Micoud

In 1866, Micoud had two of the first schools in the island, each with about 60 pupils. One was started by the 'Lady Mico Trustees' of England to 'promote education among the black and coloured population of the West Indies.' The other was a Catholic school. Today, Micoud has an Infant School attended by 460 children a Primary School with over 500 pupils, and a Secondary School with 650 students.

TOWARD THE YEAR 2001

Will Micoud still be dependent on agriculture and fishing in the 21st century? Or will the development of industries in the south provide jobs of a different kind? Some attempts have already been made, like the canning factory and the jams and pickles made from local produce. There was even an idea for removing the fibre from banana stems and shipping it away to be made into rope. None of these were very successful, and although the village has grown, nothing much has changed.

Jobs are still scarce. There is talk of development at Troumassee, a hotel perhaps or a clinic. The talk is nothing new. So far the only things to be seen in the fields are the slow, heavy cattle. They stop to drink at the pool with the water lilies by the road. Behind them, in the grass, stalk white cattle egrets on long thin legs, picking up the insects the cows disturb with their hooves.

Just before the turning to the village, a narrow, well-paved road runs off to the right. It passes through fields of bananas, through miles of well farmed land, stopping just a short distance from the edge of the central rainforest. Buses drive along it, full of tourists who have paid to walk the forest trail. They hope to see the rare Saint Lucia Parrot. In the forest the clouds hang low and rain falls almost every day. All three large rivers that carry water to Micoud's agricultural land start here.

The forest of the Central Reserve is protected by law. Outside its boundary however, much of the forest has already been cleared. The water in the rivers is not as deep as it was in the past. The future of Micoud's farmers hangs in the balance. Good land management is the only answer. The huge trees, once cut for the saw mill at Patience, were specially selected. Others were left so that the forest could regenerate naturally. Clear-cutting, or removing all the trees from one place disturbs the forest ecology for a very long time.

Forests are important for water as well as wood. Properly managed, they will provide Saint Lucia with a supply of both, now and in the future. The people of Micoud have always relied on the land. They understand how important it is to look after it.

Troumassee Falls near Fond St Jaques

Pigeon Island

Pigeon Island

THE OFFSHORE ISLAND

The island lay just a short distance from the mainland. It was narrow with two small hills, one at either end. It was lit by the fiery red of the setting sun as it spread its colour across the western sky. The glow was caught by the puffy, slow-moving clouds and reflected onto the sea below. From the beach, a canoe slipped into the water and headed out into the bay.

The canoe had been shaped from the trunk of a tall gommier tree. In it were two men from one of the Arawak villages on Iouanaloa, the big island. In their language, the name meant 'Land of the Iguanas'.

The men had spent all day fishing and exploring. They had a small catch of fish and some juicy red fruits they had gathered from the cactus bushes on the small island. They also had a few large shells that they had taken from the seagrass bed close to shore. Now they were ready to go home. Their women would be waiting with a tasty stew made from the crabs they had caught in the mangrove swamps the night before. They would eat well. Then they would throw herbs on the fire, climb into their hammocks and sleep. The herbs would make a thick, sweet-smelling smoke that would drive the mosquitoes away.

Behind them in the dusk, the little island was only a black shape against the darkening sky. Small, quick, black bats swooped from a cave high up on one of the slopes. They swirled through the sky, making a meal of the insects that were there in such numbers. The evening air was perfumed with the scent of wild frangipani and filled with the noise of crickets and tree frogs. Far out, in the dark waters of the channel, a school of porpoises passed. They leaped and turned, sometimes somersaulting clear out of the water, as they made their way north.

There was no one there to see them. The little island was uninhabited. There was no fire to cast its warm light against the shadows. Only the fireflies, flickering through the bush, lit up the scene with their pinpoints of light.

LE GROS ILET

Another group of Amerindians called the Caribs came to Iouanaloa from the islands further south. Some of them made a camp at the southern end of the small island. From here they paddled their canoes across the bay to raid the Arawak villages on the mainland.

However, after many conflicts, the Caribs moved on. Their camp in the cave on the small island was abandoned. The bats that hung high in the craggy corners and the crabs that hid among the stones, now had it to themselves. Many years later some pieces of broken pots and a few

Yacht racing off Pigeon Island

discarded tools were found. The artefacts are the only proof that the Caribs were in Saint Lucia.

On old French maps the little island is called 'le Gros Islet'. Many birds once nested in its steep cliffs. There were egrets and boobys, frigate birds, pelicans and long necked, long legged blue herons. The bay between the island and the mainland was full of fish. Boobys and pelicans could be seen swooping over the surface of the water and diving into its depths after them.

The herons and egrets preferred to fish in the mangroves on the big island. Here, they could walk around on their stilt-like legs sifting through the mud for tidbits.

In the 16th century the Spanish arrived in their many-sailed galleons. Soon they were followed by the English, French, Dutch and Portuguese. The Spanish ships, loaded with the plundered gold of South American cities, were often waylaid and boarded by pirates.

One of these pirates was a big, bearded Frenchman called Francois Leclerc. He had lost a leg in one of his fights. In its place he wore a wooden stump and so he was known as 'Jambe de Bois'. When he sailed into the bay one day, he liked what he saw. He set up camp on le Gros Islet, in a cave up on the hill. Then he posted a lookout to watch the channel.

Whenever a Spanish ship was sighted he would pull up his anchor, unfurl his sails and slip out from the bay ready to do battle.

PIGEON ISLAND

Like the Caribs before him, Jambe de Bois eventually moved on. He may have decided to go somewhere else or he may himself have been overtaken by a bigger and faster ship. We will never know. Once more, the bats took possession of the cave on the hillside. No trace of the pirate's treasure was ever found.

Fierce battles were now taking place between the French and the English. The booming of their cannons became a familiar sound. The big island that the French called Sainte Lucie, changed hands many times.

In 1778, after defeating the French at the Battle of Cul de Sac, the English established a base in Gros Islet Bay. They hauled guns to the small island, making a fortress on the top of one of the hills. On their maps the main island was now marked Saint Lucia, the smaller one was 'Pidgeon Island'.

In 1780, the island was struck by a terrible hurricane that sunk or damaged many of the English ships. But by 1782, there were so many boats at anchor in the bay, it was almost possible to walk across it without getting your feet wet! When the lookout reported a fleet of French warships leaving Martinique, Admiral Rodney set sail with more than a hundred ships.

The two navies met in the historic Battle of the Saints. The battle was so named because it took place near the islands of the same name. Admiral Rodney brilliantly outmanoeuvred the French and sailed back in victory.

Another hurricane hit the island in 1817. Some of the buildings on Pidgeon Island were damaged. They were later repaired, and others added to make barracks for several hundred men. Many of the soldiers that occupied them died, not in battle but from disease. They died of malaria and yellow fever, carried by the bite of the mosquitoes that bred in the mainland swamps.

The garrison was finally abandoned and the guns removed. For a while the buildings were used to house indentured labourers brought in from India to work on the estates. Then in 1901, troops from the Morne moved in, to escape yet another epidemic of yellow fever. When they left, the island was given over to the bats, the birds and the goats.

THE DEVELOPMENT OF RODNEY BAY

During the early part of the 20th century a whaling station was set up on the island. The little dock where Rodney and his men had once stepped ashore now served a different purpose and saw bloodshed of a different kind.

A small fleet of whaling schooners was based there. They would come in with their catch of porpoises or pilot whales. Sometimes they even managed to catch a gigantic hump-backed whale. These unfortunate, intelligent creatures were butchered on the beach. The water in the bay ran red with their blood. Their flesh was cut up and boiled in large vats to extract the oil. There was a heavy, unpleasant smell of whale oil everywhere.

Fortunately, this did not persist for long. The laws that controlled whaling were changed and the station was closed down. Once more, the island became the peaceful domain of bats, birds, crabs and goats.

An Englishwoman called Josset Legh came to the island just before the Second World War. She had been an actress and was a lover of animals and plants. She had a vision of how beautiful the island could be. Soon, the green fronds of coconut palms shaded the sand. The brilliant blossoms of flamboyant and hibiscus coloured the landscape. Houses thatched with dry grass were built upon the ruins of the old barracks. Once more the bay was filled with yachts at anchor.

At the back of the beach was a small restaurant where people ate meals of lobster, sea eggs or fish, fresh from the fishermen's nets. They washed it down with bottles of wine brought over from neighbouring Martinique. At night the bar was lit by the soft light of hurricane lanterns. Bats swooped through the open shelter and soldier crabs, clumsy in their borrowed shells, rattled about the floor.

After a while, Josset retired, to live in peace in her little house by the cemetery at the end of the beach. Then, in 1971, a causeway was built

...he steep slopes of Pigeon Island
...ade it the perfect strategic point
...om which to defend Rodney Bay

to carry a road from the mainland out to the small island. To the north, the new road was lined with boulders and feathery casuarinas. On the other side was a wide sandy area fringed with palms. Now people no longer needed a boat to visit the island.

The area was renamed Rodney Bay in honour of the famous Admiral who had once had his base there.

PIGEON ISLAND NATIONAL PARK

The care and protection of the 40 acres that once made up Pigeon Island is the responsibility of the Saint Lucia National Trust. On February 23 1979, the first day of Saint Lucia's independence, the park was officially opened by Her Royal Highness Princess Alexandra. Now, visiting Pigeon Island National Park is like taking a step back in time. Paths have been cleared, steps repaired and a lookout point built on the way up to the fort. At the top, there are guns in place, just as they might have been in Rodney's time.

The remains of the old barracks, the kitchens and the guardhouse can still be seen. The Officer's Mess, built in 1808, became the foundation for a private home. It now houses a museum, full of reminders of the island's past, and a gift shop.

Pigeon Island is perhaps best described as an open-air historical museum

The cemetery, long neglected and weed-infested, is now well kept. On the crumbling tombs only two inscriptions remain. One records the death of a two-year old infant. The other is for Mary Nicholson, *"Beloved Wife of Dr Nicholson, who departed this world on February 5, 1892 at the age of 29 years."* No other stones remain. Some modern pirate, more interested in the marble slabs than the tales they told, has taken them away.

What is happening on the island today is every bit as important as anything that went before. It is all part of Saint Lucia's history, part of her people's heritage. The Amerindians, the one-legged pirate, Rodney and his fleet, are all woven into this rich, historical tapestry.

The old stone walls are bright with splashes of bougainvillea. Pink and red oleander and hibiscus blossoms dot the pathways. Up on the hills, clinging to the bare rock, wild frangipani and 'eyelash' orchids scent the air.

Egrets and herons still nest on the steep cliff and boobys and frigate birds still skim the waters of the bay, but the pelicans have gone. Sometimes, as well as the sandpipers and turnstones, an American dowitcher can be seen on the rocky shore. At night the soft shuffling of waves onto the sand sends little yellow ghost crabs scuttling up the beach. The waves wash away the footsteps left by daytime visitors. The memories and the footsteps of the island's past are locked away in the deserted ruins.

Rodney Bay viewed from Pigeon Island's fortifications

Pigeon Island

Soufriere

THE PEOPLE OF SOUFRIERE

Soufriere

Soufriere became a town in 1746, almost a hundred years after the small community was first established. The people were mostly of French or African descent with just a few Britishers. The landowners, tradespeople and clerks were white. The domestic servants and the labourers on the estates were black. There were also mullatos who were a mixture of Europeans and Africans.

The mullatos were the ones usually chosen to be overseers or to hold other positions of trust and responsibility. For this reason they were despised and disliked by the slaves. It was not until 1838, when emancipation freed them, that the slaves were able to own property and land of their own. Many continued to work on the estates where they had once been slaves. Others, wanting to be properly independent, tried to make it on their own.

The Caribbean Sea was full of fish and some of the former slaves became fishermen. Their life was hard, but at least their families had food to eat. When the catch was good they even had fish to sell. Others scratched a living from the land, growing vegetables and raising livestock. As the town grew there was more need for shops and other services. Some former slaves became merchants.

French and Patois were the languages spoken. Even after the island became British, the descendants of the early French families continued to speak French. Although English was the official language of the island, the French-based Patois remained the language of the people. Soufriere kept its French character.

Some famous Saint Lucians have come from the town of Soufriere. Josephine Tascher de la Pagerie, who would one day become Empress of all France, spent much of her childhood there. Dr Beausoleil, the island's first Saint Lucian doctor, was from Soufriere, so were the family of R Belizaire who wrote Saint Lucia's first geography book. Queen Elizabeth II set foot on Saint Lucian soil for the first time in 1966. She landed, not in Castries, but on the jetty at Soufriere.

Before Soufriere was supplied with electricity from the power station at Vieux Fort, residents had lights powered by a local hydro-electric system. It was operated by the flow of the water in the Soufriere River. Today there is a road running north through Canaries and on to Castries. Before this road was completed a regular boat service left the jetty at Soufriere carrying people and their produce up to the city to do their marketing.

Soufriere has several small guest houses and hotels and excellent restaurants. Each year more and more visitors make the trip, by road or sea, to this very special part of the island.

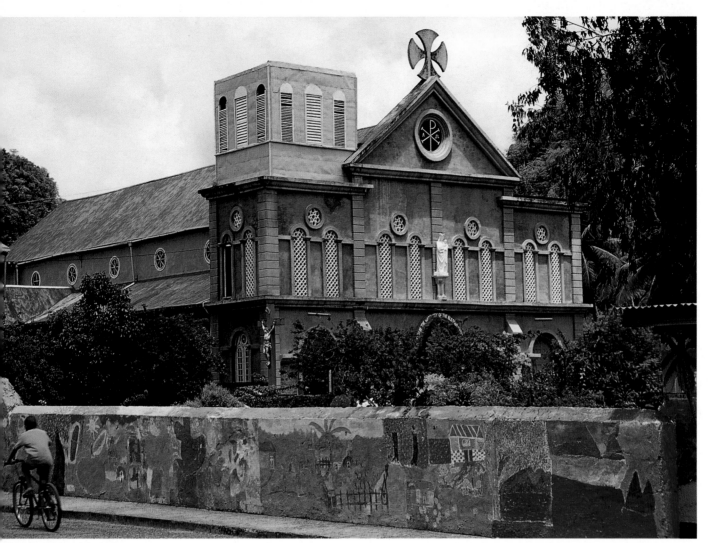

Soufriere village church

THE AGRICULTURAL ENVIRONMENT

Agriculture in Soufriere began with the arrival of the French in the middle of the 17th century. The Amerindians had tended their plots of corn and beans, their peppers and yams. But their gardens were planted for their own use, there was seldom any surplus. Now, large areas of land were cleared to plant crops like cotton and tobacco to be sold and shipped overseas. Sugar was introduced later and soon became the most important crop of all.

The rivers that watered the land came from high up in the rainforest. The estate owners brought in machinery and built large water wheels that were powered by the flowing water of these rivers. As the wheels turned they operated mills that crushed the cane, squeezing out the juice. By 1842, there were twenty sugar mills working in the Soufriere area alone. The labourers who worked in them were paid just one shilling and sixpence a day (36 cents).

Toward the end of the 19th century, the sugar market began to drop. The planters were forced to turn back to crops like cocoa and coffee that they had abandoned in favour of cane. New crops were introduced, like citrus fruits and nutmeg, then coconuts and, later still, bananas.

Many of the workers on the estates had their own gardens. In them they grew fruit and vegetables for their own families and also to send to the market in Castries. Everything grew well. The soil was rich and well watered. From the estates came coffee, cocoa, oranges, limes, spices, coconuts and a variety of vegetables. Soufriere soon became known as 'the garden of Saint Lucia'.

A lime press was installed on Soufriere estate and lime oil and juice were exported to England. Another crop that was becoming more and more important was copra. In the early 1950s the Coconut Oil Factory began operating in Soufriere. For thirty years or so copra remained the main crop for the area.

Then, in 1980, Hurricane Allen destroyed many of the trees and those that were left were severely attacked by the coconut mite. Copra production dropped from 6,483 tons in 1980 to 2,433 the following year. By 1990, however, production was already back to 5,000 tons and still climbing. The factory still produces oil, margarine and soap for local use and for export.

Today, the land around Soufriere is mainly planted with bananas, cocoa and fruits like citrus and avocado. Although bananas are the island's main export crop, copra is still a major industry. In some places, especially on the Windward coast, bananas are now being inter-cropped with coconuts.

Soufriere village

THE PHYSICAL ENVIRONMENT

The Pitons, rising from the sea at Soufriere, are Saint Lucia's most famous landmark. Saint Lucia is a volcanic island. At Soufriere the signs of the tremendous activity still churning and boiling beneath us are clearly visible.

Way back in time, before man appeared on earth, this area erupted with a terrible force. The explosion left behind a crater many miles wide. From its still molten floor, rose two huge plugs of lava. These gradually cooled and took shape to become the Pitons. Not far away, hot gases bubbled up through the thin crust, filling the air with clouds of steam. This is the spot known as the Sulphur Springs, Saint Lucia's drive-in volcano.

The water in the bubbling pools is full of minerals. The ground around them sparkles with crystals of silica, calcium carbonate and bright yellow sulphur. This sulphur gives the gas its horrible, rotten-egg smell, but it is also a valuable chemical and medicine. At one time it was mined and exported.

The Amerindians thought this was a frightening place with its boiling cauldrons and smelly steam-filled air. They called it 'Qualibu', the place of death. The French were more knowledgable. They understood the healing powers of the waters. King Louis XVI ordered baths to be

Soufriere wharf

built on Diamond Estate, for his troops to soak in the mineral waters. The baths were fed by an underground flow that came directly from the hot springs. Behind them is a waterfall where the mineral waters, mingled with the water of the Diamond River, streak the rocks with copper coloured patches.

Soufriere lies in a wide, fertile valley. At the back are the mountains that form part of the island's central watershed. Their upper slopes are covered with tall trees, their heads buried in the clouds. From them spring many rivers, Soufriere, Troumassee, Doree, Canelles, Choiseul and Vieux Fort. These are the rivers that supply Soufriere and most of the southern part of the island with water.

Then there is Soufriere Bay, wide and deep, its blue waters reflect the steep cone of the Petit Piton, rising from its southern side. Fishing boats and houses fringe the inner curve of the bay. Beyond the headland that marks its northern limit lies Anse Chastanet with its silver speckled beach and fascinating underwater world of reefs and coral gardens. From the seashore to the rainforest, Soufriere is an area of unique splendour.

THE HISTORY OF SOUFRIERE

ufriere village

Like most parts of the island, Soufriere shows signs of Amerindian occupation. Until recently however, there was little evidence to show that they had been there in any numbers. Now, the discovery of the terraces and carved rocks at Belfond and the exciting new find of the petroglyph near Jalousie indicate that Soufriere was perhaps one of the most important sites of all.

After the Amerindians, the first permanent settlers to arrive were the French who came around the end of the 17th century. Already well established in Martinique, they realised that the rich, fertile soil of Soufriere would be ideal for farming. The island changed hands fourteen times between the British and the French, but these early estates remained largely in the hands of descendants of these French immigrants. They brought in slaves from Africa to work the land. In 1746, Soufriere was officially recognised by France as a town, the first in the island.

With the last years of that century came the French Revolution. Its effects were felt throughout the French Antilles. In Martinique and Guadeloupe, many royalists were beheaded. It is said that the ship carrying the guillotine sailed into Soufriere Bay. The awesome machine was taken ashore and set up in the Town Square in front of the church, to continue its work. The revolutionaries declared that slavery in the French islands was at an end. But under Napoleon slavery was reintroduced. The island was taken by the British again. Many of the freed slaves, as well as French soldiers who had deserted, took to the hills. From their hideouts they organised raids on the town. They destroyed or damaged many buildings including the baths on the Diamond Estate.

During Soufriere's history, the town has been shaken by storms many times. There was the Great Hurricane of 1780, followed by others in 1817, 1831 and 1898. In 1839 an earthquake shook down the church steeple and more recently, in 1955, half the town was destroyed by fire. Hurricane Allen in 1980, was another blow. And, in 1991, Yokahu woke up, giving the whole island a good shake just to remind people that he was still around.

In spite of all these upheavals, Soufriere continues to grow. It will never be the island's capital but it has produced men who have been important in the fields of law, commerce and politics. Towards the end of George Charles long term as Prime Minister of Saint Lucia, more than half the members of the House of Assembly were Soufriere men, including him. Soufriere is still a centre for agriculture but tourism is slowly gaining in importance.

THE WILDLIFE AND THE FOREST

While it is true the Pitons and the Sulphur Springs attract visitors to Saint Lucia, more important than either of these are the forests that surround them. They provide a large percentage of the island's water. They are the home of the Jacquot, Saint Lucia's national bird. They also provide shelter for lesser known species like the Saint Lucia blackfinch and the rufous-throated solitaire.

The Amerindians went to the forest to cut the gommier trees to make their canoes. The settlers, who came later, cut timber for houses, furniture and fuelwood. The freed slaves cleared the forest to plant gardens to feed their families. In 1887, over a hundred years ago, a forester, E D Hooper, wrote a report condemning the clearing of Saint Lucia's hillsides to plant cocoa and other crops.

The Ministry of Agriculture was aware that the forest was being destroyed at an alarming rate. In 1938, they introduced mahogany to the island. Some trees were planted along the Murray Road, others were given to Andre Duboulay, owner of Soufriere Estate. Later, teak was introduced and in the early 1950s Mr Duboulay planted this species all along the Anse Chastanet Road. But in spite of these efforts, there was no forest reserve as we know it today.

Soufriere Anglican Church

No-one needed a licence to cut down a tree. People went freely into the forest, chopping down the best woods like the gommier, the balata and the laurier and hauling them away. Then, in 1958, Colonial Development and Welfare started a reforestation programme in the Edmund Forest. Areas that had been cleared were replanted with blue mahoe and mahogany.

Hummingbird Beach Resort and Restaurant provides excellent food and accommodation, as well as a superb close-up view of the Pitons

The reforestation programme continued through the 1960s and 1970s under Gabriel Charles, head of the Forestry Division from 1975 to 1990. Twenty-five years later those same trees were being harvested for fence posts, pickets and timber.

New trees are still being planted to replace those that have been cut. Trees are also planted to reclaim forest lands destroyed by people thinking only of their own profit. The Forest Reserve today covers 16,388 acres. If the indiscriminate felling had been allowed to continue, what a sorry heritage we would have handed on to future Saint Lucians. The heart of Soufriere does not lie buried beneath the Pitons. It beats high in the rainforest where the water, its lifeblood, springs.

Vieux Fort

As far as we know, the first inhabitants of Saint Lucia were Amerindians from South America. They arrived in canoes after making their way slowly north up the chain of Caribbean islands. The Arawaks came around the year 400 AD or even earlier. They probably landed at the southern end of the island, where Vieux Fort is today. As they steered their boats through the reefs into calmer waters, they would have seen shores covered with a heavy growth of mangroves. Behind them the land was flat, but in the distance it rose up into jagged mountain peaks. From these mountains, wide sparkling clear rivers ran down to the sea. There were fish, crabs and shellfish in the mangroves and flocks of brightly coloured birds in the forest. Everywhere there were berries, fruits and roots that were good to eat. The Arawaks were only too happy to stay.

Unfortunately for the peaceful Arawaks, the Caribs who followed them were reportedly less peaceful. They waged war on the Arawaks, killing the men and taking the women and children into their own camps. For many years they ruled the island. Then, in 1605, some Englishmen came ashore in small boats in the area of Vieux Fort. Their ship had been blown off course and they needed food and water. At first the Caribs were curious. They went to meet the strangers carrying fruit and vegetables that they exchanged for knives, beads and other trinkets. When they realised the Englishmen intended to stay they were no longer friendly. They attacked the camp, setting fire to the rough shelters that the men had built and killing many of them. The survivors were forced to escape in a small boat.

Once more the Caribs were in command, but not for long. Soon other foreigners arrived, French, Dutch and more English. Although the Caribs usually started by being friendly, they always ended up killing the new arrivals or chasing them away. More strangers came, they had guns and they built forts to protect themselves from the Carib's raids. One of these forts was at Point Sables. It was built by some Dutchmen to protect their ships when they came in to get wood and water. After a while they abandoned it, but the ruins remained. That was how Vieux Fort got its name, for in English Vieux Fort means 'old fort'.

Vieux Fort

THE FIRST SUGAR MILL

During the 17th century, the English and the French had both tried to settle in the Vieux Fort area. They cleared land and cut trees to build their houses. They planted tobacco, cotton, cassava, ginger and other crops for their own use. And they fought with and finally defeated the Caribs. Then, for the next hundred years, they fought each other for possession of the island.

In 1764, Saint Lucia was made a dependency of Martinique and the French planters introduced sugar cane to the island. The first sugar mill in Saint Lucia started working at Vieux fort that same year. By 1775,

Picking plums near Hewanarro Airport

there were 61 estates in the Vieux Fort area alone and although cotton, cocoa and coffee were still grown, sugar became the most important crop of all.

Most of the estate owners and their families were French. Their labourers were black slaves shipped from Africa. When slavery was abolished in 1838, many of the slaves left the estates. Some went to work in the town, others took up fishing or worked on their own small plots of land. The estate owners brought in people from India to replace them. By the year 1898, there were 336 Indians working on the Vieux Fort estates. They were not slaves but indentured labourers, contracted to work for the person who had paid their passage money. When their contract time was finished they were given the choice of money or a piece of land. Some took the money and went home, but most chose to remain.

Until the end of the 1914-1918 World War, sugar was still an important export crop. Vieux Fort was still one of the largest producing areas on the island. Then the world market price for sugar dropped. Vieux Fort's Central Sugar Factory, one of the first in the Caribbean, suffered badly.

The estate owners, the workers, even the businesses in town saw some hard times. In 1939, the Saint Lucian Government sold about 700 acres of land belonging to the Sugar Company to the Government of Barbados. This opened the doors for quite a few Barbadians to leave their island and settle in Saint Lucia.

That was also the year of the beginning of the Second World War. Soon after the war started, the US leased over 1,000 acres of land at Vieux Fort to build an airport and a military base. This meant plenty of jobs for everyone. People came all the way from Castries to work in Vieux Fort.

Vieux Fort

BOOM TOWN

The US base at Vieux Fort brought jobs and other improvements. A new dock was built for ships to tie up alongside. New, well-surfaced roads were constructed to service the base, and a big, modern hospital. Wounded servicemen were brought there, on their way back to the US. When Beanefield was handed over to the Saint Lucian Government in 1960, the hospital was included in the deal. Now it is run by the Sisters of the Sorrowful Mother. People from Vieux Fort and the rest of the island go to St. Jude's for treatment.

By 1960, sugar had lost its importance as a crop. The world market price was still low and most estates were concentrating on coconuts or bananas. In the Vieux Fort area were many Indians, whose ancestors had been brought in as indentured labourers to work on the sugar estates. Some now owned and worked their own land. A few grew rice for their own use. Herds of cattle grazed the fields, providing fertiliser for the gardens and meat for the local market.

For the small farmer, bananas seemed to be the best crop. They produced fruit all year round and brought in a regular income. The banana industry grew very quickly and Vieux Fort became the port for shipping all the bananas grown in the south. The Geest banana boats would come alongside the new dock to load before going on to Castries.

In 1961, the 'Heifer Project' brought in new cattle to improve the local stock. There were enormous red bulls of a breed called Santa Gertrudis. They had been chosen for the amount of beef they could produce. Others were handsome, white brahmins with wide horns, humped backs and long, loose folds of skin hanging down from their necks. Like the zebu cattle, already brought in by some of the estates, the brahmins were originally from India. In that country, they were not eaten but kept for their milk and as working animals.

The East Coast Road made transportation of people and goods between Vieux Fort and Castries much easier. This attracted more business to the area. With the help of two million dollars donated by Canada, the old Beanefield airstrip was reconstructed. In 1971, it opened as an International Airport and was renamed 'Hewanorra'. The biggest hotel in the island, the Halcyon Days, was built in Vieux Fort around this time. New buildings went up in town. New schools were built and factories opened, making clothing, electrical equipment, cardboard boxes and Heineken beer.

It looked as if Vieux Fort was all set to become the southern capital. Then, in 1980, Hurricane Allen struck. The dock, the flour mill, the factories and many of the houses were badly hit. But, like Castries after the fires, Vieux Fort soon started to rebuild.

Church at Vieux Fort

VIEUX FORT HAS IT ALL

As well as the growth in agriculture and business, Vieux Fort grew in other ways. People became aware that it was one of the truly unique natural areas in Saint Lucia. The Maria Islands, lie just off the coast. They are the home of a colourful ground lizard and a harmless snake called the couresse. These creatures are found nowhere else in the world. To protect them, and the many seabirds that nest there, the islands have been made a Nature Reserve. In the Interpretative Centre, on the beach opposite the Maria Islands, are photographs and other exhibits.

There are many reminders of the people who lived in Vieux Fort in the past. At Black Bay and la Tourney there are Amerindian sites. At Savannes Bay and Pointe Sables are the remains of estate houses. The ruins of old sugar mills can be seen at Pointe Sables, Anse Noir, la Tourney and Black Bay.

Vieux Fort also has one of the last large mangrove swamps left on the island. At one time it was in danger of disappearing like so many others, cut down for coals or development. It was saved by an Organisation of American States (OAS) project, managed by the Forestry Department, that planted Leucaena trees at nearby St. Urbain. These trees grow taller than a man in one year, over 30 feet in three years! They provide quick

School of Medicine, Vieux Fort Industrial Estate

growing timber for charcoal and so help to reduce the pressure on the mangroves. They also enrich the soil and their leaves make good animal fodder.

The Fisheries Department also started a project at Vieux Fort. With a group of local fishermen they began to farm seamoss. It is grown on long cords attached to frames that float in the sea. When it is cut, the roots are left behind and so the seamoss grows back. It can be gathered from the same place again and again.

The seas around Vieux Fort are full of fish. But they still need to be 'farmed' if there are to be enough to feed the growing population. Reefs and mangroves are the breeding places and nurseries for many marine species. In the past they were thoughtlessly destroyed. Now, the fishermen understand their importance and are doing all they can to preserve them.

A community is made up of people who have different ways of earning their living. They have to understand and respect each other's needs if they are to live happily together. The Caribbean Natural Areas Resources Institute (CANARI), the Saint Lucia National Trust, Forestry Department and the Department of Fisheries, are working together to teach the people how to manage their resources wisely for the future.

FUTURE GROWTH

Vieux Fort

The early Amerindian settlers called Saint Lucia, Hewanorra. In their language that meant 'Land of the Iguana'. Today, iguanas, like the Arawaks, the Caribs and the sugar plantations, have disappeared from Vieux Fort. The inhabitants of the town come from many places. Among their ancestors were English and French settlers, Africans slaves, Indian indentured labourers and immigrant Barbadians.

The herds of cattle have grown. Animals can now be seen wandering freely, even along the roadside. Not only cows, but pigs, sheep, goats and horses. Among them move the cattle egrets, long-legged, long-necked white birds that nest in the mangrove swamps. At Beausejour, the Government Agricultural Station, new planting methods are studied. There is also a herd of black and white Holstein cows, imported to improve the local milk supply.

Vieux Fort fishing community

Many visitors are attracted to Vieux Fort's beautiful sandy beaches. They come to swim in the sea, laze in the sun and enjoy the fresh seafood and the tropical fruits. Like the island's very first settlers, nearly all the tourists arrive at Vieux Fort. Most of them travel by road to stay at the hotels in the north. Wherever they stay, when they fly out of Hewanorra, their last glimpse of Saint Lucia will be the Maria Islands and the lighthouse at Moule a Chique.

The money brought into the island by tourism is an important part of the economy. So is the growing foreign investment from the development of the Vieux Fort industrial estate. Large jets fly into Hewanorra International Airport every day bringing tourists from Europe and North America. They also provide strong business links between Saint Lucia and the rest of the world. The new jobs that are being created will help

St Lucia's volcanic origins clearly illustrated at Cape Moule-a-Chique, site of the world's second highest lighthouse

the people of Vieux Fort build up their town and the communities around it. They will no longer have to move away from home to find work. Vieux Fort has so much to offer, beautiful beaches, some of the world's rarest reptiles and room for industrial growth. There are also the people who can make it happen. People who are no longer French, English, African, Indian, Bajan or American, but Vieux Fortians and proud of it!

How to swim on a mountain top!

Sir John Compton Dam provides a valuable water resource in times of need

Agriculture

By the early 19th century sugar had superseded export crops like tobacco, cotton and ginger. Over time bananas became the leading crop, particularly after the collapse of sugar markets in the late 1950s released large areas of land for banana cultivation.

By 1965, bananas formed nearly 90 per cent of the country's exports, making St. Lucia the first Caribbean country dependent on the monocultivation of bananas.

Even though St. Lucia diversified into tourism, service industries and light manufacture, agricultural output was still important, accounting for just under 17 per cent of GAP in 1986. Together with forestry and fishing it provided 30 per cent of the jobs.

Unfortunately, agricultural land patterns used during the colonial period have not been easy to change, and even presently these contribute to the continuing land deterioration. The monoculture production system was never appropriate for a naturally diverse tropical environment capable of supporting more mixed agriculture. The consequent environmental costs have been high, despite the present economic gains. Entrenched practices of land tenure, preferred cropping systems and farming methods have made it difficult to implement new policies or directions.

Rainfall is generally less along the coasts, particularly on the windward side and often substantially higher in the interior, with local variations dependent on topography and elevation. The extreme south of the island is notably lower in elevation, flatter and drier than elsewhere. Seasonal variation produces a dry season between January and May, sometimes with periods of drought lasting over six weeks. Irrigation is therefore required to ensure high production levels throughout the year. At present only about 200 hectares of land are irrigated, consuming an estimated 300 million gallons of water per year. However, more than ten times this amount - 2,000 hectares of prime agricultural lands - has the potential to benefit from irrigation.

When low cost water is available in large quantities, irrigation provides the highest rewards of any agricultural investment and is especially important for accelerating the import substitution and new regional and extraregional markets for St. Lucia.

Irrigation may well be a major argument against the small farm strategy as it requires large scale public, rather than private, development of irrigation which requires sophisticated management, something which small farmers generally lack. On the plus side, however, land use practices associated with irrigation are very good, especially in terms of erosion control and sediment reduction.

Like many other Eastern Caribbean countries, land tenure in St. Lucia is a complex blending of British common law and local traditions, some imported from Africa. Further problems arise from the surviving elements of the French civil code, in particular, the laws of intestate succession and inheritance whereby a deceased's land is frequently divided among many heirs in the extended family tradition. While many indi-

Papaya/Pawpaw

Coco Pods

viduals own land, the pattern of ever increasing fragmentation deprives the agricultural sector of the benefits from economies of scale.

However, studies show that fragmentation does not necessarily have to lead to less efficient resource management or production. If access to credit, capital and management expertise is provided, the subdivision of large agricultural estates can actually result in a market increase in productivity. This may follow from aggressive, intensive exploitation and, in large part, to higher individual incentives associated with private land ownership.

It is clear, however, that agricultural production in St. Lucia has changed from a plantation system, dominated by large sugar and banana estates, to small-scale agricultural expansion characterised by small holdings controlled and operated by rural farm households or families.

The decline of the traditional estate system is a strong trend and is expected to continue. While this pattern is generating a core equitable distribution of land, it is important that redistribution is not achieved at the expense of land resources. Government efforts to address some of the negative impacts of estate subdivision are encouraging.

The Small Farm System: Most St. Lucian farmers are classified as small farmers. More than 83 per cent of 1986 holdings were under five acres, and over 93 per cent under 10 acres. However, all holdings of less 5 acres account for only 21.3 per cent of the total agricultural land. The land in the latter figure is of relatively poor quality compared to the large estates.

Still, despite these handicaps, small farmers contribute roughly 60 per cent of the income of the agricultural sector. This may be even high given the increased involvement of small farmers in banana production. Traditionally the small farming sector was subsistence based with the

Fishermen play a vital role in the life of Saint Lucia

emphasis on food crops. This has gradually changed as many small farmers have turned to cash crops, like bananas for example, particularly in relatively higher land capability. Where land is less fertile, especially along the borders of the estates, and on the worker's own plots, this is not the trend. In general, the extent of cash cropping within the sector has been variable, increasing when economic conditions have been favourable, as they have been for banana cultivation until the troubled 1990s.

ST. LUCIAN AQUACULTURE

Aquaculture may be described as the rational rearing of fish, lobsters, prawns and so on. They are cultivated in specially devised freshwater ponds for the domestic and regional market. They also replenish depleting stocks in lakes and rivers.

Aquaculture has been practiced for thousands of years starting with the ancient Egyptian and Chinese civilisations.

St Lucian aquaculture has a very bright future. Overfishing has either led to the disappearance of many species or to depleted stocks. This has, in turn, inflated prices. The demand for supplies of seafood, has intensified, with scientific backing for fish as a healthier alternative to red meats.

Seamoss cultivation is an expanding part of aquaculture

IS IT STILL WORTH THE METAL?

*Banana Day is my
special day
I cut my stems and
I'm on my way.
Load up the donkey,
leave the land,
When the truck comes
down I take a ride
All the way down to
the harbor side.
That is the night when
you, tourist man,
Would change your
place with a banana
man*

(Except from the poem
'Song Of The Banana Man'
by Evan Jones of Jamaica)

Song Of The Banana Man" was writ-
en in the days when banana was king
crops. Those were the days when
very farmer, man, woman and child
anted bananas on their inherited or
ased plot of land, be it flat, slopping
hillside land. Those were the days
hen bananas were by far the invinci-
e crop, the number one foreign
xchange earner (oh yes, those were
e days when the pound had weight)
nd the Caribbean national felt a
nse of security, so why entertain
e 'rumor', the unforeseen need for
versification of agricultural produce.

The island's aquaculture is expanding to help meet some of this demand. This has created opportunities for business and employment. Training schemes are in place and the response has been enthusiastic. With their famed work ethic, the industrious and productive St. Lucians, can be expected to consolidate and expand the significant gains made in aquaculture. The region, too, will be a beneficiary, with regular supplies of a variety of seafood at sensible prices.

HISTORY

By the end of the 19th century sugar cane production was on the decline in St. Lucia, as a result of the successes of mechanized sugar production in Cuba and the growing of beet in Europe. Then other crops such as arrowroot, cocoa, nutmeg, limes and bananas were experimented with. It turned out that these crops blended perfectly with the small estates and required a minimal amount of capital investment. In effect, the small-scale landowners gained a certain measure of autonomy from the established plantocracy and became established farmers in their own right.

However, the banana with time, was to become the major export crop of the Windward Islands: (Dominica, Grenada, St. Lucia and St. Vincent & The Grenadines). With the emergence of banana becoming "King", the large plantation owners moved swiftly to establish and assume the monopoly of the banana market.

In 1925, a subsidiary of United Fruit Company called Swift Banana Company, bought land in St. Lucia for banana production. This episode in our agricultural history characterizes the commencement of domination by large-scale planters.

Although the Swift Banana Company was liquidated in 1927, many other ventures of a similar nature were tried. The next major enterprising venture occurred in 1933 when the Caribbean Buying Company yet another subsidiary of United Brands, presented a deal to the small banana growers of the Windward Islands.

This deal was a five-year contract to acquire bananas on condition that the small growers banded together into an association of their making which would be responsible for the collection and loading components.

In the early 20th century, banana production was affected by disease, inadequate transportation, World War 11 and the decreased trade following the War. By 1941, these factors had forced the banana trade into liquidation.

The banana trade sought a new lease on life in 1948, when a UK based company called 'Foley & Brand' signed a fifteen-year contract to acquire all the bananas from the Windward Islands. St. Lucia at that time, was a colony of Britain and the Colonial Office had the responsibility of the island's internal and external affairs.

In an attempt to make the colony self-sustaining and less dependent on the Mother Country, the Colonial Office vigorously pursued consolidation and expansion of the banana trade. The St. Lucia Banana Growers Association (SLBGA) was established as a private company in 1951, with the help of the Colonial Office and technical experts from London.

The 1950's in St. Lucia was the era in which banana production expanded. The Roseau and Cul-de-Sac Valleys situated on the western side of the island and used formerly to grow and produce sugar, were acquired by the Van Geest family in 1961. Geest immediately turned these two estates to producing bananas.

By the 1960's, bananas became a well respected cash crop. By the mid-1960's a research unit was established at Roseau to investigate research on the varying components of the crop. This research unit, still in operation today, is known as The Windward Islands Banana Growers Association (WINBAN). It also provides the marketing and shipping co-ordination of banana exports for the Windward Islands.

During the 1960's, low wages and generally poor conditions on the banana estates led many young persons to migrate to the city, Castries or overseas to the metropolitan countries such as Britain, the US and Canada.

Although there are many small-scale producers in St. Lucia, over seventy-five per cent own only ten acres of land and in many cases even less. Much of this land is marginal land situated on hillslopes. Thus, low yields and generally poor quality fruit plagues the small-scale farmer.

The 70's witnessed prolonged drought and the banana industry was severely affected. Banana exports declined by as much as fifty per cent in 1977 and the industry resorted to aid and credit for its daily survival.

The banana industry has become known as 'social transformer'. This emanates from the fact that feeder roads have been build all over the island, the ports have expanded to receive the banana volume and trade, more vans are imported and the trade has generated foreign exchange.

In 1980, the arrival of Hurricane Allen devastated the industry. Production was drastically reduced and the banana farmer had to begin from almost scratch. Hurricane Allen did in fact cripple the industry for a period of time.

However, the era of the late 1980's and 1990's can be described as an era of the 'banana boom'. The farmers by then, had retrieved themselves from the effects of the hurricane loss. But a new problem emerged.

The whole question of preferential access of the Caribbean bananas into the European market is today a politically contentious issue. Politicians, banana farmers, everyone is preoccupied with this new development. Whilst the negotiators exchange words over their tables, the question emerges 'Banana, is it still worth the metal?'

The banana plant is classified as a herb and attains a height of up to 25 feet. The tree bears fruit once producing one bunch. The fruit usually appears when the plant is about 12 months old and could be reaped

BANANA CAKE

12 ripe bananas
1 lb flour
1 lb sugar
3 eggs
Half lb butter
2 tsp vanilla
2 tsp baking powder
1 Cup honey
1 Cup grapefruit juice
2 tsp unflavoured gelatine
1 Cup milk

Cream butter and sugar. Add eggs and blend well. add sifted flour and baking powder alternately with milk. add one cup mashed banana. slice remaining bananas lengthwise and arrange in greased cake tin. Mix gelatine, grapefruit juice and honey. Boil. Pour over sliced banana. Pour cake batter over all. Bake in oven 20 minutes at 400 degrees F. Cool. Turn out on platter with banana side up. decorate with whipped cream. (Serves 8 -10 persons)

SCRATCH - ME - BACK COCKTAIL

1 ripe banana
Half slice pineapple
Half slice pawpaw
Half slice watermelon
3 oz sweetened condensed milk
3 oz evaporated milk
3 oz rum
Ice
Nutmeg

Peel banana, pawpaw and pineapple. Slice them and blend together in blender. Add milk and rum, then add ice and blend again. Serve sprinkled with grated nutmeg. (Serves two persons)

Lucia is more than self sufficient
fruit and vegetables and is a
...ding banana exporter

in three months. The entire tree is cut down and as it falls to the ground the banana bunch is severed by one stroke of the machete.

It is difficult to make a choice selection of banana recipes, there are hundreds. The banana can be used in a variety of ways, namely in soups combined with fish, meats and vegetables and in salad both sweet and savoury. It lends itself to any form of desert, as well as being delicious in beverages and as a preserve. Banana wine and liqueur are superb.

Perhaps what really distinguishes the banana in this part of the world, is the inclusion of banana in what the locals call **'Fruit Punch'**. This feature is unique to the Caribbean folks ! Or perhaps should we say it is *endemic*? The banana has no doubt added to the versatility of our local foods.

Banana Plantation

Travellers Tree - a palm-like tree, its leaves are like those of the banana which shredded by wind action form an enormous rotating fan. The cupped shape depression at the base of each leaf can hold up to a pint of water, hence the name. Common throughout the Westindies.

A PRICELESS NATURAL DIVERSITY

St. Lucia offers panoramic scenery of its mountains, rolling hills, indented bays and rugged coastline. These are natural, geophysical characteristics. However, the plants and animals also form an essential, though subtle, part of the island's mosaic, whose beauty is easily recognised and appreciated.

Some people still retain the impression that natural vegetation consists mainly of weeds and bushes and should be destroyed to make way for agricultural crops. This profoundly mistaken view stems from the perceived need to convert forested areas into agricultural lands, and from the fact that exhausted, abandoned lands do indeed contain much bush and some weeds, but very little wildlife.

St. Lucia still has a remnant tropical plant kingdom supporting a variety of wildlife, with some interested endemic species of plants and animals; a fact that often goes unrecognised, meaning that much of the remaining wildlife is becoming seriously endangered, with most species feeling the effects of habitat destruction.

Loss of habitat is reflected in a decline in the quality of life, for example. more noise, less tranquillity; more congestion, less open space; more pollution, less beauty; more construction, less shade; more deforestation, less drinking water.

The natural environment supports the biological diversity of the earth, along with the natural processes and resources upon which all living things depend for their survival. The perceived need to perpetuate economic growth has resulted in the reduction of natural resources into a taxable cash base. This activity is carried out at the expense of future options, with the bountiful gifts of nature being destroyed without first being assessed for their potential value, on the short sighted assumption that 'non-profitable' eco-systems should be converted to economically 'profitable' uses. The results are clearly visible worldwide in the wasting of natural forests, the depletion of top soils and a decline in biodiversity.

While humanity has decreed that nature must be used for its own benefit, one needs to question such an anthropo-centric or self-centered view in a natural world, prefigured on the time, perfected diversity of nature. One needs to ask the question; 'Who speaks for nature, where is nature's place in humanity's scheme of things?'.

THE FORESTRY ENVIRONMENT

Following emancipation in 1838, displaced slaves, in order to survive, moved from coastal villages in large numbers to Crown Lands in the interior to cultivate land as squatters. This practice of shifting cultivation gradually devasted more and more of the forest land.

As the effects of deforestation began to have a serious impact on stream flow and water control, an officer of the Indian Forest Service in 1886 recommended a series of reservation forests. These recommendations went unheeded until 1916 when St. Lucia adopted a Crown Lands Ordinance followed by a Timber Protection Ordinance in 1918, designed to prevent the unlawful felling of timber on Crown land.

Forest and people

A census in 1991 revealed that the total population of St. Lucia had reached 136,000 inhabitants. Compared with 1980, there had been an increase of almost 21,000. The districts whose populations increased most were: Castries, Gros-Islet, Micoud, Vieux-Fort, Laborie and Soufriere. A decrease of population was noted in the districts of Canaries and Choiseul.

Historically, most of the so called 'common property resources' of St. Lucia have been under an open-access regime that led too often to excessive exploitation of the natural resources, including the forest and forestry products. The constant use of these products for construction and fuel, combined with the clearing of the forest for agricultural purposes, is largely responsible for deforestation. Although people's needs and uses of forestry products are changing, the increase of population, and the demand for agricultural land still account for much of it. Recently, the development of residential construction and an access road network are becoming a major factor in the process of deforestation.

Charcoal: Uses and needs

According to a 1992 sociological survey the use of fuelwood to make charcoal is still the most important domestic use of forestry products by rural people. St. Lucia households were using charcoal on either a regular or occasional basis as the main energy source for cooking, and firewood was used in only four per cent of all units

Rural people have experienced important changes during the last decade due to the expansion and provision of national infrastructure. More primary and secondary roads, the availability of passenger transport, electrification, provision of pipeborne water and access to telephone lines have reduced the social distance between the capital city and the outer/rural districts. These developments permit the spread of commercial activity to those areas, thereby gradually transforming the domestic lifestyles of rural people.

One area in which change is evident is the source of energy supply for cooking. Charcoal is being quickly replaced by propane (gas) stoves.

However, it is still used on an occasional basis, when the households' propane supply runs out or when certain types of food are cooked on special occasions.

The gradual substitution of gas for charcoal has resulted in a reduction in the annual consumption of fuelwood per household.

On the other hand, the increase in the population would call for an increase in the figures of total fuelwood consumption.

The rural household consumes on average 400 to 600 lbs of charcoal per year. Asssuming that it takes about 8.6 pounds of fuelwood to make one pound of charcoal, then on an annual basis, a rural household would consume approximately 3,500 to 4,500 pounds of firewood.

Other products: Uses and needs

In addition to the use of fuelwood as an energy source, other forestry products are being used by the rural people for different purposes. According to their specific economic activity, farmers, fishermen and artisans have different needs for trees, timber and other biomass resources.

Farmers

Seventy four per cent of the farmers use trees as windbreaks. Mango, glory cedar, coconut, blue mahoe and mahogany are the main species commonly used.

A large percentage of rural families still occupy timber houses. Ninety-nine percent of those houses are constructed with imported timber, mostly pine. But there are few instances where houses are constructed with both imported and local timber.

Fencing of farmland is not a common practice in St. Lucia. But while the use of poles for fencing is rare, and accounts for very little in the utilisation of forestry rsources, many farmers use particular types of trees to make natural fencing for their Land-holdings. Glory cedar is a common species used in this way. In some cases these trees are utilised as boundary markers, especially when Land-holdings are bounded by other privately owned lands.

Fishermen

Unlike the farmers, the fishermens' use of trees is closely related to their means of production. In the context of fishery operations along the coast and off-shore, a majority of the boats and fish pots are still made of wood. Gommier is by far the preferred species in the making of boats. This material, which is found in the rainforest, is becoming rare and expensive.

Red and white cedar are also used to make oars and fish pots are usually made of bamboo. Most of the fishermen buy the wood they need to make fish pots, but some get it from scrubland. The landing site in some fishing settlements also features particular species of trees. For example, glory cedar is used to build the frame for thatched shelters for boats. Other species are used to trail the boat from the shore and also to form the support base for parking purposes.

Artisan - craftsmen

The needs of the craftsmen and other resource-based activities (haker, boatmaker, carpenter) depend very much on the type of activity they are engaged in. Various forms of activities utilise particular types of trees. For example, mat-making would require kus kus grass. The majority of people who are engaged in this activity do not own the source of supply of the raw material. Carpenters and joiners also use local forest products. The main local species are mahogany and blue mahoe. These are used to manufacture household furniture.

Tree production - farms & homesteads

Rural farmers demonstrate a preference for particular types of trees. More female farmers prefer fruit trees in general (citrus, mango, avocado, and plum were the ones mentioned) more than their male counterparts, while more male than female farmers prefer mahogany and blue mahoe trees.

Importance of trees

Traditionally, the forest has been a major source of livelihood, fuel energy and recreation for many rural folk. The dissemination of information on the importance of the forest and its place in the environment has been the focus of the local government, in association with regional and international agencies. Generally, people agree that protection of forests against the indiscriminate felling of trees ensures water supplies.

Ownership of the forest

Approximately two-thirds of the rural people see the forest as a resource that belongs to Governement or State, while the remaining third see it as belonging to all St. Lucians. Very few people perceive the forest as belonging to the community or to rural people living near the forest.

Forestry economy

The direct contribution of the Forestry sector to the overall economy is minimal. Almost all the wood for construction is imported. Seventy three per cent of the imported wood is from coniferous species, while the remaining 27 per cent is from non-coniferous species.

There is a small amount of locally converted wood available in the country, the milling of it being done on a small scale using environmentally sound techniques and equipment. The Government is fully aware of the role that forest conservation plays in watershed protection, water supply, soil conservation, protection of the flora and fauna, and the provision of recreation for both the residents and visitors to the island.

Pigeon Island National Park is regaining its trees, plants and wildlife

HERBARIUM

A herbarium is a place where a collection of dried specimens of plants are kept and all the known information concerning these plants is stored. In Saint Lucia, the Herbarium is a part of the National Trust and is located in the lower part of the Trust's building at Vigie. In it are dried specimens of all the plants presently known and identified in Saint Lucia.

The Saint Lucia Herbarium was established in 1984, when the Saint Lucia Association for the Promotion of Natural Products was launched. Among its members are pharmacists, medical practitioners, agricultural scientists botanists and traditional herbalists. One of the organization's objectives is to collect and identify local plants. The specimens collected are placed in a plant press and dried. They will form part of the collection of the plants of Saint Lucia. The Saint Lucia National Trust provides laboratory and storage space at their Vigie headquarters

PLANT RESEARCH

Although rainforests cover only 2 per cent of the earth's surface, they contain half of all the world's wild plants. In a typical four-mile square patch of tropical rainforest it is possible to find as many as 750 species of trees and 1,500 species of flowering plants. The rainforest is a huge genetic storehouse of information on the many plant and animal species that inhabit it.

More than half the prescribed medicines in common use today come from plants. One in four of these medicines comes from a plant in a tropical rainforest, yet only about 1 per cent of all rainforest species has ever been studied. According to the National Cancer Institute of the United States, 1,400 rainforest plants are believed to offer cures for cancer. The rosy periwinkle, is found growing all over Saint Lucia. This plant has already provided a cure for leukaemia in children.

Other products, like quinine, curare and rubber have all been developed or harvested from plants. Many more plants have yet to be identified and studied. Scientists believe that among them are some that could help in their search for a cure for diseases like AIDS and cancer

BOTANIC GARDENS

A botanic or botanical garden is a place where plants from all over the world can be seen growing in their natural state. The garden is usually arranged like a park.

In the Tropics exotic plants can be seen growing in their full beauty as nature intended. However, no botanic graden will have a natural climate that can support all the different plant types. Orchids and bromeliads, for example, require the specialized environment of the tropical rainforest. These plants can be seen growing naturally in Saint Lucia. In temperate zones the conditions they require have to be artificially created.

Saint Lucia's first botanic garden was established in 1887 in what was then called the George V Park. It was one of these original gardens in the Westindies, following after those in Jamaica and Saint Vincent. Unfortunately, the offices of the Town Council had to be moved to the Gardens after the 1948 fire. This, as well as pressure from encroaching development caused rapid deterioration of the area. Today, the garden occupies a fraction of its original space and very few of the original trees remain.

BEAUTIFICATION

Ever since the time when humans gave up their wandering existence and settled in one place, they have used plants to make their homes more beautiful. At first a herb or a bush might have been planted near the house because it was useful. Perhaps it was a cure for a certain ailment, or maybe it added flavour to food. later, the seeds or fruit of a plant may have been brought back from an expedition into the bush simply because it was beautiful to look at.

Rainforest

FLORA

1. Allamanda *(Allamanda Cathartica)*
   Buttercup flower, Golden Trumpet,
   Yellow Allamanda, Yellow Bell

2. Amaryllis *(Hippeastrum puniceum)*
   Barbados Lily, Lent Lilly

3. Angel's Trumpet *(Datura Candida)*
   other names: Angel's Tears, Daturas

4. Anthuruim *(Anthuruim Andraeanum)*
   Flamingo flower, Heart flower

5. Bermuda Lily *(Lilium Longiflorum)*
   Easterlily

6. Bird of Paradise flower *(Strelitzia reginae)*
   Crane flower, Queen's Bird of Paradise flower

7. Bougainvillea *(Bougainvillea spp)*
   Paper flower

8. Canna *(Canna generalis)*

9. Castor Dil *(Ricinus communis)*

10. Cherulle Plant *(Acalypha hispida)*
    Monkey Tail, Red Hot Cat Tail

11. Chaconia *(Warszewiczia coccinea)*
    Water Well Tree, Wild Poinsettia

12. Crown of Thorns *(Euphorbia Splendens)*

13. Cup of Gold *(Solandra nitida)*
    Chalice Vine, Golden Chalice, Golden Cup

14. Firecracker *(Russelia Juncea)*
    Fountain Plant

15. Ginger *(Alpinia purpurata)*
    Ostrich Plume Ginger, Red Ginger

16. Hibiscus *(Hibiscus spp)*

17. Heliconia *(Heliconia spp)*
    Lobster Claw, Wild Banana

18. CoralHibiscus *(Hibisais schizopetalus)* Dissected Hibiscus, Fringed Hibiscus

19. Ixora *(Ixora macrothyrsa, Ixora coc cinea)* Flame of the Wood, Jungle Flame, Jungle Geranium

20. Lantana *(Lantana camara)*

21. Morning Glory Bush *(Ipomea fistulosa)*
    Potato Bush

22. Mexican Creeper *(Antigonon Leptopus)* Chain of Love, Coral Vine

23. Passion Flower *(Passiflora spp)*

24. Periwinkle *(Catharanthus roseus)*
    Ramgoat Rose

25. Petrea *(Petrea volubilis)*
    Blue Petrea, Bluebird, Vine, Purple Wreath Vine

26. Plumbago *(Plumbago capensis)*
    South African Leadwort

27. Poinsettia *(Euphorbià Pulcherrimà)*
    Fire Plant, Painted Leaf

28. Shrimp Plant *(Justicia Brandegeeana)*

29. Spider Lily *(Hymenocallis caribaea)*

30. Thunbergia *(Thunbergia grandiflora)*
    Bengal Clockvine, Bengal Trumpet, Skyflower

31. Turk's Cap *(Malvaviscus arboreus)*
    Pepper Hibiscus, Sleeping Hibiscus

MEDICINAL PLANTS

The range of plants that are used medicinally in Saint Lucia is very large indeed, but the number of people who are truly skilled and practiced in their use is declining. Almost all of the plants used medicinally can be toxic if taken without proper knowledge of their individual properties. Below is a list of some of the more common medicinal plants and the complaints they are used for:

Aloe vera -Lalwye
Known as the medicine plant, aloe is taken internally for colds and asthma and applied externally to heal wounds.

Bryophyllum pinnatum - leaf of life
Also known as Kalanchoe pinnata, the leaf is used for teas and as a poultice.

Catharanthus roseus- kaka poule
Used as a tea for diabetes. Now considered to be a cure for certain types of leukaemeia.

Chenopodium ambrosioides - simen contwa - zeb a ve
This plant is used for intestinal worms, throughout the Caribbean. It is also used as a cooling tea.

Commelina diffusa - zeg gwa
Used as a cooling infusion and in teas for 'flu'.

Cymbopogon citratus - citwonelle
Used in hot teas for colds or chills.

Eryngium foetidum - chadoni beni
Used for fevers and chills. Also rubbed on the body for fainting and convulsions and in cases of vomiting and diarrhoea.

Leonotis nepetifolia - Gwo pompom
Leaves boiled as a tea for 'flu and fevers, or sometimes as a bath for prickly heat.

Peperomia pellucida - shining bush
Used in cooling teas and as a tea for colds. Sometimes used as a diuretic for kidney ailments.

Portulaca oleracea - koupye
Can be cooked and eaten or used in salad. Used in teas for worms and flatulence, and as a poultice for back ache.

Sambucus canadensis - flewi siwo
Flowers are used in teas for colds and fevers.

Stachytarpheta jamaicensis - vevenne latchay wat
Used in teas for colds and fevers, sometimes also for worms.

Wedelia trilobata - zeb a fam
Leaves are pounded and used as a poultice, or as a tea for coughs and colds.

NATURE PLANT CRAFTS

PLANTS FOR CRAFTS AND OTHER USES

Many of the grasses and reeds that grow wild in Saint Lucia provide material for local craftsmen and women. Khus khus grass is cut and laid in the sun to dry. It is then woven into fine mats and baskets. Pandanus is dried and plaited to make hats and baskets. The Roseau reeds from which the Roseau Valley got its name, have strong, heavy, stems. They are still gathered and dried to be used as a roofing material or to make a decorative covering for walls

The long aerial roots of some vines are gathered from the forest and soaked in water to remove their skin. they are then dried and woven to make strong linen baskets and market baskets. The people of Choiseul are well known for this craft. The awali, on whose fruits the rare Saint Lucian parrot feeds, is one of the creepers whose roots are used in this way.

The seeds of some plants are used for traditional games like warri where the seeds take the place of more conventional counters. Seeds and other parts of plants are also dried and used for decoration. For example, the dried fruits of the loofah vine are used for a variety of craft items including artificial flowers and the soles of slippers.

Screw Pine leaves are used for making hats, place mats and bracelets

Plants provide us with many of the ingredients for cosmetics. For years coconut oil has been widely used particularly in suntan lotions. Now the gel from the aloe vera plant is becoming even more popular. It turns up in face and hand creams, suntan lotions, shampoo and hair conditioners. The pulp from the flat, fleshy leaves of some cactus and the crushed leaves of the hibiscus, are also used as shampoos. Even hot peppers have their cosmetic use mixed with other ingredients they are said to make a great hair tonic!

WILDLIFE

Wildlife covers all forms, flora and fauna, in an uncultivated or undomesticated natural state. The average St. Lucian is no longer reliant on the wilderness for his daily sustenance, and almost all are of the view that depleted natural resources impoverish a nation, not just environmentally but socially, culturally and economically.

Like most countries in the world, even the developed world, St. Lucia has realised the dangers to the environment by a variety of practices ranging from pollution, to the destruction or defoliation of the natural habitat.

In the 1970s, the plight of the Jacquot, the St. Lucia parrot shook the nation. There were a hundred birds left from a population of thousands, and they seemed destined to the same fate as three species of the Amazon Parrot which have become extinct.

Government acted quickly to save the Jacquot. The Forestry and Lands Department in the Ministry of Agriculture established a sanctuary for the parrots, passed enabling protective legislation for severe penalties against transgressors, and raised public awareness through systematic environmental education.

These measures paid off handsomely. The Parrot, designated St. Lucia's National Bird, recovered from its endangered species status to register an increase of 150 percent at 250 birds in the 1989 census. While this was a cause for considerable pride, St. Lucian's were reminded by their experts that St. Lucia's National Bird was not still out of the woods. They were told that the bird was vulnerable and that they, too, had a duty to protect it from 'hunters' and other vandals.

Other creatures, too, are threatened, especially by habitat destruction. The Grand Anse Estate is one of the most prominent refuges for wildlife species which have been on the brink of extinction. The area is rich in endemic birds which were identified and documented in the 1920s by James Bond, the respected ornithologist. Species such as the white-breasted Thrasher and the St. Lucia Nightjar were once thought to be extinct. But though threatened by livestock roaming freely around the estate, they appear to be adapting well to their new circumstances.
The Grand Anse Estate is also a temporary, but welcome, refuge for a variety of migratory birds escaping the fierce North American winter.
A variety of ducks, plovers, sandpipers, herons and other waders occupy the ponds and the mangrove.

The Grand Anse Beach, with its deep sand, is the ideal nesting place for the Leatherback Turtle, one of the world's endangered species.

FAUNA

1. Mongoose (Herpestes Auropunctatus)
2. Agoutic (Dasyprocta)
3. Couresse (harmless bush snake)
4. Grand Gorge (Brown Pelican)
5. Ground Lizard
6. Iguana

Offshore island's are also under wildlife management. The Maria Islands are the only habitat of two endemic reptiles, the St. Lucia Whiptail and the St. Lucia Racer .

The St. Lucia Whiptail project has benefited through cooperation with the Jersey Wildlife Preservation Trust. Studies of Maria Island led to the establishment of alternative satellite islets for a second colony for the Whiptail. The Maria Islands are also the prime nesting ground for thousands of terns which nest there during the months of September. The Island is protected by the St. Lucia National trust.

A key, indispensable element in wildlife management is the involvement of the St. Lucian people in protection and conservation. Proceeding on the principle that only an intelligent, aware and well-informed people can be the best custodians of their environmental treasures, the conservation message has been taken into every home and school with highly encouraging results.

SAINT LUCIA PARROT

First described in 1776, this beautiful parrot is, and always has been, found only on St. Lucia.

It is predominantly green in colour, and a typical specimen has a cobalt blue forehead, merging through turquoise to green on the cheeks and a scarlet breast. There are no visible differences between the two sexes.

Mating for life and maturing after five years, these long lived birds are cavity – nesters, laying two to three white eggs in the hollow of a large tree during the onset of the dry season between February and April.

St. Lucia Parrots are birds of the forest canopy. Despite their large size and bright plumage, they are difficult to detect among the dense foliage as they clamber about in search of fruits, nuts, seeds and berries from a wide variety of trees, including gommier, chatagnier, bois pain maron and aralie.

Over the years a combination of hunting, habitat destruction and the illegal bird trade resulted in a rapid decline in numbers and by the mid 1970's the St Lucia Parrot faced extinction.

Commenting on the hunting of this species, a Lady Thompson wrote in 1902: "Unfortunately, dead birds may be found almost every week in the market of the little town of Soufriere, and they are eaten as a delicacy by both black and white Creoles."

In 1968, someone observed that "as many as forty parrots are probably shot each year in an attempt to catch them alive for sale".

In 1978 the Forestry Division of the Ministry of Agriculture launched a campaign to save the parrot from extinction.

In 1979, the St Lucia Parrot was declared the island's National Bird and, in 1980, wildlife legislation was revised accordingly.

Today the parrot, and most other forms of wildlife are absolutely protected all year round and anyone found hunting, keeping or trying to trade in these birds is liable to a fine of $5,000 or one year in jail.

Forestry laws were also revised to protect watersheds as well as wildlife habitats, and illegal clearing of forest is punishable by fines of $2,000.

During the last decade, protected areas have been set aside and educational programmes initiated. These are having the desired effect. By 1988, the St. Lucia Parrot was slowly increasing in numbers, and today its population stands at about 250.

It may be seen flying across the forests of Quilesse, Millet and Edmund Forest, symbolic of the island's beauty and uniqueness.

In 1982, the first ever successful captive breeding of the St. Lucia's Parrot occured at Jersey, in the Channel Islands, and in 1989 two young parrots were returned to St. Lucia St. Lucia's National Bird, however, remains an endangered species and should be treated and cherished accordingly.

BIRDS

ENDEMIC BIRDS

SEMPER'S WARBLER
Leucopeza semperi
Pied Blanc

Found only in St. Lucia where it is probably very rare and possibly extinct. Little is known of this small (5.5") Warbler. It has dark grey upper parts and a whitish-underside. A bird of the mountain forest.

SAINT LUCIA BLACKFINCH
Melanospiza richardsoni

5.5" This small finch is restricted to St. Lucia where it is uncommon but more widespread than formally thought. The male Blackfinch closely resembles the Lesser Antillcan Bullfinch, being predominantly black in color. the Blackfinch however lacks the red chin and has pale pink, rather than dark legs. The females of the two species also resemble one another although the female Blackfinch has a grayer crown and lighter underparts found in the forest and coastal woodlands.

SAINT LUCIA ORIOLE
Icterus laudablis
Carougc

Found only on St. Lucia this Oriole is widely distributed being found from montane forests to the coast.
Males and females are mainly black in color. Males have orange wing patches; in the females these are yellow. Orioles are insectivorous and weave basket-like nests that are suspended beneath a palm frond or Heliconia leaf.

SAINT LUCIA PARROT
Amazona versicolor
Jacquot

Oriole

Found only on St. Lucia this species is mainly green in color and has a blue head, red neck and maroon belly.
Twenty years ago the Saint Lucia Parrot flickered on the edge of extinction being threatened by forest destruction and capture for the pet trade. Thanks to vigorous efforts by the Forestry Department its numbers have now increased to 250. Restricted to the Central Forest Reserve is St. Lucia's national bird.

RAINFOREST BIRDS

FOREST THRUSH
Cichlherminia lherminiere
Grieve Pieds Jaune

10.5" This bird is found only on Dominica, Montserrat, Guadeloupe and St. Lucia.
A large, dark Thrush with a chocolate-brown back, black and brown spotted breast and grey-white underparts.
Bill, legs and eye ring are yellow.
This rainforest-dweller feeds on insects and fruit.

ANTILLEAN EUPHONIA
*Euphonia musica Peruche, Mistletoe
Bird Blue-hooded Euphonia*

5" A shy, seldom seen little bird that spends much of its time in the forest canopy where it feeds on mistletoe and other berries. This small finch-like bird has a Pale blue or violet crown, a yellow forehead and chin, greenish-yellow back and under-parts.

ANT. CRESTED HUMMINGBIRD
*Orthorhyncus cristatus
Fou fou: small Doctorbird*

3.5" One of the region's smallest yet common-est birds. Male and females look similar being green above and grey below. They have a straight bill and bluish iridescent crest which is more distinct in the male.
Antillean crested humming birds feed on nectar and make a tiny nest from lichens and grass.

Blackfinch

TREMBLER
*Cincloerthia ruficauda
Trembleur*

At 10" this slender attractive bird gets its name from its habit of trembling. it has a down-curved bill orange-red eye, and olive-brown upper parts.
Tremblers are birds of the rainforest where they feed on insects and small animals as well as fruits.

LESSER ANTILLEAN PEWEE
Contopus latirostris

This small 6" long, largely grey-brown fly-catcher has a Pale throat and buff or rufous belly and lives in humid forest habitats.

SCALY-BREASTED THRASHER
*Margarops fuscus
Grieve*

This medium-sized bird (9") of the woodland and forest is dark grey-brown above and whitish grey below. Its breast is heavily flecked with grey giving it a scaled appearance.

ADELAIDE'S WARBLER
*Dendrocia adelaidae
Sucier Babad*

This small attractive Warbler is restricted to Barbuda and St. Lucia as well as Puerto Rico and Vieques.
This largely grey warbler has yellow under-parts and eye stipes and two white wing bars. (5"). A bird of the coastal woodlands: although in St. Lucia this species can also be seen in the rainforest.

PURPLE-THROATED CARIB
*Eulampis jugularis
Colibri rouge, or Large Doctorbird*

A large dark iridescent hummingbird with a pur-ple throat, blue-green rump and vivid green wings. The Purple-throated Carib is most frequently seen at higher elevations in wet forest habitats.

RUFOUS-THROATED SOLITAIRE
Myadestes genibarbis
Mountain Whistler
Siffleur de Montagne
Soufriere Bird

One of the region's most attractive birds and a beautiful songster. At 8" this species has a greyhead, back, wings and tail: the latter edged with white. Its underparts are pale grey with a rufous throat and belly.

MIGRATORY BIRDS

CARIBBEAN ELAENIA
Elaenia martinica

A plain grey, fairly nondescript bird with two white wing bars and an inconspicuous crest. The underparts may be a pale grey or yellow. (7") The region's commonest flycatcher occurring throughout the Eastern Caribbean.

BLACKFACED GRASSQUIT
Tiaris bicolor
See See Zeb; Sparrow
Grassbird

4.5" This little finch is found throughout the region in open areas, grasslands, scrub and gardens where it feeds on seeds. The male is dark green above with a black head and breast and grey belly. The female is grayish-brown with paler underparts.

GREY KINGBIRD
Tyrannus dominicensis
Pipiri, Pipirit or Pitiwick

9" Grey above, white below and having a black eyestripe; this bird is a familiar sight along roadsides and in open country where it perches on wires and branches. The Grey Kingbird is found throughout the Eastern Caribbean.

CARIB GRACKLE
Ouiscalus lugubris
Blackbird or Merle

Measuring 9.5-11 inches, the male is easily recognized by its glossy black plumage, yellow eye and V-shaped tail.
The female is smaller and more variable in color being dull black in Barbados and pale brown with a whitish throat in the northern Antilles.

Sempers Warbler

GREEN-THROATED CARIB
Sericotes holosericeus
Large Doctorbird
Colibri vent

At 5" this bird can be distinguished by its large size and long curved bill. Both males and females are iridescent green with a violet breast and black tail.

LESSER ANTILLEAN BULLFINCH
Loxgilla noctis
Pere Noir/Moisson,
Sparrow, Red-breast

At 6" the male is black with red on the eye, chin, and throat and has orange under the tail. The female is brown with a greyish underside and also has orange under its tail.

BROAD-WINGED HAWK
Buteo platypterus
Chicken hawk or Malfini

This broad-winged, medium-sized, largely brown hawk has light brown barred underparts with a dark brown and white barred tail. it feeds on repitles, rodents and small birds.

St Lucia Parrot

PURPLE-THROATED CARIB
Eulampis jugularis
Colibri rouge, or Large Doctorbird

A large, dark iridescent hummingbird with a purple throat, blue-green rump and vivid green wings.
The Purple-throated Carib is most frequently seen at higher elevations in wet forest habitats where it feeds on nectar as well as insects.

BANANAQUIT
Coereba flaveola

Sucrier, Bananabird, Yellow breast
In general Banaquits have greyish upperparts and a yellowish breast, belly and rump. Adults have a white eye stripe below in the young.

La Savanne near Vieux Fort

MANICOU

The 'Manicou', also known locally as the opossum, was introduced into St. Lucia from Dominica in 1902. Because of its close similarity to Didelphis marsupialis, it is thought that the species in Dominica was introduced into that island long ago by the Caribs from South America.

The Manicou is a survivor par excellence. During it's short life span of two to four years it usually breeds twice, producing litters of at least a dozen young. It is arboreal, but tends to move about extensively, covering one or two miles per night in search of food, which, in its case, means anything edible. If it shows a preference, it is usually for well decayed meat. However, this is supplemented by such things as fruits (fresh or decayed) birds' eggs and sometimes small birds, berries, nuts, slugs, fish and small snakes.

The Manicou is an excellent scavenger, so don't be surprised if you find your garbage being raided at night. If it is not the neighbours dog, it may well be an Opossum. If chased, it cannot run very fast, as it normally moves awkwardly on the ground, but it will stand and fight. However, it is no match for a large dog.

HOW THE MANICOU CAME TO ST. LUCIA

The Opossum was not found in St. Lucia before the turn of the century. Breen and other historians and early writers made no mention of the manicou in St. Lucia. Handbooks for the period 1900 to 1903 do not mention it either. However, the handbook of 1924 states: 'The Manicou or Opossum, of late introduction, is fairly common in wooded places.'

A search of the St. Lucian newspapers for the years 1900 to 1910 reveals that Major Cowie, who was attached to the Royal Engineers stationed at The Morne, arrived in St. Lucia in 1900. His hobby was collecting live animals, to set up a menagerie. Before Major Cowie left St. Lucia in February 1902, he disposed of his collection. The British Museum agreed to take the insects. Thus, in February 1902, Major Cowie unceremoniously released the animals, including a female Manicou with nine healthy mature young into the bushes at the back of Morne Fortune.

The following letter sheds some light:-

'The appearance of the Manicou in a wild state in this colony, to which our attention was called by a correspondent, whose letter was published in the last issue of *The Voice* is no doubt due to the fact that Major Cowie R.E., before his departure, about a year ago, gave its liberty to a female Manicou, which he had got from Dominica, which he was keeping in a cage. The Manicou had a family of nine young ones which were enfranchised with the mother.'

Voice, January 22 1903.

Obviously, the Manicou has thrived in the lush environment of St. Lucia, where it now appears to be quite plentiful. This may however, be a misconception, as the Manicou is being driven out into the open by rapid deforestation, leading to the disappearance of the natural forest in the wake of banana cultivation.

SECTION 14. WILDLIFE PROTECTION ACT NO.9 OF 1980

GECKOS

The Caribs called them mabouia, evil spirits. The unfortunate myth persists that these small, inoffensive reptiles will attach themselves to a person's skin and can be removed only by killing them with a hot iron.

There are three types of geckos on St. Lucia: Heidactylus; The cadactylus; and Sphaerodactylus. The distinguished characteristics are based on the structure of the toes.

Geckos are mostly nocturnal and have highly specialised eyes for night vision; they are covered by a transparent scale and have no moveable eyelids. In Sphaerodactylus which is not strictly nocturnal, the pupils are broad ovals, which contract only slightly.

Their ability to cling to smooth surfaces may have given rise to the unfortunate myth attached to them. The underside of the toes are covered by a series of flap-like scales, which bear minute projections which act as hooks.

Among reptiles, geckos are unique in being truly vocal : their calls vary from bird-like chirps to rapid clicking.

All members of the group are insectivores.

SEA TURTLES

Seven species of sea turtle occur around the world. Of these, thress species (possibly four) occur in the seas around St. Lucia, namely the Green Turtle, the Hawksbill Turtle, the Leatherneck Turtle, and possibly the Loggerhead Turtle.

Sea turtles spend most of their lives in the ocean although the females come up every year to lay their eggs on the island's sandy beaches. After about 50 days from laying, the babies (or hatchings) head directly for the sea. Upon reaching maturity they will return, usually to the beach where they were born, to desposit their eggs. They may lay more than once during a season.

SNAKES

Five species of snakes have been recorded in St. Lucia. Of these, the cribo, is extinct. Three others, fer-de-lance, boa constrictor, and worm snake, live on the mainland. The fourth, the St. Lucia Racer, is found only on Maria Islet, but was probably common on the mainland before the introduction of the mongoose.

IGUANAS AND LIZARDS

Two types of iguanid lizards have colonised St. Lucia: Iguana and Anolis the tree lizards.

*The Iguana (Iguana iguana), is the largest on the mainland. Iguanas are tree dwellers but are frequently seen on the ground. Their skin is basically green, with brown or black markings. Along the necks is a crest of spines which gives it the look of a prehistoric monster.

The Iguana grows up to six feet in length, about half of this being a strong whip like tail. If surprised in the top of a tree, it may escape by crashing to the ground and running off. They are also excellent swimmers.

The females lay up to seventeen eggs in the ground which takes about fourteen weeks to hatch. Iguanas feed on leaves, shoots and fruits.

Iguanas are mostly found along the Northeast coast.

TREE LIZARDS

The generic name for the tree-lizards Anolis comes from "anole", an old French creole term.
Three species of ancies live on the island but only

one, (Anolis luciae) is indigenous. The others, (Anolis extremus) and (Anolis wattsi) come from Barbados and Antigua respectively.

*Anolis Luciae is the largest of our anoles. The general colour may be brown, olive or bright green; the head is usually brown. These lizards are very abundant in the lowlands and especially in cultivated areas; they are comparatively rare in the rainforest.

*Anolis extremus is the tree-lizard most commonly seen in Castries township. Males are bright green with mottling on the head. They are easily recognised by intense black pigmentation around the eye.

*Anolis wattsi is the smallest and most attractive anole. In males, the back and tail are coloured cinnamon brown; sides are green; lower jaw bears green and white markings and there is a blue patch below the eye.

Tree lizards are basically insect eaters but seem to enjoy very ripe fruit, especially mangoes.

GROUND LIZARDS
St. Lucia has two types of ground lizards: Gymnopthalmus and Cnemidophorous.

*The small Nxoli tere (Gymnophalmus), commonly seen on the ground running through leaves and grass is sometimes mistaken for a small snake as its tiny legs are not obvious. This insectivorous lizard moves with mercurial ease on the round and is frustratingly difficult to catch.

The St. Lucia Whiptail (Cnemidophorus vanzoi), known also as Zandoli terre, was unknown to science before 1958 when it was collected on Maria Island by Gregor Williams and Earl Long.

It is considered one of the world's rarest lizards and is the only cnemidophorus lizard found in the West Indies. the lizards are restricted to two islets, Maria Major and Maria Minor and have not been reported from elsewhere. However, it seems probably that it once occurred on mainland St. Lucia.

Males are very dark grey brown with a pattern of charcoal grey dots and fine lines running from the neck to the base of the tail. Bellies are a brilliant sulphur yellow. Under ribs of hind legs, vent area and entire tail are a brilliant sea blue patched with turquoise. When fully grown an adult male measures 14" from snout to the tip of the tail.

Females are smaller reaching 10 inches. They are and browner than males with a pattern of stripes running laterally from the neck to the base of the tail.

In 1982 the Maria Islands were declared a wildlife reserve. As with all other protected wildlife, the Maria Island Lizard is absolutely protected under the 1980 Wildlife Act of St. Lucia.

The biggest threat to the lizards are from the activities of visitors to the islands. Empty bottles can easily trap lizards where they eventually die. A fire escaping into the vegetation on the Island can cause widespread damage and jeopardize the lizards' very existence.

LAND TORTOISE
The local Land Tortoise (Geochelone carbonaria) commonly called the Molocoy, was introduced to St. Lucia many years ago.

The hard shell of the Molocoy is divided into large scales with a row of small ones around the edge. The shell forms the only protection for the Molocoy and it withdraws its head at the first sign of disturbance.

In the cool of the evening or after a shower of rain, they emerge from their burrows to feed on fruit, succulent grasses and carrion. They mate throughout the year and the female may lay, in a shallow hole which she digs in soft earth, up to 3 clutches of white round eggs a year. The eggs hatch in about 6 months and the little ones crawl out of the loose soil. The adults grow to about 2 feet in length, taking many years to attain this size.

TURTLE WATCHING

ST. LUCIA NATURALISTS' SOCIETY
The St. Lucia Naturalists' Society (SLNS) is a non-profit making organisation which was established in 1978. Its primary purpose is to protect and conserve the natural and cultural environment of St. Lucia through education. Most of its activities are funded by subscription fees and from donations of Society members and local businesses.

The Society is small, only 180 members. The club holds a monthly general meeting where talks on environmental matters are given and projects and field trips are planned and reviewed. The Society also publishes a quarterly newsletter *The St. Lucian Naturalist*, which discusses subjects of local, regional and international relevance. Specific projects are undertaken as part of the contributions to environmental education and conservation. These projects almost always involve field trips islandwide. Society members thus have broad exposure to their local environment.

Projects presently undertaken by the Society include:
• Study and documentation of mangroves. The Society reports on the state of the island's wetlands which ones are, for example, under threat of destruction, which ones are flourishing, which once require replanting and/or other forms of protective and corrective measures.

• Identification and documentation of waterfalls. A report on the location and description of the island's waterfalls and their overall suitability for development as sources of enjoyment and areas of protection.

• Bird watching and assistance in recording migratory patterns of certain species. The Society's bird specialists teach participants how to identify the indigenous birds of St. Lucia and their respective bird calls, nesting and feeding habits. Especially under study is the white breasted thrasher.

• Turtle watching, tagging and recording of nestings (primarily of leatherbacks) is done annually between March and August. This is a great favourite and many St. Lucians spend their Saturday nights camping with the Society on the lookout for nesting turtles.

• Beach cleaning and monitoring of garbage accumulation on beaches is a relatively new project. It is intended to increase public awareness of the growing need for proper garbage disposal in St. Lucia.

In the last 12 years, the SLNS has been involved in other activities, such as forest walks and trail identification; the study of orchids; the study of St. Lucian birds, visits to Brigand caves, and other sites of natural and cultural significance. The Society has also been responsible for organizing a national school quiz on the environment, hotel and school lectures, and environmental beach fairs.

TURTLE WATCHING
The St. Lucia turtle watching progamme is run primarily by the St. Lucia Naturalists' Society (SLNS), whose primary purpose is to protect and conserve the country's natural and cultural environment through education. With permission and assistance from the Departments of Fisheries and Forestry, of the Ministry of Agriculture, Fisheries and the Environment, the Society conducts turtle watches on a one mile long beach on the north-east coast.

The Grand Anse beach is relatively isolated. A small farming community of under 500 persons is located 4-5 miles away in the hills overlooking the beach. The area is extremely rural, with the very minimum of urban conveniences. Every year, from March to July, the Grande Anse beach is visited repeatedly by members of the largest species of marine turtle, the leatherback. This beach is in fact believed to be the location of the largest population of nesting leatherbacks on the island and is there an ideal choice for the turtle watching programme.

The Turtle Watching Programme:
The monitoring of marine turtles during their nesting, was started in 1983 by the Department of Fisheries. Turtle watching was expected to facilitate the collection of data which would then guide the department in the planning and management of its marine turtle programme.

Regular turtle watching was also considered necessary as a protective measure against slaughtering of the females whilst on land and against the poaching of the turtle eggs. Unfortunately, in recent years, the Department of Fisheries has had to reduce the magnitude of its beach monitoring due to limited manpower and thus has happily encouraged the growth of the watches by the SLNS. Turtle watching, tagging and recording of nestings (primarily of leatherbacks) is now carried out annually between March and August, almost exclusively by the SLNS. With few exceptions, all watches take place on the Grande Anse beach.

The trip down to the Grand Anse Beach takes about one hour. On arrival at the beach, the group splits into two, with most persons walking the beach to check on the locations of nests laid earlier in the week, and on any evidence of slaughters or hatchings. The second group assists in the setting up of the tents for the night. There are normally 3 watches, each 3 hours long, from 8 pm to 5 am. The beach is split into two sections (the north end and the south end) and each watch group patrols a section once every hour. When turtles come in to lay, the entire camp is notified, normally with the assistance of mobile radios. Turtles are left completely undisturbed until laying commences. Once laying commences, participants move in and conduct certain tasks. Some people are asked to lie on their bellies and count eggs as they are dropped into the funnel shaped nest, others assist in measuring the length and maximum width of the turtle. Others make notes of any distinguishing marks visible on the female and others take photographs. Of course, there are always one or two reliable persons to record all the data collected. Towards the end of laying, the front flippers of the turtle are tagged with stainless steel tags. Tagging does not hurt the turtle and, if done properly, is undetected by it. Once laying and covering of the nest is completed, the turtle returns to the sea.

Turtle watches have led to the sensitizing of St. Lucians to the plight of the sea turtles, to the wonder of their existence, and have served to encourage Government legislation for the protection of turtles and their eggs during the breeding season. As of 1996, due in part to pressure by the Society, a moratorium on the fishing and trade on all sea turtles and their bi-products was established by the Fisheries Department. It is hoped that a hatching programme may eventually be set up.

The primary objectives of the Turtle Watching Programme are to:

- Reduce the incidence of slaughter of maritime turtles during nesting;
- Collect and record relevant nesting data (for example, size of female, time of nesting, number of eggs laid, location of nest);
- Educate the general public on turtles and their nesting patterns;
- Sensitize persons to the plight of turtles in general, especially nesting turtles;
- Facilitate public experience of a natural phenomenon;
- Develop and increase public fondness for one of the world's oldest living reptiles

Are these objectives being achieved?

Over the last five years, particularly in the last three, a significant contribution to the protection of marine turtles, especially the leatherback has been made. The regular public response via newspaper articles, telephone calls and the generous donations of time to assist in the running of turtle watches, all suggest that many St. Lucians are becoming more aware of and concerned about the plight of the marine turtle and its environment. Participants are now often motivated to speak out against the slaughter of nesting turtles, the disturbance of nests and removal of eggs. Participation in the turtle watches have increased significantly in 1997, from the average of 15-18 persons per watch in previous years to an average of 30-40 persons at present. Similarly, the number of turtles sighted has also increased from an average of 1 per night to 3 per night.

With well-managed and self-financing marine protected areas in three territories of the region - Saba Marine Park, Bonaire Marine Park and the marine protected areas of the British Virgin Island - the Caribbean is leading the way in local financing of coral reef conservation, yet another large step in the direction of self-reliance.

Revenue is obtained by fees levied on scuba divers and, in the case of the British Virgin Islands, yacht charters as well.

As the negative effects of these activities, and overfishing, and most critically, improper controls over coastal and watershed development threaten the well-being of the picturesque coral reefs, other countries in the Caribbean are planning the development of marine protected areas.

In 1995, the Caribbean Natural Resources Institute held a regional workshop on strategies to raise revenue for protected areas. Of the 14 participants from nine Caribbean countries, 12 were involved in the development of coastal and marine protected areas.

In St. Lucia, a collaborative management arrangement has been instituted between the government and a community body capable of managing the protected areas and levying and collecting fees. Fees are placed in a separate government fund from which payments are made quarterly to the community body managing the protected area.

The important and encouraging fact is that St. Lucia, acutely aware of the consequences of ignoring unwitting damage to its coastline, is taking practical and positive steps to protect its precious and irreplaceable marine resources.

PRECIOUS CORAL REEFS

Jim Bohinsack, the National Fisheries Services biologist, likens artificial reefs to saltwater crack house: 'They attract a lot of fish, but it may not be healthy for them. They build, em like mad but they don't spend any money to study them. A lot of these things are strictly for public relations. Other times, they're building artificial reefs because no one's catching fish like they used to. But it is probably not going to help the problem of depletion, and if they're not done properly, they could actually cause harm. At the very least, it takes a lot of money that could be better spent elsewhere, on studying and preserving seagrass or mangroves, for example.'

REEF construction, which is gathering speed, is a controversial issue. The question being asked by many St. Lucians is: Do these man-made structures really improve the marine environment? Do they improve sport and commercial fishing? Are some of the reef-building efforts a public relations exercise?

There are a variety of objections, some of the most disturbing being the use of truck tyres, toilet bowls, shopping cards, rubble, metal dredge pipes, oil rigs, smokestacks and even military tanks, airplanes and other equally damaging pollutants in their construction.

The fact that man-made reefs attract fish is not in dispute. The question is whether artificial reefs are a discrete ecosystem, spawning ground and nursery that add to the overall fish population, or do they merely draw fish from elsewhere, concentrating them in a place where they can be more easily viewed and killed by fishermen.

Most experts maintain that an artificial reef cannot be a fishing spot, a diving spectacle and a scientifically sound maritime habitat all at once. That view appears to be shared by the St. Lucians themselves.

New Southeastern University Professor Richard Spieler is also in no doubt about the negative impact of artificial reefs: "I think the aggregation-versus-production question is mainly of historical interest. We had a lot of people putting in artificial reefs that weren't correct. It pointed out a need for research. Now there's a real research impetus, and the result is a belief that it's going to depend a lot on the species, the location and the natural history as to whether you're going to get production or aggregation of a particular animal in a particular session at a particular site. I don't think there is a general answer to that"

INDUSTRY

St Lucia like many of its neighbours has a very small light manufacturing sector, contributing less than 20 per cent to Gross Domestic Product (GDP). It has essentially developed only over the last 30 years. In recent times, the sector's growth has been helped by fiscal incentives from government for the development of industrial estates and infrastructure.

The government has established the Small Enterprise Development Unit (SEDU) to facilitate growth and development with special focus on youth and the unemployed.

Preferential access to overseas markets has been secured such as CARIBCAN, the Caribbean agreement with Canada; the United States' Caribbean Basin Initiative (CBI), the Lomé agreement with the European Union (EU), and the Caribbean Common Market, CARICOM.

Manufacturing in St Lucia is to be found mainly in the following areas:- agribusiness, garments, electronic assembly, chemicals, industrial gases, handicraft, paper products, plastic products and beverages. Most of the companies can be considered as small or micro enterprises. Over 50 per cent of those operating in the agribusiness sector are cottage- type businesses.

Production methods are generally labour intensive and owner-operated. Due to the small size of the local and regional markets, many firms operate below capacity.

St Lucia's manufacturing is set to face a challenging period in the next five to ten years, primarily because of the wave of trade liberalisation and globalisation which is sweeping the world.

St Lucia is a member of the World Trade Organisation (WTO) and has committed itself to adhering to the rules of free trade. Marketing will have to assume greater importance for companies along with research and development so that they may become and remain competitive.

Companies must realise that preferential market access is becoming a thing of the past and that restructuring is needed if they are to survive into the next century. Niche marketing and product differentiation will be the key to this process.

ST LUCIA'S PORTS

Port Vieux Fort

The St Lucia Air and Sea Ports Authority (SLASPA) has earned a deservedly impressive reputation for servicing the needs of the country's port users along with a healthy increase in port traffic.

This growth has been partly due to the higher demand for imports needed to support a burgeoning population. The expansion of tourism has also brought significant increases in shipments of construction and luxury items. The growth in traffic levels has also been spurred by the

Vieux Fort
Fishing community

Vieux Fort Marine Terminal

heightened capability and reputation of St Lucia's main port, Castries, for the efficient handling of transshipment cargoes. Indeed large numbers of containers are handled on the island en route from the Far East to Caribbean countries both north and south of St Lucia.

The competitive environment in which transshipment cargoes enter the region has ensured that the port authority offers a high standard of services to complement its ideal location and protected harbor. An ongoing development program ensures that these facilities match the increasing demand and offer enhanced benefits to users.

Modern data communications and equipment, strategic location, and a cadre of skilled and committed staff are among the factors behind the attraction of both Port Castries and Port Vieux Fort as viable transportation routes.

Over the years, SLAPSA has registered impressive improvements in its operations, with resulting productivity gains and benefits to all port users. In particular, it has been recognised as the highest performing port authority in the Organisation of Eastern Caribbean States (OECS) sub-region on three consecutive occasions, from 1988 to 1990.

SLASPA has kept waiting time to a minimum through careful planning of schedules. Necessary work is carried out at night or on weekends so that goods can still be discharged promptly.

The great strides taken in container traffic operations since their inauguration in the late 1970s are also indicative of the authority's high levels of service. From an annual total of less than two thousand units during that decade, the total amount of containerised traffic increased by more than 60 per cent by the mid-1980s. The efficiency of operating conditions is clear from the increased tonnage of ships calling at the port: up nearly 400 per cent between 1970 and 1980. Container movements over the same period also rose fourfold, with transshipment traffic making up about 25 per cent of the total of nearly 8,000 movements. Nearly 60 per cent of domestic cargo is now containerised.

The level of success achieved in the 1980s stemmed from SLASPA's global objective of providing the best service to accommodate users' requirements. The same formula of dedication and commitment to customer needs has been applied to all St Lucia bound international freight operations during the 1990s, with facilities being expanded and upgraded.

The sole finder pier at Port Vieux Fort was constructed in the early

1940s as a US naval facility. The structure had deteriorated over the years and the piled substructure was in urgent need of repair, while the fendering system was inadequate.

The Vieux Fort area has been designated as the island's industrial zone. One of the requirements of such an area is the availability of wide-ranging port facilities.

Accordingly, the pier rehabilitation programme was extended to include the provision of a container handling capability at Vieux Fort. The project was conceived in 1986 and centred around minor dredging, pier rehabilitation and the construction of a roll-on/roll-off container berth. When the relatively high mobilisation cost of dredging equipment and the future needs of the Vieux Fort area were taken into consideration, the project was revised and enlarged to take full advantage of the availability of a suitable offshore marine contractor. A contract was signed with Diate Kogyo Co Ltd, of Japan in May 1990 and work commenced the following month.

astries Harbour, early 1900's

Pointe Seraphine

Pointe Seraphine was the first duty free complex of its kind in the Caribbean. Opened in 1986, the complex owes its name to the French family that owned the land on which it was built.

The government bought the derelict site in the mid-eighties, construction began in 1985 and just one year later the terminal was officially opened.

In 1987, the first cruise ship arrived. In that year there were 104 such arrivals bringing over 500,000 visitors. In 1990, the number of arrivals and tourists had more than doubled. In 1989, a tender jetty had been added to the facility and this enabled passengers to disembark directly from ships to pleasure boats.

Duty free shoppers must present their passports, air tickets, or cruise passes to qualify for duty free purchases. The shops at Pointe Seraphine have a wide range of merchandise and some of the best buys - in spirits, fragrances, crystal, china, porcelain, leather, tropical fashions, handicrafts, gifts and souvenirs.

The Cruise Industry

The cruise industry is a highly significant area of tourism in St Lucia. The Caribbean in general accounts for around 60 per cent of all international passenger cruises.

St Lucia is well placed to benefit from this development. The port of Castries is equipped to accommodate up to five cruise ships at the same time.

St Lucia's rich history, engaging people, varied attractions and excellent facilities are guaranteed to maintain its reputation as a foremost cruise destination.

Vigie Marina, home to the Co_ Pot Restaurant and Unicorn tall ship

St Lucia's Airports

The St Lucia Air and Sea Ports Authority oversees the operation of two airports. Hewanorra International Airport in the industrial town of Vieux Fort caters primarily to international traffic, while the smaller Vigie Airport in the capital city of Castries is used mainly for regional traffic and charters. The airports are about 40 miles apart and a charter service for traffic between them is available.

Management structure allows for increased flexibility and customer awareness, resulting in a positive impact on airport growth and development.

Hewanorra and Vigie play a critical role in the growth of the burgeoning tourism sector. Arrivals by air account for around 98 per cent of all tourist arrivals.

The airports also help promote the development of manufacturing industry and foreign investment. Hewanorra is very close to the Free Zone facility in Vieux Fort, so a number of companies utilise air services for 'just in time' imports of raw materials as well as the export of finished goods.

*gie Airport - less than five minutes
om centre of Castries*

FISHING

This intelligently environmentally conscious and protective island attaches as much importance to its exceptionally diverse marine life as it does to its almost limitless botanical assets.

In a bold move that will contribute to a greater knowledge about some rare and important species of marine life, the St. Lucia Department of Fisheries, in association with CARICOM Fisheries Resource Assessment and Management Project (CFRAMP) and the St. Lucia Game Fishing Association, have produced a Fish Tag and Release Tournament for four migratory pelagic species, the first of its kind in the Caribbean. CFRAMP's prime concern in assessing the living marine resources of the CARICOM region is to determine fish migration patterns. The conservation and sound management of fish resources in the CARICOM seas are also high priorities.

In a highly original exercise, applauded by conservationists the world over, a Fish Tag and Release Tournament in St. Lucia on May 19, 1997, released four commercially important fish to determine their migration patterns throughout the Caribbean. These were dolphin fish, wahoo and king mackerel, known locally as kingfish, and blackfin tuna, called bonito by the islanders.

The information gathered is proving most useful in furthering fishery development and facilitating management decisions in CARICOM countries.

The Tag tournament has earned St. Lucia enormous goodwill for its practical contribution to conservation. The sports fishing fraternity, too,

245

have been delighted with the results. The future of eco-tourism is extremely bright, with the international environmental movement, alarmed by recent catastrophes, such as that in south east Asia, intensively lobbying for more effective monitoring of abuse, and a new set of enforceable international laws to deter countries which, in their unrestrained pursuit of 'industrialisation', have given little thought to the serious consequences of riding roughshod over nature. Certainly, where St. Lucia is concerned, it makes every effort to preserve the natural balances.

MANAGING FISHERY RESOURCES IN ST LUCIA

Marine life is as diverse as bird and wildlife, characterised by the same interdependence between the creatures of the deep on their environment, as animals and humans, on the rainforests.

St. Lucian marine biologists carefully and conscientiously strive to ensure that the delicate balance of nature in the seas is preserved despite unfriendly intrusions. Hence the meticulous attention to several sea plants, especially Seamoss and Seagrass.

Seamoss is a group of sea algae, a plant belonging to the Gracilaria family. Seamoss consists of branched fronds generally attached to a rock. Seamoss may reproduce naturally and also be grown by taking a cutting from another plant and using it as a seedling. Since the technique of cultivating seamoss was introduced in 1985, many St. Lucians are earning a livelihood from a humane industry, which is ingeniously safeguarding marine life. Its cultivation meets the heavy demand for the product while lessening the burden on wild stocks.

Seagrass beds are inshore or offshore, formed from flowering plants with roots, stems and leaves. Seagrass beds provide a home for white sea eggs, conch and young fish, and food for animals and turtles. The roots of the plants hold the bottom of the substrate together and prevent sediment from causing murky waves.

Port of Castries container trans-shipment facilities

DISTILLERIES

The switch from the export of sugar to bananas in the early 60s affected the viability of the smaller distilleries. They could only survive by merging with larger and more profitable enterprises.

This proved to be the case with the Barnard family who had made rum for three generations in St.Lucia. They merged with the larger Geest Distillery and the Dennery Factory Company to become St. Lucia Distillers Ltd., which is on the site of the old Geest Distillery, just south of Marigot on the west coast of the island.

There was yet another merger in 1987 creating the East Caribbean Distilleries, a joint venture with Duncan, Gilbey and Matheson

*Lucia's Distilleries produce a boun-
of favourite tipples*

International Limited. The new company introduced gin, vodka and brandy, opening up new markets for St. Lucian distilled and bottled liquor. Profitable bulk exports of alcohol to Europe and Africa followed this expansion.

Under another agreement between the Martinique-based company of G & P Dormoy and the newly formed West Indies Liquer Company, the famous La Belle Creole liquers are being made and botttled in St. Lucia.

St. Lucia Distillers bottles a rich and rare variety, from white fresh to aged and blended rum. The most popular white rum is known locally as Denros or Strong Rum. At 80% alcohol by volume this is one of the most potent overproof rums in the Caribbean.

Five-gallon plastic containers of this white rum are prominent in the small rum shops, where it is blended with fruit and spices and is simply described as 'spice'.

The premium white rum, Bounty Crystal White, with its blue and silver label is much admired by connoisseurs for its smooth qualities. At 40% alcohol by volume, Bounty Crystal makes a pleasant cocktail base, and the rum-based drinks so popular in America and Europe.

The best-selling rum in St. Lucia is the blended Bounty Rum at 40% alcohol. Those wanting a heavier taste turn to Buccaneer at 43% alcohol.

The premium rum from St. Lucia Distillers is Old Fort Reserve Rum. Bottled at 40% alcohol by volume, Old Fort Reserve Rum is the smoothest product of Distillers. Rum lovers visiting St. Lucia will find it difficult to resist Old Fort Reserve.

St. Lucia Distillers has the largest product line of any distillery of comparable size. As their directors continue to diversify their strong market base they can be counted on to produce even more exciting varieties of rum, and other liquors and liqueurs.

Visitors to St. Lucia, especially those with a bacchanalian tendency, are strongly advised to do the Spirit of St. Lucia Tour which takes in St. Lucia Distillers and the West Indian Liqueur Company housed in verdant Rouseau Valley, 7 miles south of Castries. Walk through the old distillery which has been producing excellent rums for over 50 years. The guided tour takes you through the only fully operational distillery in St. Lucia. Here is the fascinating opportunity to see how fine rums and liqueurs are made and prepared for distribution throughout the region and internationally. Quench that irrepressible thirst with a generous tasting of the Distillery's range of treasures.

The British visitor, appreciative of the cultured rum of St. Lucia, have created another most welcome dimension. Varieties of St. Lucian rum, vodka etc. now proudly occupy valuable but profitable shelf space in some of the large supermarket chains. Although British visitors are warmly welcomed to St. Lucia, they need no longer go there especially to savour the island's irresistible rums.

St. Lucia's encouraging, indeed spectacular success as an exporter of spirits, is due to the highest standards of quality control. Even the pernickety Japanese who have the most demanding quality control standards in the world will probably acknowledge St. Lucia's own faultless standards in this particular regard. St. Lucia will not deviate from this policy, not only because spirit exports are a valuable foreign exchange earner, but because of the island's strong commitment to moral and ethical practices in all walks of life.

INVESTMENT

Like most forward looking nations, St. Lucia welcomes investments for the obvious reason that they help improve living standards by creating more job opportunities and enriching the treasury.

The attractions of St. Lucia are its considerate tax system, industrial zones, political and economic stability, attachment to democracy, a friendly, honest, intelligent and diligent workforce and experienced and skilled managers. The island also has a modest but sound infrastructure. There is also another unusual St. Lucian asset - its beautiful climate, limitless sunshine and gentle breezes, inviting beaches, fitness and sports facilities, some of the finest restaurants in the region and an exciting nightlife. Besides, St. Lucians are a hospitable, law-abiding people warm and welcoming to outsiders. Crime is a negligible factor in this island of God-fearing, devout people.

Investors not only seek profit but they like to operate in safe, stable conditions. They also want to enjoy their leisure in privacy and comfort, indeed luxury, which comes at a fraction of the price charged by the more advanced nations of western Europe and North America

modern brewery produces
e Piton beer

St. Lucia also has that rare quality - it is by its very nature, an unspoiled, sublime other Eden, an unrivaled stress-free zone. Western business executives who want to strike the right balance between the work ethic and the pleasure principle have to look not further than serene and sublime St. Lucia.

The incentives are also characteristically generous. Below are listed the main features of the St. Lucian investment strategy:
Free Trade Zones: There are two of these strategically located zones, the Hewanorra and Vieux-Fort.
Industrial Zones: The St. Lucia National Development Corporation has set up five industrial estates for manufacture and assembling.

A Data Entry Park has also been created for information processing. Manufacturers are entitled to duty free imports of all raw materials, machinery, plant equipment and spare parts with a 15-year tax holiday and unrestricted repatriation of all profits and capital.

Under the Caribbean Basin Initiative, St Lucia provides duty free access to specified products into the US. The island benefits similarly from CARIBCAN (Canada) and LOMÉ 1V (Europe), which also provide duty free and preferential access for products manufactured in St. Lucia to agreed markets.

The Tax Information Exchange Agreement (TIEA) under the CBI entitles St. Lucia to below the market rate financing for projects. US executives can claim tax deduction on convention expenses incurred on the island.

TAXES

Tax concessions of up to 15 years in the manu-facturing, information processing and tourism industries. A double taxation agreement is in effect with the US

For information on Free Trade Zones and Industrial Estates, contact:

St. Lucia National Development Corporation

TELECOMMUNICATIONS

Direct dial telephone to all part of the world. Fully automatic telex services. International tele-graph. Facsimile. Fully digital earth station. Fibre optic lines.

TRANSPORT

996 kilometers of roads

AIRPORTS

Major international airport (South) 2743 meters
Regional airport (north) 1737 meters

SEAPORTS

North
Roll-on/roll-off capacity
Storage facility for 3000 containers
226 cubic meters of cold storage facilities
Simultaneous berthing for 6 vessels, 213-244
1 Cruise ship facility; capacity: 2 vessels

South
Capable of handling container traffic
Roll-on/roll off capacity
Simultaneous berthing for 3 vessels

UTILITIES

Electricity
Diesel generated.
Power outage: Infrequent
Cost per kilowatt hour: US$0.15

Water
An abundant supply. No shortages. Treated to conform to WHO standards
US$3,80 per 1000 gallons for industrial use

Sewage
Septic tanks and sewage treatment facilities

Work permits
Granted on a case by case basis

Residency
Non-immigrant persons who reside in St. Lucia for over 6 months must apply for an extension of their stay through the immigration authorities. Persons wishing to apply for residency must apply to the office of the Prime Minister.

NATIONAL DEVELOPMENT CORPORATION

Establishing a Business in Saint Lucia

Trade Licenses
All foreign individuals and companies who intend to conduct business in St. Lucia require a trade licence which is issued by the Ministry of Commerce, Industry and Consumer Affairs. The application is considered by the Trade Licence Advisory Board. The trade licence is an annual one and expires on December 31 in the year it was granted. Applications for renewal must be made every year. Approval of trade licences may take one to three months. Licence fees are one thousand Eastern Caribbean dollars ($1,000 ECD) for a period of one year, and renewable thereafter.

Work Permits

Under the Foreign National and Commonwealth Citizens (Employment) Regulation, No. 3 of 1971, all persons who are not St. Lucian nationals or citizens require a work permit to engage in any form of occupation on the island. This can be obtained from the Labour Department of the Ministry of Legal Affairs, Home Affairs and Labour, John Compton Highway, Castries, St. Lucia.

Establishing a Company

Incorporating a company must be done through a lawyer registered in St. Lucia. Documents required are:
Declaration of Compliance;
Memorandum of Association;
Articles of Association.

These documents are to be filed with the Registrar of Companies and a fee of two thousand Eastern Caribbean dollars ($ ECD 2,000.00) paid to the same. Upon incorporation, the company is issued with a Certificate of Incorporation.

Local Taxes and Fees

Depending on its location in St. Lucia and the nature of its business, the company would be required to pay fees to the Castries City Council (located on Peynier Street, Castries) or the respective town or village council. These relate to taxes on property and trading fees, which are payable on an annual basis.

Other Regulations

If a company wishes to develop land, it must apply for permission to do so from the Planning department of the Ministry of Finance, Planning, Information Services and the Public Service (First Floor, Block C, New Government Buildings, John Compton Highway, Castries). The application, which must be made in triplicate, should be accompanied by maps and plans. Failure by authorities to give a decision for development approval within ninety days may be deemed a refusal. The applicant, however, has the right to appeal.

In cases where the proposed development may have environmental implications, the Development Control Authority (DCA) of the Ministry of Finance, Planning, Information Services and the Public Service would authorise the conduct of an Environmental Impact Assessment (EIA), the results of which would determine approval.

In the case of food operations, these would require a permit from the Division of Public Health of the Ministry of Health, Human Services, Family Affairs and Women (Chausee Road, Castries). These permits are granted on an annual basis.

Fiscal Incentives

The Government of St. Lucia provides incentives to manufacturers as a reward for investment in plant and machinery. See below

Industrial Estates

The government has a number of industrial estates on the island which are managed by the National Development Corporation. Further information on rental fees can be obtained by contacting their offices in the Monplaisir Building, Brazil Street, Castries. Tel: (758) 452-3614, Fax: (758) 452-1841.

INCENTIVES TO INDUSTRY FOR INVESTMENT

Objectives

Fiscal Incentives are granted to enterprises under the Fiscal Incentive Act of 1974 to facilitate local and foreign investment into the productive sectors of the economy. Export oriented manufacturing enterprises are especially encouraged to apply for fiscal incentives.

Fiscal Incentives Offered To Industry

Waiver of Import Duty and Consumption Tax on imported plant, machinery and equipment.
Waiver of Import Duty and Consumption Tax on imported raw material and packaging.
Carry forward of losses.
Export Allowance - tax relief on export earnings.

Criteria

The enterprise must be incorporated and registered in St. Lucia and must contribute to the economic development of St. Lucia. The country's human and natural resources must be utilised. The enterprise must train local personnel and upgrade its plant through technological transfer. The enterprise must form linkages with other economic sectors and the enterprise must contribute to earnings in foreign exchange.

Other Services

Duty-free concessions on machinery, raw materials and packaging are also granted to enterprises which do not qualify for the full range of fiscal incentives.

Administration

The Ministry of Commerce, Industry and Consumer Affairs has the administrative responsibility for fiscal incentives offered to industry.

TRADE LICENCES ACT NO. 5 OF 1985

All foreign individuals and companies who conduct or intend to conduct business in St. Lucia require a trade licence issued by the Officer with the approval of the Minister of Commerce, Industry and Consumer Affairs. This requirement became law with the passing of the Trade Licences Act No. 5 of 1985.

In considering applications for the award of licences, the Board and the Minister will be guided by the Government's policy with respect to areas of commercial activity to be reserved for St. Lucian nationals.

The St. Lucian Government recognises that there is insufficient investment in certain critical areas of productive activity. This can be due to several factors, including unavailability of venture capital, the lack of appropriate technology, or skills. The Government intends to use the licensing mechanism, among others, to direct foreign investment and enterprise into those areas which will be most beneficial to the development of the country.

At the same time, the Government recognises the adequacy of investment in certain areas and the need to ensure the realisation of the full benefits to St. Lucians of their investment in those areas which they satisfactorily service. Such areas will be specifically reserved for nationals.

It is important that all persons and companies required to hold licences make the necessary applications for doing so. The legislation makes adequate provision for the summary conviction, fining and imprisonment of those who contravene any of the provisions of the Act. However, the Ministry would prefer not to have to prosecute anyone for contravention. It should be noted that Section 15 of the Act places the onus on anyone who considers that he or she is not liable to take out a licence under the Act to prove such non-liability. Consequently, those who are in doubt as to their liability are to **contact the Ministry**.

It is expected the trade licencing arrangements will prove of significance in the economic development of St. Lucia and the cooperation of all concerned is urged by the Ministry of Commerce, Industry and Consumer Affairs and the Licencing Board.

AREAS OF INVESTMENT ACTIVITY RESERVED FOR NATIONAL

~Distribution, both retail and wholesale, except where conducted ex-factor, wholesale;
~Import for the purpose of trading;
~The operation of agencies and distributorships;
~Operation of restaurants, with the exception of top class specialty type;
~Rental agencies for home, villas and apartments;
~Real estate;
~Construction, (excluding ad hoc contracts)

Modern developments appear all around St Lucia

repairs and maintenance of buildings and other facilities;

~Landscaping;

~Services which nationals have the capability to provide, including secretarial, clerical, hairdressing services, laundry, internal hire, transportation, vehicle and other repairs;

Advertising, except where local technology is not sufficiently advanced;

~Entertainment on a protracted basis;

~Operation of guest houses of less than 10 rooms or with an investment of less than EC $ 500,000;

~Operation of a manufacturing or processing plant in an area in which there is already adequate local productive capacity and in which the investment in the plant is below EC $ 250,000 and employment is offered to less than ten (10) nationals;

~Printing, except where local technology is not sufficiently advanced;

~Production of the following exclusively for the domestic market:

- agricultural goods- handicrafts
- handicrafts
- furniture
- soft drinks - carbonated and non-carbonated
- bread and pasta
- quarrying
- games of chance and lotteries
- warehousing where capital investment is below EC $ 500,000
- heavy equipment, hire and leasing
- tyre retreading and repair
- road maintenance and repair

Despite the reservation of the above areas of business for nationals, a licence could, nevertheless, be awarded to non-national companies of persons in cases where local investment has not sufficiently been forthcoming or where the appropriate technology is not available locally.

The St. Lucia National Development Corporation was established by an act of the St. Lucia Parliament, No. 9 of 1971. The main functions of the Corporation as laid down by the Act are to stimulate, facilitate and undertake the economic development of St. Lucia, and to promote the development of land and industry in St. Lucia.

Corporation policy is determined by the board of directors, appointed by the minister, acting under the general authority of Cabinet. The minister appoints the chairman and deputy chairman from among the board members of the corporation.

The day-to-day administration of the corporation is the resonsibility of the manager, who is accountable to the board for the implementation of its policies. The organisation is divided into four functional divisions, namely Personnel and Administration, Finance and Accounts, Engineering and Estates, and Investment Promotions.

NATIONAL DEVELOPMENT CORPORATION

NDC Vieux-Fort Office

The general functions and objectives of the Vieux-Fort office include:

• The upgrading of the Vieux-Fort master plan and the monitoring of its implementation.
• The identification of specific regional physical projects and programmes consistent with NDC's development strategy.
• Responsibility for the control of all lands in Vieux-Fort vested in the corporation.
• To conduct squatter relocation and resettlement exercises.
• To conduct land surveys for lots approved by the Devleopment Control Authority.

To date, 35 companies lease factory space from NDC, of which 21 are foreign-owned. Approx. 3,500 St. Lucians are employed within NDC's Industrial Estates.

Fiscal Incentives

For manufacturing establishments, both local and foreign, the Government grants a number of Fiscal Incentives.

1. Up to 15 years tax holiday
2. Duty Free concessions on the importation of both equipment and raw materials needed for the operation
3. Repatriation of profits for foreign companies

It must be noted that the extent of the fiscal Incentives will vary in accordance with export business outside the Caribbean Community, Caricom, local value added content, and the degree of capital intensiveness of the investment.

Commercial and Residential Lands

With the demand for commercial lands in Vieux-Fort on the upswing, the corporation has undertaken the following:

1. The completion of Black Bay III
2. La tourney Phase IV-Residential
3. La tourney Phase V-Residential
4. Beanefield I - Combination of commercial & residential
5. Derriere Morne Phase I-Residential
6. Beausejour

Commercial development includes:

- New Dock extension - 3 lots remaining
- Commercial Block, La Tourney V
- Garage and Church Complex
- Beanefield Commercial Extension
- Black Bay III Commercial Block

Industrial Estates

Presently, there are eight industrial estates with Beauchamp (Micoud) being the most recent addition:

1. Bisee Industrial Estate
2. Dennery Industrial Estate
3. Hewanorra Airport Freezone*
4. Odsan Industrial Estate
5. Vieux-Fort Industrial Estate
6. Vieux-Fort Industrial Freezone
7. Union Industrial Estate
8. Beauchamp Industrial Estate
*(Industrial Estates situated in Vieux-Fort)

Tourist Lands

Recognising the importance of providing sites for tourism-related development, the Corporation has identified specific areas for that purpose. These sites include:

Black Bay   L'au Piquant   Anse de Sables

Government Investments and Corporation Subsidiaries:

An often forgotten aspect of the corporation's function is the execution of its tasks as the custodian of Government's investment and its responsibility to create development companies, so as to facilitate the growth and development of specific projects which have commercial possibilities.

Such projects include:

Beausejour Dairy Farm (St. Lucia Livestock Development Co.)
Duty Free Pointe Seraphine
Dennery Farm Co.
St. Lucia Fish Marketing Corporation

Trade Shows

In order to maintain a strong presence in the international arena, the NDC has been participating annually in a number of international trade shows, conferences, exhibitions and expos. It is through those shows that a number of leads are generated, for example:

Coil Winding Electronic Trade Show
Miami Conference
Association for Information and Image Management International (AIIM) Show
Bobbin Apparel Show
Electro Electronics Show

NATIONAL DEVELOPMENT CORPORATION

Objectives

The NDC develops and implements programmes with a view to:

- Encouraging investments in St. Lucia by both foreign and local concerns

- Creating employment

- Developing the small business sector through the provision of technical assistance

SERVICES PROVIDED BY THE NDC

The NDC focusses on the following major areas:

- Investment Promotion

- Trade/Export Promotion

- Technical Assistance

- Business Information

IDENTIFICATION OF LAND AND FACTORY SPACE

The NDC owns and manages seven industrial estates, with factory shells, ranging in size from 3,800 to 30,000 square feet. These shells are available for rent at attractive rates.

The NDC also liaises with private landowners on behalf of parties interested in leasing or purchasing land for development purposes.

AFTERCARE SERVICE

The NDC will assist in business development and expansion by sourcing technical assistance and financing new markets.

BUSINESS COUNSELLING

The NDC, through its Small Enterprise Development Unit, will provide the following services to micro and small entrepreneurs:

- Development of a Business Plan

- Preparation of a financing proposal

- Identification of sources of finance

- Setting up of proper accounting systems

Pope visits St Lucia

MARKETING

The NDC will undertake market research for export ready companies and, through collaboration with the Ministries of International Trade and Industry, Commerce and Consumer Affairs, attempt to gain access to new markets for exporters.

TECHNICAL ASSISTANCE

The NDC will try to obtain technical assistance for micro, small and medium sized enterprises from bilateral and multilateral agencies, in areas such as quality control, packaging, product design, and so on.

Lady in 'National Costume'

OVERVIEW OF TOURISM

Tourism is fast becoming the bedrock of the St. Lucian economy. Backed by its tremendous natural resources, St. Lucia has also intelligently created a first rate infrastructure with a political and social stability to match.

The world associates tranquillity, order and safety with what some knowledgeable travel writers use as a synonym for St. Lucia, The Other Eden. Sizeable investments have gone into the expansion of the airport, harbour and road systems. The country's close proximity to North and South America is also helpful.

Keep fit while on holiday

In a highly competitive tourist market, St. Lucia cannot rest on its laurels, hence the continuous search for new pastures. While the traditional delights, sun, sand and sea are still hugely popular, attention is also being devoted to relatively unexplored territory. The island's own well informed and helpful promotional literature on the distinctive French Creole culture and history is bound to appeal to the historically and culturally minded. Health conscious, nature loving tourists are soon to have easier access to the health-enhancing sulphur springs at Soufriere. "Taking the waters" in continental spas, once so beloved of the aged and ailing privileged classes of Europe, is no longer fashionable on the continent as many spas crumble through neglect. Soufriere sulphur springs, still as pristine as when they were first created, are not only a classless luxury but an eminently affordable one.

Sailing has also been given a new dimension. From St. Lucia, as a base, international trans-atlantic yachts muster after the ARC race and plan trips south through St. Vincent and the Grenadines, and north to Martinique and Dominica.

Thanks to one of the most serene climates in the region, St. Lucia has an all-year round attraction. It is one of the few destinations in the world without the off-season syndrome. There is, to be sure, a slack season but even then the ubiquitous package tours fill the hotels, beaches, restaurants and nightclubs. St. Lucian promotion campaigns never lose sight of the fact that there is an enormous tourist potential in the Caribbean, and this has paid off handsomely with more and more visitors from all social backgrounds to the island.

Estates

MAIN ESTATES

Although much has been written about the plantation system in the Westindies, there has been virtually nothing about the individual estates. Some of the more famous or important ones are in St. Lucia.

Estates in St. Lucia were not named before 1763, when the Treaty of Paris assigned the island to France. Prior to that, they were simply known by the owner's name. After the Treaty, however, French planters felt somewhat more secure and this led to the expansion and development of the plantations, which then acquired more elaborate names.

An estate located on Morne Paix Bouche was given the name la Cauzette by its new owner, Joseph Tascher de la Pagerie, father of Josephine - the future Empress of France - who was born at la Cauzette on June 23 1763. That estate is now fragmented into small housing plots and little remains of the original estate house, which is barely visible at ground level.

An estate on the eastern side of the island was named **Marquis**, after the Marquis de Champigny, who landed there in 1723. With a small army of Frenchmen, he marched across the island and dislodged the British from St. Lucia, forcing the signing of the Treaty of Choc, which declared the island neutral. This estate is now a tourist attraction. The ruins of the sugar works still survive.

Soufriere Estate, on the outskirts of the town of Soufriere, was part of a larger Crown Grant, one of the earliest grants made. Around 1713, the Estate was given to the Devaux family, who were living in Martinique at the time, and who took up residency in St. Lucia in 1742. This estate is now a popular tourist destination. The old water wheel that once turned the rollers for grinding cane has been restored.

Balembouche Estate, on the southwest coast of the island, is one of the flattest and most fertile in the whole island. It was named after the quick sand bar or Ba l'an bouchwie which occasionally forms at the mouth of the river. This estate is now a small tourist resort. Ruins of the water mill can still be seen.

Morne Courbaril Estate in Soufriere was once part of a larger land grant. It was named after the great number of courbaril trees or Westindian locust tree, that once grew on the estate. This estate is now a tourist attraction. Part of the old sugar works can still be seen.

Roseau Estate on the east coast was once a productive sugar cane valley, with a large central sugar factory. The valley was later converted to banana cultivation. The refinery has been developed into a fine modern distillery, which now attracts numerous visitors. The abandoned factory ruins can still be seen.

Fond Estate, formerly known as Fond Devaux Estate, on the east coast is one of the most productive and diversified estates in Saint Lucia. The estate is managed and operated on a scale unmatched locally. The ruins of the old aquaduct, chimney and water wheel from the sugar era can still be seen.

Migney Estate in the interior highlands, at 2,000 feet above sea level, has the distinction of being at the highest elevation of any estate in Saint Lucia. With its cool climate and high rainfall, the estate has the best citrus orchard in the island. It faces the highest mountain range and borders on the central forest reserve, where parrots abound.

St. Joseph Estate in the Errand Valley is a typical small family estate that has remained with the traditional crops of cocoa, coffee, coconuts and, more recently, bananas. Sugar cane was also grown there. The Canot River divides the estate and keeps it well watered, but also well drained.

Mahaut Estate in the Micoud District is a typical banana estate, where the traditional crops have been replaced by the quick growing, but labour intensive, banana plant. There is a banana boxing plant on this centrally located estate in the banana belt of the island.

CAP ESTATE

Cap Estate was one of the earliest estates in St. Lucia to be established on a relatively organised basis. This was largely due to the fact that it was owned by Baron de Longueville, a wealthy Frenchman who came to St. Lucia in 1744 as Civil Commandant. Prior to this, the area of Cap Estate was a magnificent wilderness of gently rolling hills covered with lush xerophytic vegetation. Apparently there was little or no human interference other than a track from the beach on the north-west coast, which led up to a small clearing on Morne du Cap. Pirates from nearby Pigeon Island used this hill as a lookout to observe the movements of ships.

Only two Amerindian sites are known in the area. An Arawak village once existed more or less where Gros Islet town now sits and a Carib village once existed near Anse Epouge.

HISTORIC FORTS

CHOC FORT. Built in 1664, as a safe haven for the English colonists. The fort was intended to defend the colony from a possible invading French force from the seaward side as well as Caribs from the landward side. The few English survivors burnt and abandoned the fort in 1666. The site is now under private ownership.

MORNE COURBARIL BATTERY. Built by the French about 1744, for the defence and protection of Soufriere Bay and Town. The fort was situated on the high point of Morne Crabier on Morne Courbaril Estate, which was owned by Philippe Devaux, Captain of the militia. It is now being promoted as a tourist attraction.

Old water wheel that once turned the rollers for grinding cane has been restored

Places of Interest

VIGIE BATTERY. Built by the French in 1744 and used alternatively by the French or British when in possession of St. Lucia. The fort is accessible only through a tunnel. It was abandoned in 1898 when a new 2-gun battery was built on the hill above, known as Meadow's Battery. The original fort below was re-activated during the Second World War, when a three-inch anti-aircraft gun was installed there. It is under private ownership.

VIEUX FORT BATTERY. Built by the French in 1763 for the protection of Vieux Fort Bay and Town. It was situated a little to the south of the town on a promontory overlooking the sea. Recent harbour developments have destroyed the earthworks and dry stone walls of this historic site.

FORT RODNEY. The fort was built in 1779 on the lower of two peaks on Pigeon Island while Admiral George Rodney had his Naval Headquarters and Convalescent Hospital on this tiny 44 acre island. The fort was armed with three 24-pounders and two 16-inch mortars. The island, now joined to the main by a causeway, has been turned into a well preserved historic site.

MORNE FORTUNE CITADEL. Built in 1784, as the Military Headquarters of the French while they were in possession of St. Lucia. The Citadel was destroyed by the British Army during new military construction about 1890, and was replaced with military barracks. The Citadel was defended by a ring of five redoubts. Only one, Prevost Redoubt, has survived, as a nearly landscaped park.

APOSTLE'S BATTERY. Built on the western spur of Morne Fortunè by the Royal Engineers in 1888 and manned by the West India Regiment Fortress Company and, later by the St. Lucia company Royal Artillery. The fort boasted four 10-inch RML (rifled muzzle loading) armour piercing guns, with a range of 12,000 yards, and two 6-inch mobile Howitzers. Each half of the fort is inter-connected by a tunnel and underground magazines. The fort was abandoned in 1905. It is being restored as an historic site.

LA TOC 2-GUN BATTERY. Built by the British about 1890 as one in a system of ten defensive batteries around Port Castries. It was originally designed to carry two 9-inch RML (rifled muzzle loading) guns, but was modified to take two modern 6-inch BL (breech loading) guns. The fort is on three levels underground, with an access tunnel below. It is now a tourist attraction.

THE CALYPSO CRUISE. St. Lucia in a different light. This evening cruise takes you along the northern coastline. Barbecue buffet, free bar and calypso music are all featured. In addition to the Calypso Cruise at

Vigie Marina, home to the Coal Pot Restaurant and boarding po for the Unicorn Tall Ship

various times throughout the year other boats offer a romantic sunset cruise. These usually include drinks and dinner. Check with your hotel desk.

THE CARRIAGE RIDE. Taking a horse drawn carriage ride is a novel way to see Pigeon Island. This tour also includes a drive through Cap Estate and Gros Islet Village.

National Cultural Foundation

CASTRIES. A bustling capital of some 60,000 inhabitants, Castries has one of the largest and busiest ports in the Caribbean. In the harbour, you will see just about every kind of floating vessel, from banana boats to cruise liners, cargo ships and yachts. In the town itself you can walk, explore and enjoy the dozens of boutiques, craft and gift shops, photo services, pharmacies and other attractions.

Unfortunately, very litte of the "old" Castries remains. In 1927, a fire destroyed half the town, then again in 1948, an even bigger blaze destroyed all but a very small part of the town. In fact, if you stand in Derek Walcott Square - once called Columbus Square - you can see the "old" on one side of the square and the "new" on the other.

Places to look for in Castries includes Castries Central Market, Cathedral of the Immaculate Conception (with spectacular paintings by a local artist inside) and Derek Walcott Square.

THE ERRARD PLANTATION. This tour takes you across the interior of the island, along the east coast road to Dennery and then through the countryside to Errard Plantation. The personable owner will escort you around the estate by 4-wheel drive, explaining the many fruits you will see and the complete processing of cocoa beans, including the traditional dance used to polish them.

FREGATE ISLAND NATURE RESERVE. This tour takes you to the Atlantic Coast and offers fantastic scenic views. The one mile nature trail encircles the park to the observation point overlooking the small Fregate Islands.

As the fregate birds nest here only in summer, do not expect to see too many of these magnificent creatures at other times of the year. But along the walk there is a wide variety of vegetation, from species requiring little water to the seaside mangrove. A large selection of birds have made their homes within the reserve, including the scarce Ramier Pigeon, the St. Lucian Oriole, the Trembler, and several types of herons. It is also the natural habitat of the timid boa constrictor. Tours are coordinated by the St. Lucia National Trust and can be arranged by hotels and local ground handlers.

HELICOPTER TOURS. See St. Lucia in an unusual and thrilling way - by helicopter! A unique opportunity to see what the country has to offer in the shortest time possible. A great way to get superb photos.

A choice of North Island or South Island Tours or Airport transfers. There are two helicopter companies: St. Lucia Helicopters, Tel. 453–6950; and Eastern Caribbean Helicopters, Tel. 453–6952.

LAND AND SEA. This is a popular tour for those keen on seeing the landscape but who do not want to spend a whole day in a bus. This tour to Soufriere, home of the Sulphur Springs and Pitons, allows you to drive one way and return by boat. Lunch is included in this full day tour.

LA SIKWI SUGAR MILL. This old sugar mill, located in the village of Anse La Raye, has been restored and is now a major tourist attraction. The site belongs to a local family who also run a restaurant there. Tours to the Sugar Mill are available.

MARIA ISLANDS. These are two small islands off the coast of Vieux Fort which have been set aside as a nature reserve and are home to two species found nowhere else in the world – the Kouwes snake and the Zandoli Te, a ground lizard, of which the male exhibits a splendid tail of brilliant blue. Maria Island Tours are coordinated by the St. Lucia National Trust and can be arranged by the hotels and local ground handlers.

MARIGOT BAY. Towards the south, Marigot Bay was a vital wartime base. A British Admiral once launched an ambush from this picturesque bay by camouflaging his fleet with palms. Today a yacht haven, Marigot remains one of St. Lucia's most beautiful spots.

MARQUIS ESTATE. Marquis Estate is located on the north-east coast of the island on a very historic spot, a short drive from Castries. The route passes through the countryside and reaches heights offering excellent views. You will be greeted at the estate house by one of the owners with a refreshing tropical drink. Escorted to the fields, you will follow the production of St. Lucia's main export crops – banana and coconut-copra, coffee and cocoa.

MORNE FORTUNE. Morne Fortune, or the "Hill of Good Luck", presiding over Castries. Panoramic views look north over Castries Harbour, Vigie and Pigeon Island, with Martinique on the horizon. To the south, look for the needle points of The Pitons.

NEIGHBOURING ISLANDS. Day tours are also available to the neighbouring islands of Barbados, Bequia and Mustique, Dominica, The Grenadines, and Martinique.

PIGEON ISLAND. In 1970, Pigeon Island was linked to the main land by a causeway. Today, the Island is run by the St. Lucia National Trust and visitors can walk or drive across, to wander amongst the historic ruins and visit the small museum. History aside, the sedimentary rock formation of Pigeon Island is a geological phenomenon. Pigeon Island is also the home of the St. Lucia Jazz Festival.

THE RAINFOREST. This full day tour must be done accompanied by a guide from the forestry department. The walk begins at the entrance in Dennery and passes through the natural habitat of the St. Lucia Parrot.,

SOUFRIERE. Soufriere in the south, boasts St. Lucia's oldest surviving architecture in the oldest settlement nestling in the midst of the island's most famous natural attractions. These include the Sulphur Springs Volcano, the Diamond Mineral Baths (constructed in 1784 from funds granted by King Louis XVI for the good health of his French officers), the Diamond Waterfalls and Tropical Gardens, and the twin peaks, the Pitons, which have come to symbolise St. Lucian's untamed beauty.

SPECIAL INTERESTS. Other special interest tours, focussing on horticulture, zoology and ornithology, can be arranged through the Department of Forestry or the St. Lucia National Trust.

THE SPIRIT OF ST. LUCIA. The tour takes you to the tropical heaven of Marigot Bay, the famous yachting harbour. From there you'll visit the Roseau Valley with its acres of bananas. You will be taken on a tour of the island's rum distillery for some sampling!!

UNION NATURE TRAIL. The Union Nature Trail, located at Union in the north of the island, is run by the Department of Forestry. The first stop is the mini-zoo where a few species of St. Lucia's native animal wildlife can be observed. The next stop is the medicinal garden which exhibits a variety of local herbs.

An entirely different view of his tropical paradise

VIGIE LIGHT HOUSE. The Vigie Light House was built in 1914 and has lovely views north and south. The small foundation ruins here are from a Power Magazine built around 1890, as was the Officer's Mess, now St. Mary's College, and the Officer's Quarters. On the outer side of the airport, in Vigie Cove, you will find a canon salvaged from the 74 gun battleship HMS Cornwall, abandoned after the battle of Martinique in 1780.

VIGIE PENINSULA. Located near Castries, the Vigie Peninsula is the site of many historical buildings and ruins.

VILLAGES - ANSE LA RAYE / CANARIES. Small fishing villages located on the west coast of St. Lucia, where fishermen can be seen on afternoons bringing in their daily catch.

WEDDINGS/HONEYMOONS. Most of the hotels in St. Lucia provide special facilities for couples getting married on the island. Some hotels will provide a private room or suite for the ceremony if you prefer it to the outdoors. They will cater to your every need, providing the wedding cake, champagne toast for the bride and groom, and if necessary even the services of the Best Man. Honeymooners usually also get special treatment in most hotels with a basket of fruits and flowers or a bottle of chilled sparkling wine on arrival.

DOCUMENTS REQUIRED: The following original documents are required to be produced in person before the local Registrar *(foreign documents must be translated officially into English)*:

* Passport
* Birth Certificate
* If one of the parties is a divorcee, proof of Decree Absolute is required.
* In the case of a widow/widower, a Death Certificate of their first spouse is required.
* If a name has been changed, a Deed Poll is required.
* If one of the parties is under the age of 18, evidence of consent of parents is required in the form of a sworn affidavit stamped by a Notary Public.

RESIDENCY: Application to be married in St. Lucia must be made by a local solicitor to the Attorney General who prepares and signs the licence after a two-day residency period in St. Lucia. The Attorney General should receive the application at least four working days before the Wedding date.

FEES: On application

OTHER: The hotels can usually arrange any other requirements - bridal bouquet, button holes and other floral arrangements, photos, video, steelband music etc. Prices vary.

Hotels that offer special wedding packages include: Anse Chastanet, Club St. Lucia, Green Parrot Inn, Le Sport, Royal St. Lucian, Sandals, St. Lucian and Windjammer Landing.

Nature Trails

The island of St. Lucia is home to a number of magnificent scenic coastal areas, beautiful mountains and a rich legacy of cultural sites. These attractions can be viewed by means of a series of hiking trails. A well-planned and constructed trail can be a thing of beauty, giving enjoyment and excitement to the hiker at every turn. It is worth remembering that a nature trail will only be successful if it is designed with the eye of an artist and the heart of a sculptor

ANSE L'IVROGNE RIVER WALK. L'Ivrogne River is still one of the cleanest rivers in St. Lucia and has a strong flow. The river bed is strewn with boulders making it attractive as a nature walk. The walls of the canyon are quite high, especially on the north side below Gros Piton where there is a sheer wall of at least 70-meters.

The ideal way to access the valley of L'Ivrogne is to approach from the sea. This would enable a full day's tour, perhaps with a picnic lunch on the beach and a chance to do some snorkelling. A convenient landing may be made right up to the beach, where people can disembark without getting wet, due to the presence of a deep Sink Hole right against the shoreline. This amazing feature attracts a great variety of marine life and is ideal for snorkelling and scuba diving.
Length of Trail: 0.25 Miles.

GROS PITON CLIMB (Soufriere). Gros Piton is approximately 2600 feet above sea level. Unless one begins climbing from the coast, the best approach is to begin from the village of Fond Gens Libres, located about 300 feet above sea level. This is the most popular route.

The trail provides a rich insight into the St. Lucian people's history of resistance to slavery and oppression. Shortly after leaving the village, the climber passes through the ruins of a 'Brigand Camp' where numerous rock caves and parapet walls can still be seen. A little further up, the climber will pass a small 'Brigand' lookout, with a commanding view of the entire south west coast of the island.

The summit of Gros Piton is surprisingly large, for a peak of such apparent steepness, and as a result some effort must be exerted if the elusive but incredible view is to be enjoyed.
Lenght of Trail: Approximately 0.75 miles.

MORNE SOUF CLIMB (Soufriere). Morne Souf is a gently sloping Volcanic Cone, with an exposed western face covered in grass and ferns. This slope provides an unobstructed and dramatic view of the Sulphur Springs below, Soufrière valley to the north west, the Pitons to the west and St. Vincent's Soufrière Volcano on the horizon to the south west.

In addition to the fantastic scenery, there is a 'Brigand' Camp Site near the top. A great deal of evidence remains concerning their life style.
Length of Trail: Approximately 1.25 Miles

MORNE TABAC CLIMB (Soufriere) There is a breathtaking view from Morne Tabac which, overlooks Soufrière bay, town, valley and the Pitons. It is possible to see the outline of the Qualibou Caldera and the collapsed volcanic crater, that contains Soufrière below. This is possibly the only place where this can be observed.
Length of Trail: Approximately 2.5 Miles

MORNE GIMIE CLIMB (Canaries). There are four main peaks: Gimie, Piton Canaries, Piton Dame Jean, and Piton Troumassée. All are about 900 meters high. Surrounding this massif are several other lesser peaks, some of which had 'Brigand' Camps. The most direct approach is from Canaries, but the longer traditional route is via Fond St. Jacques. These mountains can also be approached from the south east via Troumassée or from the north via Millet.
Length of Trail: Approximately 8 Miles.

Walks

BARRE DE L'ISLE TRAIL. The Barre de L'isle Forest Reserve gets its name from the fact that it is a ridge that divides the eastern and western halves of St. Lucia. It takes approximately one hour to walk this one mile trail and another hour to climb Mt. La Combe ridge.

The Barre de L'isle trail provided panoramic views from four lookout points along the trail. Observe the ragged Mount Gimie, and the blue-green mountain rainforest, Cul-de-Sac valley, the Caribbean Sea, and the community of Aux Leon. View the expansive Mabouya Valley and Fond d'Or beach on the Atlantic coast.

BIRDWATCHING. Birdwatching tours can be arranged with the Forest and Lands Department. Visitors can observe some of St. Lucia's rare indigenous species - the colourful St. Lucia Parrot, St. Lucia Oriole, White Breasted Thrasher, Lesser Antillian Peewee, St. Lucian Wren and many other tropical birds. The following areas are designated for birdwatching excursions:

Piton Flore Reserve	*North*
Grand Anse	*North*
Edmund Forest Reserve	*West*
Bois d'Orange Swamp	*North*
Eau Piquant Pond	*South*
(Boriel's Pond)	

ACCESS TO TRAILS. No one is allowed on these trails without express permission from the Forest and Lands Department. It is an offence under the Forest Soil and Water Conservation Ordinance Act. For more information, call the Forest & Lands Department at telephone 450-2231/2078. Alternatively, your tour representative may be able to book your tour.

UNION NATURE TRAIL. Spend time with nature on a looped trail which passes through a secondary dry forest in just about an hour. Many tree species which thrive here, are still used island wide. Pretty birds can be spotted along the trail, including humming birds, finches, warblers etc.

Discover the unbelievable magic and wonders of the medicinal herb garden. Bush medicines are becoming an increasingly popular form of alternative treatment. To complement your trail experience, satisfy your curiosity with close-ups of some indigenous and a few exotic wildlife species in the Union Mini Zoo.

An Interpretive Centre provides information on endangered species, vegetation zones and the forest by night and day. It takes ten-fifteen minutes drive from most hotels in the north to get to this trail. This is a half day tour.

George V Recreational Gardens

DES CARTIERS RAINFOREST. Experience a botanical paradise, at Mahaut, St. Lucia's most hidden lush rainforest. Drive six miles inland from the east coast main highway through a secondary road. Hope to see the rare St. Lucia Parrot *(Jacquot)*. Trek through the rainforest and view the wonderful verdant forest, discover some of St. Lucia's endemic wildlife on this two kilometres trail. It takes one and half hours from Castries to get to this reserve and is a full day tour.

EDMUND FOREST RESERVE. In just over three and a half hours, a guide from the Forest and Lands Department would have taken you through the heart of the island into Edmund Forest Reserve on the western side of the island, to experience some of nature's pristine opportunities.

Numerous plants, such as bromeliads, orchids, mushrooms, lianes and others can be seen attached to their hosts, sitting on large buttress roots or branches, on the spongy forest or even cascading the sides of the trail. Continue westward for a magnificent view of Mt. Gimie, St. Lucia's highest peak.

On completing your walk, it's now time to head back home on a long journey by bus, with lasting memories and experiences of the Edmund Forest tour. It takes one and a half hours by bus to drive from the northern part of the island to the Edmund Forest on the west. This is a full day tour.

Waterfalls

As a small volcanic island, St. Lucia is best known geographically for its twin mountain peaks of Gros Piton and Petit Piton, which are believed to be the highest coastal elevations in the world as well as for it's drive-in volcano, one of the very few, in the world. Many St. Lucians and most visitors are completely unaware of the real beauty of the country. In fact, among the many hidden, natural beauties are a host of delightul and spectacular waterfalls.

ABBASSEAU WATERFALL. A 30 minute drive from Soufrière town, up through Fond St. Jacques and along the road leading into the rain forest.

ANSE LA RAYE WATERFALL. This fall is located in the Anse La Raye area, approximately 15 minutes drive inland from the village and 15 minutes easy walk off the main road.

CANARIES WATERFALLS. There are at least four falls along this river. The closest point off the river is about 20 minutes drive inland from the Canaries village.

CLAUZIER WATERFALL. Access is via the Roseau dam. Take a two minute boat ride across the dam to the right arm of the watercourse. This takes you to the Clauzier river.

DENNERY WATERFALL. A half hour drive inland from the village along the river road past Errard Estate. The waterfall is reached by climbing down a steep slope along a mud path, immediately off the main road,

FOND FALLS. This fall is located off the side branch of the Fond River. Reaching it involves a 45 minute drive along a rough country road, which first runs parallel to the river, crosses it, and then runs back towards the coast.

L'OUVETTE WATERFALL. It is a difficult one hour drive (with a four wheel drive vehicle) from the community of Aux Leon (from the southern end) or from the community of Des Barras (from the northern end) to the L'ouvette beach. From there, a 15-20 minute walk inland along an abandoned road leads to the river.

MILLET FALLS. One must follow the road to Tet Chemin, in Millet. At Tete Chemin, there is a secondary road branching off to the right. At the very end of this road there is a footpath through at the river.

SALTIBUS WATERFALLS. There are at least five falls located along the main Saltibus River. They can be approached either from upstream or downstream. However, it is considered less strenuous to approach from the top.

SOUFRIERE FALLS. There are several falls reported in the Soufriere area. It is, however, only possible to visit a few, owing to the remoteness of most of them.

MALGRETOUTE JALOUSIE. This is located off the main access road to the Jalousie Plantation, and is then an easy hike of 20-minutes.

DIAMOND FALLS. This is probably one of the best known falls on the island. It is located at the Botanical Gardens, 15-minutes drive from Soufriere town. This fall is noted for its rich mineral content. A fee is charged for entry into the botanical gardens.

ZENON WATERFALL. This is a 15-minute drive along the Soufriere/Fond St. Jacques main road, and a five minute climb off that road.

RAVINE CLAIRE. This is about 20 minutes drive from Soufriere town along the Soufriere/Fond St. Jacques road, and then a half hour walk and climb along a dirt path, crossing private property.

Sport

'97 Olympic contender -
ichelle Baptist

St. Lucians are generally sports loving people and in recent times the island has adopted a more conscious outlook with regard to that sector of social life.

Cricket, football, netball and track and field are among the popular sports. Volleyball has made a significant mark at the sub-regional level, but administrators of the sport are still trying to spread its popularity islandwide.

Football is undoubtedly the largest crowd puller and the unofficial 'sport of the people'. St. Lucians seem committed to the game, and whenever the national team plays, the island's premiere venue, the Mindoo Phillip Park, is generally filled to capacity.

St. Lucia national teams compete in various competitions and at various age groups. There's the Windward Islands Football Tournament, the Shell Umbro Caribbean Cup and World Cup and Olympic qualifying fixtures. The game is administered by the St. Lucia Football Association whose affiliates meet in regular congresses.

Despite not having a player ever to reach test level, St. Lucia continues to strive for excellence in cricket. Perhaps the players to come closest to selection in recent times have been wicket-keeper Ignatius Cadette and middle order batting stylist John Eugene.

Eugene once led a West Indies under -23 squad; Julian Charles captained the Windward Islands at junior and senior levels; while Cadette was one of the best keepers of his time and a no-nonsense batsman. The leading competition is the Piton Inter-District competition, played among parish teams.

Netball and more recently Volleyball are the sports with greatest attraction for women. St. Lucia participated in the 1997 American Federation of Netball Association (AFNA) tournament played in Grenada, with mixed fortunes. Female volleyballers too have held their own at the sub-regional and regional levels.

Women also play active cricket, with three St. Lucians, Eugena Gregg, Roslyn Emmanuel and Verina Felicien having been selected to represent the Caribbean Womens' Cricket Federation in the 1997 Womens' Cricket World Cup in India in December.

Karate at Sealy's Martial Arts School

St. Lucian athletes competed at the 1996 Atlanta Olympics. The island did not pick up a medal, but the country shared the joy of being part of the Games for the first time. The National Individual Championships is the main event of St. Lucia's Track and Field Calender. St. Lucian athletes also compete in regional and international meets sanctioned by the International Amateur Athletics Federation (IAAF).

Road running is also a very popular form of athletics, and St. Lucia has a long tradition here. Some of the runners now making their mark are Mohiki Bikila, the winner of the first ever OECS half-marathon, Gilbert Actie, Tony Fessal and Victor Ledgers.

Boxing and cycling are two sports that are currently facing a lull, but efforts are underway to revive these disciplines. However, events in tennis and squash have brought considerable interest in the area of sports tourism. St. Lucia is entering the Davis Cup on its own, having previously played as part of an Eastern Caribbean squad.

The Legends Cup, an innovative event put on by the St. Lucia Racquet Club at the end of each year, to boost visitor arrivals has been regarded as a huge success, with the island being graced with the presence of former greats of the game, like Roy Emmerson, John and David Lloyd, Yohan Kriek and Ilie Nastase, among others.

Squash, too, has had its share of success and popularity, with the Elite section of the St. Lucia Open attracting some of the top names in world squash. The air conditioned courts at the St. Lucia Yacht Club are the best on the island and have become the venue for local and regional squash competitions. Charlie Sonson is the island's top ranked player.

Golf continues to be played on a regular basis. There are two golf courses on the island. One is located on the property of Sandals St. Lucia and the other is the St. Lucia Golf and Country Club at Cap Estate in the north of the island.

St. Lucian golfers are often selected to participate in Eastern Caribbean teams at the Caribbean Golf Championships. Countries of the OECS usually host open tournaments, which are used as the main criteria for selecting the sub-regional team.

The advent of the Atlantic Rally for Cruisers (ARC) has brought some interest in yachting, with a spin-off for the tourism industry. The only St. Lucian boat to have participated in the ARC so far has been the *Breeze Away*, making the Atlantic crossing from Las Palmas to the Rodney Bay Marina.

The Ministry of Youth and Sports has overall responsibility for the island's sports. Various disciplines are run by elected executives and most are affiliated to the relevant international bodies. There is also the National Olympic Committee headed by Richard Peterkin. Alfred Emmanuel, President of the St. Lucia Amateur Athletics Association, also serves as General Secretary of the NOC.

Indoor events, like table-tennis and dominoes, are also played competitively in St. Lucia. Table tennis is struggling for a regular venue, while dominoes continues to be popular with St. Lucians, who have won world titles as team and pair champions.

Basketball is currently administered by an interim committee. It has had some trying times, and is yet to be established as a major national competitive sport in terms of participation from all districts.

Adequate funding of sports has been a bane of life in St. Lucia. But the new Minister of Sports, appointed in 1997, has announced that funding has been identified for the construction of a sports stadium and the St. Lucia National Lottery says it will formulate a policy on how its funds can be drawn on for sports development.

GOLF

ST. LUCIA GOLF & COUNTRY CLUB. This golf course is currently a nine-hole located at Cap Estate in the northernmost part of the island. The course, which can be played as eighteen from a variety of tees, winds its way through lush tropical surroundings and has beautiful views of the Caribbean Sea and the countryside around Cap Estate. Water already comes into play on three holes, but there will be three new holes open for play from late 1997 with water a factor on two of these as well. The club house has a bar with a variety of snacks available and visitors are always welcome. There is a fully stocked proshop. Instruction is available, as are caddies and power carts for those golfers feeling a little less energetic.

tch & Putt - Rodney Bay

Club competitions are held regularly and visitors are welcome to participate. Corporate outings and cruise-ship visitors are also catered for.

The course is presently being expanded to eighteen-holes under the supervision of Love Enterprises, the design company of famous PGA tour pro Davis Love III. The new championship course, expected to be playable in late 1998, will command views of both the Atlantic Ocean and Caribbean Sea and will be a challenge to all levels of golfer.

SANDALS LA TOC. This is a nine-hole course located just south of Castries at the Sandals St. Lucia Hotel, a couples only, all-inclusive resort. This course, always maintained in top class condition, can be tight in places and requires precision shot making. Although it is essentially for guests of the hotel, visitors are often welcomed for a modest green fee. Tee times should be booked in advance by calling the golf shop at the hotel.

ROTARY CHARITY SCRAMBLE. This event takes place in early November each year and is organised by the Rotary Club of Gros Islet. This is a great fun event open to teams of four with a host of fabulous prizes. Golfers and guests are guaranteed a good time at this well-organised charity event. It was first held in 1992 and has raised an average of EC$50,000 each year. The tournament has grown in stature over the years, attracting entries from all over the Caribbean and even teams from as far afield as Ireland. Players and guests are treated to a welcome reception on the Friday evening, which is a great chance for the players to become acquainted, both with each other and with the rules of the tournament. The tournament proper takes place on the Saturday, followed by a prize giving dinner, with entertainment, on Saturday night.

ST. LUCIA OPEN. The annual St. Lucia Open usually takes place in June each year, with prizes being played for in all handicap categories for men, women and seniors. The first day is a practice day, followed by a welcome reception in the evening. The tournament proper commences on Saturday morning, with the final day on the Sunday. The presentation of prizes takes place on Sunday evening. The tournament attracts entries from most of the local players, plus some players from around the region. Fees for the tournament include the practice round and welcome reception, the tournament rounds, plus lunch on both Saturday and Sunday.

SQUASH

St. Lucia is slowly becoming a squash haven, with the country's Squash Open attracting some of the world's best athletes to play at the St. Lucia Yacht Club's courts on the magnificent half mile long Reduit beach in Rodney Bay.

The 1995 tournament saw the entry of Steve Richardson, the Irish No.2 and the first really world class player to grace the event. He eventually went on to win the 1995 St. Lucia Squash Open, beating the Caribbean's No.1 and previously world ranked player Max Weithers.

The St. Lucia Squash Open is now established as one of the game's major international events.

Frank Mindoo, St Lucia's first international cricketer

Sandals La Toc

NATIONAL NETBALL ASSOCIATION

The St. Lucia National Netball Association was formed in 1953 and was headed by President Euralis Bouty. In the same year, St. Lucia participated in the first tournament in St. Vincent organised by the West Indies Netball Board. In 1954, the Windward Island Championship was hosted by St. Lucia. Since that period, St. Lucia has participated in almost every Netball Tournament held by the West Indies Board and later the Caribbean Netball Association.

In 1988 the national squad journeyed to the Cayman Islands for the 10th CNA tournament, where St. Lucia jumped from seventh position in 1986 to fourth position. In 1989 St. Lucia placed joint third with Barbados and St. Vincent in Trinidad & Tobago, the country's best placing since 1971.

HORSEBACK RIDING

Horseback riding in St. Lucia is an activity not just for enthusiasts. Many horses in St. Lucia are kept by individuals for their own riding pleasure, as is evident by the sight of young local men testing their bareback skills along the beautiful shorelines islandwide. However, there are also several riding stables which offer organised tours, off the beaten track. From Trim's Riding Stable in the north of the island, to Club Aquarius' in the south, there is plenty of variety for the nature lover to see and explore.

The local horse breed, called the Creole, which has Arab roots, is generally the mount of choice, though there is also a widespread Thoroughbred influence form the country's Caribbean racing neighbours of Barbados, Trinidad and Marinique. In Vieux-Fort, in the south of the island, one can see the Creole roaming free in the rich grazing lands of the area. Trim's Riding Stable, the oldest riding establishment in the island, has a miniature race track, where the boats of young men and their trusty Creole steeds are tested in a fun-filled atmosphere.

Back to nature on horseback

Several of the stables, including Country Saddles and International Riding Stables, offer treks down to windswpt Atlantic coastlines. With a greater influence on eco-tourism, horseback riding can offer an opportunity to visit out of the way places, often inaccessible even by four wheel drive vehicles, through forested areas, along rivers and through plantations.

Country Saddles offers riding at your own pace. With experienced guides and plenty of instruction, the main tour is conducted through a working plantation, steeped in history, down to the beach. The old estate buildings are the first sight, with their old sugar factory, in which one can still see the wooden vats used in the processing of the cane into sugar. A tour for more experienced riders, takes you along the edge of tropical rain forest, with spectacular mountain views. The area has plenty of bird life, with rare birds often not seen in other parts of the island. Country Saddles also has a pony club, and staged St. Lucia's first ever horse show, in June, 1997. The organisers are hoping to make it an annual event in St. Lucia's sporting calendar.

Whether riding at Morne Coubaril, which boats the spectacular backdrop of Soufriere, or the Fox Grove Inn in Praslin, with the surrounding plantations and tropical gardens, one can truly absorb the beauty of the natural country settings. Or let Trim's Riding Stables or International Riding Stables bring the lunch, when they take you on their beach barbecues. And for the romance of a tropical wedding, there's nothing like a horse-drawn carriage ride on your way to tie the knot.

Clearly, whether a 'horse nut' or not, riding is a gateway to the unspoiled beauty of St. Lucia. All you have to do is put your faith in your trusty steed and, with him, indulge in something simply beautiful.

YACHTING

The waters around St. Lucia are every sailor's dream. They are reputed to be among the best sailing waters in the world. There is little tide, constant winds most of the year, and seas that are normally calm to moderate. The yachting "season" is November to April. Although good conditions often prevail in the summer, the occasional hiccough occurs when tropical systems are in the areas.

St. Lucia's popularity with sailors is, perhaps, explained firstly by the beauty of her coastline and secondly, by the fact that she has the largest marine in the region. The marina, situated at Rodney Bay, offers good repair facilities, including haul out, a well-stocked chandlery, sail and electornics repairs. The marina also has banks, a supermarket and other shops.

The visitor to St. Lucia can enjoy boating at whatever level required. There are day trips and sunset cruises on catamarans. The full day excursion includes a visit to famous sights, lunch on board, and a chance to swim and snorkel in a picturesque bay. A similar outing on 'Unicorn', the brig used as the slave ship in the television series 'Roots', is available.

If the visitor prefers a more private scene, there are yachts operators who offer a number of alternatives such as: whole day, half-day or sunset cruise. skipper and crew are provided.

Sailing lessons on small craft can be arranged through most hotels. There is no need to be a hotel resident to take lessons or hire a sunfish dinghy from Carib Leisure, which runs the water sports off the beach by the Rex St. Lucian hotel.

Visitors can hire yachts for longer journeys either with skipper and crew provided, or on a bareboat basis. There are yacht hire companies based at Rodney Bay Marina, and at Marigot Bay.

ST. LUCIA YACHTING ASSOCIATION. All racing and other events involving keel boats are organised by the St. Lucia Sailing Club. Visiting and other non-member yachts are always welcome to take part in events.

The three main Regattas run by the St. Lucia Sailing Club each year are: The Heineken Regatta, the Round the Island Race and The Sir John Compton Trophy.

ST. LUCIA HEINEKEN REGATTA. The founders of the Regatta were determined to make this event a little different from other Caribbean Regattas. They succeeded, and the St. Lucia Heineken Regatta is now well known for its informal atmosphere and the formula of the races, which are short races 'around the buoys'. This makes for an exciting time, testing the sailing skills of the yachtsmen and not their boredom threshold!

Vigie Lighthouse

The Regatta takes place over three days and is the most important occasion on the Sailing Club's calendar.

From 1998, the St. Lucia Heineken Regatta, although remaining a separate event in its own right, will form part of a three Regatta competition. Participating yachts will enter the Barbados, St. Lucia and Grenada Regattas. Awards will be given to those who perform best overall in all three Regattas.

ROUND THE ISLAND RACE. 'The Voice' Round The Island Race was created in memory of the late Sir Garnet Gordon, one of St. Lucia's most eminent lawyers and business men. The race takes place over the third weekend in March each year. The yachts race from Rodney Bay down the eastern (Atlantic) side of the island to Vieux Fort in the south. They return north the following day up the western (Caribbean Sea) side.

SIR JOHN COMPTON TROPHY. This event is a race to Martinique, St. Lucia's closest neighbour, and back. The race was formerly known as 'the Prime Minister's Cup'. Now that Sir John is no longer Prime Minister, after more than thirty years in that office, the event's name has been changed in recognition of his support for yachting in the country. Sir John is the Commodore of the Sailing Club. This race is traditionally held on the weekend nearest to St. Lucia's National Day, December 13. St. Lucia's yachtsmen are always sure of a warm welcome and Gallic hospitality at the Martinique Yacht Club.

Sailing off Reduit Beach in Rodney Bay

ST. LUCIA YACHT CLUB This Club organises dinghy sailing, including a programme for teaching young hopefuls. The Yacht Club also offers Squash Courts, where international matches are held. The Club's premises are in a prime position on St. Lucia's largest beach and all 'yachties' are welcome to use the facilities, which include a bar offering bargain priced drinks!

ATLANTIC RALLY FOR CRUISERS ARC. The Atlantic Rally for Cruisers, or the ARC, was devised in 1986 by Jimmy and Gwenda Cornell of World Cruising Ltd., a company based in England. The ARC offers a means by which sailors who wish to make the Atlantic crossing, but prefer to do so in the company of other boats, can realise their ambition.

The ARC sets out from Gran Canaria in November each year. The fastest boats arrive in St. Lucia about two weeks later. Some 150-200 yachts participate in the ARC each year, and for the some eight years, St. Lucia has been the port of arrival and host of the ARC. The crews make Rodney Bay Marina a lively spot at this time of year.

St. Lucia makes excellent landfall for the ARC yachts. Her approaches are clear of dangers and the finish line in Rodney Bay can be easily crossed, even at night. The marina can accommodate all but those boats with very deep drafts.

OTHER INTERNATIONAL YACHT RALLIES. St. Lucia is a port of call for the tri-annual Round the World Rally. In 1997, yachts taking part in the Hong Kong Challenge stopped over in Rodney Bay, and in the year 2000 The Millennium Odyssey boats will visit these shorts.

INTERNATIONAL BILLFISH TOURNAMENT

The the St. Lucia Billfish Tournament anglers are given points based on the size and type of fish caught. They are penalised if the fish falls below a minimum weight. More than $50,000 worth of prizes are presented.

Teams consist of three-to-eight people but no more than six lines must be in the water at once. Live bait, fresh bait and artificial lures are used. The 1996 Tournament attracted 28 boats and 128 anglers, mainly from the Caribbean. Boats came from Grenada, Dominica, St. Thomas, Antigua, Martinique and Barbados.

David Ferrell, the editor of the *American Marlin Magazine* and *Sport Fishing Magazine,* wrote excitedly about the huge number of fish which showed up for the St Lucian Tournament. Ninety blue marlin were caught in three days of fishing, pretty impressive for anywhere.

Deep-sea fishing in St. Lucia is a popular pastime with tourists, even made more popular by its prestigious and highly eventful annual International Billfish Tournament. What is particularly appealing about the tournament is the large number of local entrants who participate side by side in an engaging spirit of camaraderie and conviviality with anglers from many parts of the world.

SCUBA ST. LUCIA

Scuba St. Lucia is located at one end of the sheltered bay below the Anse Chastanet Hotel. Just a short walk from the Dive Centre is the start of the beach dive, and the spectacular Anse Chastanet reef which falls quickly away from 20 feet to 140 feet.

A great range of corals, finger, brain, boulder, leaf, flower, and a tremendous variety of sponges - tube, barrier, vase, encrusting - give an unparalleled mix of colour and texture to the reef, providing shelter for the many reef inhabitants, crabs, lobster, sea lilles, basket stars, sea cucumbers, urchins, shrimps and a dramatic back drop of the schools of reef fish, chromis, Bermuda chub, bar jack, snapper, and many more.

The beach dive is a required 'first' dive to give an orientation to the area. The boat dives include dramatic walls beneath the majestic Piton Mountains, Superman's flight, a drift dive in the shadow of the Petit Piton, Coral Gardens and Jalousie under the Gros Piton, Piton Wall, Malgretoute, the Blue Hole, the wreck of the *Lesleen M*, Anse La Raye and Anse Cochon. Closer to home for the afternoon boat trips, but no less spectacular sites, the diver can explore Fairyland, Turtle Reef, Grand Caille, Trou Diable, The Pinnacles and Hummingbird Drop-offs.

Beach dives and boat dives are scheduled daily. Night dives are offered at least twice weekly, on the Anse Chastanet Reef, which really 'wakes up' at night, with many interesting crustaceans on the move, large basket stars, sleeping parrot fish, octopus, squid and bioluminescence.

All dives offered by Scuba St. Lucia are guided by one of their instructors/divemasters to maximise diver safety and enjoyment. The whole area is designated a Marine Park, so divers are asked to 'look but not touch.' These measures make diving here a paradise for underwater photographers. Scuba St. Lucia is also an ideal place to learn to dive, with warm clear waters and a shallow, protected reef so close to the Dive Centre. An introductory Dive 'n' Discover course is offered most days of the week. A full range of PADI and SSL courses such as: Advanced Open Water, Rescue Diver, Divemaster and Assistant Instructor. Specialities are available by arrangement.

DIVE SITES

The following are some of the major sites in St. Lucia.

ANSE CHASTANET REEF. This reef starts just a few short steps across the warm volcanic sand from the dive centre. The reef has three distinct areas:

SHALLOW. With many brightly coloured sponges and soft corals. Goat fish, parrot fish, chromis, and wrasse are found all over the shallow reef and there is even a school of reef squid. At the base of the cliff there is a large cavern with resident frogfish;

MEDIUM. Visited by many schooling fish. In amongst the many different corals are live crabs, lobsters, moray eels, and much more. Deep water lace corals are also found on this dive.

DEEP. Giving way to plate coral, layer upon layer of delicate porcelain-like growths stacked one on top of the other. Well worth a visit.

TURTLE REEF. This crescent-shaped reef to the north of Anse Chastanet Bay is a favourite with many divers. It drops quickly from a plateau at around 40-feet to over 150-feet. From the spectacular pillar coral and barrel sponges in the shallows to the deeper soft corals and ledges, this reef has a lot to offer. The occasional turtle has been known to visit, but even if not immediately evident, there will be plenty of other creatures to keep divers happy.

Multi-choice diving in St Lucia

FAIRYLAND. A very short boat trip from the dive centre is the beautiful dive location of Fairyland. This area is on a major headland and is subject at times to very strong currents – this has the benefit of giving the site excellent visibility, and to keep all the corals very clean so that the whole area sparkles with the vibrant colours of many varieties of corals and sponges. All over the reef are large numbers of schooling fish, particularly chromis and creole wrasse. Turtles are occasionally seen.

PINNACLES. This is probably one of the most visually stunning dive sites. Four spectacular seamounts rise dramatically from the depth to within a few feet of the surface. These are encrusted with a profusion of black and orange gorgonia, and this lacy network provides shelter for trumpet fish, filefish, and sometimes seahorses. Larger fish – grouper, jack and snapper – can be spotted around the Pinnacles.

fect conditions for snorkelling

SUPERMAN'S FLIGHT. A fifteen-minute boat trip south from Scuba St. Lucia, across Sourfière Bay, brings divers to the base of the spectacular Petit Piton Mountain. The cliff face here was used as a setting for the film Superman II. Superman can be seen flying down the cliff – face above water, and divers can fly along it below water. There are often strong currents on this site, which help to give it good visibility. The steep slope here is covered with beautiful soft corals, and there is a great profusion of fish life.

PITON WALL
Also at the base of the Petit Piton, this dramatic wall falls from the surface to many hundreds of feet below. Sea whips, gorgonia, delicate soft corals and lots of large featherduster worms make this a colorful location.

CORAL GARDENS. Further south is the Piton Piton's sister mountain, the Gros Piton. At the base of this is Coral Gardens, a steep slope with many different species of corals and large barrel sponges. The unusual sargassum trigger fish can be spotted in the deeper areas here, and recently a large school of barracuda have taken up residence.

WRECK OF THE *LESLEEN*. This wreck is located to the north of the dive centre, and the Scuba St. Lucia dive boats take approximately 35 minutes to reach the site. The 165-foot freighter was sunk in October 1986 as part of a project by the Department of Fisheries to provide artificial reefs. Already it is covered in soft corals, spones and hydroids, and provides an ideal habitat for many juvenile fishes such as Nassau groupers, queen and French angle fishes.

ANSE LA RAYE. Close to the wreck site is the site of Anse La Raye. These two sites are usually visited on the same day, as a two tank trip followed by a barbecue lunch at the beachside restaurant at Anse Jambette. There is a shallow wall at Anse La Raye, and below this is a slope covered in hugh boulders, giving a very interesting terrain. The shallow areas have lots of brightly coloured fire corals. There is a lot of fish life on this dive, look out particularly for jacks, bermuda chub and spotted drums.

DAINI-KOYO-MARU

St Lucia's newest wreck

St. Lucia has a new wreck, the *Daini-Koyo Maru*, a 250-foot long dredger that was donated to St. Lucia as a wreck. She was put down in the water a short distance from the *Lesleen M* which was sunk 10-years ago.

As she slid beneath the surface, she tilted to her starboard and landed that way 105-feet under water. As a result there is a 45-foot high wall over 200-feet long covered with three years of sponges and soft corals. On the other side there is a pristine wreck as the entire super-structure is available to dive. The dive begins at 60-feet.

Hotels, Inns & Guest Houses

CLUB ST. LUCIA
Anse du Cap, Cap Estate,
St. Lucia, WI.
Tel: (758) 450-0551
Fax: (758) 450–0281

Club St Lucia

Club St. Lucia, set in 40 acres of tropically land-scaped and wooded grounds, with 312 rooms, restaurants, bars, entertainment lounge, 3 swimming pools and two beaches, offers one of the most extensive lists of all-inclusive features in the Caribbean.

JALOUSIE PLANTATION RESORT
PO Box 251
Sourrière St. Lucia, WI.
Phone: (758) 459-7666
Fax: (758) 459–7667
Telex: 441787 (U.S. and Canada)
U.K. call Supereps 071-242-3131

Escape to St. Lucia, the "Jewel of the Caribbean." Tucked between the Piton mountains overlooking the sea, the new, magnificent 320 acre luxury resort, Jalousie Plantation, will captivate you. Suites and cottages with panoramic ocean views. Private verandas and plunge pools. Tennis, scuba and beach watersports. Complete spa. Three restaurants, poolside snacks.

Jalousie Plantation Resort

LE SPORT HOTEL
PO Box 437
Castries, St. Lucia WI.
Tel: (758) 450-8551
Fax: (758) 450-0368

Le Sport Hotel

Located just 9 miles from Vigie Airport, LeSPORT is situated on a beautiful Caribbean Beach on the most northern point of St. Lucia. With 102 beautifully decorated air-conditioned rooms all with ocean views and private balconies, LeSPORT offers a full complement of water and land sports with body pampering treatments at our lovely Oasis facility.

Rendezvous Hotel

RENDEZVOUS HOTEL
PO Box 190
Castries, St. Lucia WI.
Tel: (758) 452-4211
Fax: (758) 452–7419
U.S. Rep: Tropical Vacations 1–800–544–2883
Canada: Ms. Judy Arkin 1–416–423–9100

Formerly Couples, St. Lucia, Rendezvous is located just minutes from Vigie Airport near Castries. A wide array of water and land sports are offered as well as beautifully appointed rooms. Swim-up Tropical Bar and great lush tropical gardens.

SANDALS ST LUCIA
La Toc Road, Castries,
St. Lucia, WI.
Tel: (758) 427–3081
Fax: (758) 453–7089

Sandals St Lucia

All inclusive and for couples only, Sandals St. Lucia is 15 minutes from Vigie and 11/2 hours from Hewanorra, and is set upon 150 acres of enchanting tropical isle surrounded by the sparkling Caribbean Sea. Largest fresh water pool

in the Eastern Caribbean. Located on the property is a nine hole golf course. Waterskiing, scuba diving, snorkeling, windsurfing, and all land sports including tennis. 60 elegant suites, some with personal plunge pools. 4 gourmet restaurants to choose from.

WYNDHAM MORGAN BAY RESORT
PO Box 2167, Gros Islet,
St. Lucia, WI.
Tel: (758) 450–2511
Fax: (758) 450–1050

Wyndham Morgan Bay Resort

Nestled in the lush tropical jungle, minutes away from Vigie Airport, is 22 acres that is the luxurious All-Inclusive Wyndham Morgan Bay Resort. 240 air-conditioned guest rooms, with private balconies, terraces, remote control TV. Morgan Bay offers everything from water-skiing, snorkeling, sailing or relaxing on our beach or near our freshwater pool.

THE ROYAL ST. LUCIAN HOTEL
PO box 977
Reduit Beach,
Castries, St. Lucia, WI.
Tel: (758) 452-9999
Fax: (758) 452–9639
Telex: 6244 ROYAL

The Royal St Lucian

Deluxe beachfront all-suite hotel located on famed Reduit Beach. 98 oceanview suites featurin bedroom, sitting room, luxury bathroom with separate shower and tub, air-conditioning, cable television, minibar, inroom safe, hairdryer and terrace. Large tropical pool complex with swim-up bar, room service, two bars, two restaurants, nightly entertainment. Shopping Arcade, watersports and tennis adjacent at St. Lucian Hotel.

THE ST. LUCIAN
PO Box 512,
Reduit Beach,
Castries, St. Lucia, WI.
Tel: (758) 452–8351/5
Fax: (758) 452–8331
Telex: 6326 LUCIAN

The St Lucian

The St. Lucian Hotel offers a variety of free daytime activities that include tennis, sunfish sailing, snorkeling and windsurfing. An unparalleled vacation experience awaits you at the St. Lucian Hotel.

WINDJAMMER LANDING BEACH RESORT
PO Box 1504
Labrelotte Bay, Castries,
St. Lucia, WI.
Tel: (758) 452–0913
Fax: (758) 452–0907

Windjammer Landing

With 114 spacious self contained 1-, 2-, 3- and 4-bedroom villas overlooking the Caribbean Sea. 38 miles from Hewanorra Airport and 5 miles from Vigie Airport and Castries. The 2-, 3-, and 4-bedroom villas have private plunge pools. 4 swimming pools, 4 restaurants and bars, mini mart, fitness center and villa shuttle service. Nightly entertainment, kid's program, extensive complimentary watersports. Scuba diving and tennis available. Golf nearby.

BEACH HAVEN (RESTAURANT & BAR)
PO Box 460
Vide Bouteille
Castries, St. Lucia, WI.
Tel: (758) 453–0065
Fax: (758) 453–6891

Beach Haven Hotel is your ideal "Home Away From Home." Situated on the island's popular northwest coast, we're right in the thick of the tourist belt. With 10 air-conditioned double rooms with hot and cold water and color TV, we offer most of the modern conveniences of the larger luxurious hotels.

Beach Haven Hotel

Caribbees Hotel

CANDYO INN
Rodney Bay,
PO Box 386
St. Lucia, WI.
Tel: (758) 452–0712
Fax: (758) 452–0774

Candyo Inn

Candyo Inn, occupies one of the most enviable locations in popular Rodney Bay. Providing the visitor with easy access to beaches. This cozy Inn boasts 8 suites and 4 bedrooms all comfortably furnished, each with its own private bathroom. Service is paramount at the Candyo Inn - anything your heart desires is just a telephone call away.

CARIBBEES HOTEL
La Pansee
PO Box 1720
Castries, St. Lucia, WI.
Tel: (758)453–1210/452–4767
Fax: (758) 453–1999

St. Lucia's finest small hotel serving West Indian/International cuisine. Experience tranquility amidst the luscious greenery of our garden-style landscape. Caribbees is ideally tucked away on the hillside of La Pansee and commands a superb panoramic view of the capital city of Castries, the harbour, the Caribbean Sea and the neighbouring island of Martinique.

CHATEAU BLANC GUEST HOUSE
Morne-Du-Don,
Castries, St. Lucia, WI.
Tel: (758) 452–1851
Fax: (758) 452–7967

Chateau Blanc Guest House

286

Enjoy the warm, friendly atmosphere that only a family-run guest house can provide. It has 7 comfortably furnished rooms with baths and ceiling fans. Food and drinks available. Located just five minutes from the center of Castries. Discover what real Caribbean hospitality means.

E's Serenity Lodge

DU BOIS GUEST HOUSE
Castries, St. Lucia, WI.
Tel: (758) 452–2201
Fax: (758) 452–7967
In U.S. and Canada: 1–800–456–3984
Charms: 1—800–742–4272A

Beaches are just a short walk away, and many of St. Lucia's most popular restaurants are easily accessible by automobile.

GREEN PARROT INN
PO Box 648
The Morne, Castries
St. Lucia, WI.
Tel: (758) 452–3399/3167/3168
Fax: (758) 453–2272

Du Bois Guest House

Cozy family-operated guest house with four comfortable guest rooms overlooking Castries and the Vigie Peninsula. The operation has won the Best Decorated Small Restaurant Award and the Ministry of Health Award for Cleanliness for five consecutive years.

Green Parrot

E'S SERENITY LODGE
Sunny Acres
St. Lucia, WI.
Tel: (758) 452–1987
Fax: (758) 451–8600

Set in quiet surroundings overlooking historic Choc Bay, E's Serenity Lodge lives up to its name. This hotel's 11 rooms are situated three miles from downtown Castries and Vigie Airport.

The Green Parrot is St. Lucia's most prestigious restaurant. Internationally acclaimed for its excellent cuisine, impeccable service and delightful atmosphere, the Green Parrot has now extended its facilities. These include a 62 room Inn, created to provide each room with a breathtaking view and the best in comfort, utility and decor.

287

Tapion Reef Hotel

HUMMINGBIRD BEACH RESORT
PO Box 280
Soufrière, St. Lucia, WI.
Tel: (758) 459–7232/7492
Fax: (758) 459–7033

Humming Bird Beach Resort

DAPHIL'S HOTEL
Marie Therese St.
Gros Islet, St. Lucia, WI.
Tel: (758) 450–9318
Fax: (758) 452 4387

Located on the Soufrière Beach just a one-hour drive from Hewanorra Airport and two hours from Vigie Airport, this resort has 10 rooms with Piton/ocean view. It has a swimming pool and scuba and snorkeling facilities available. (PADI instructors) only a 10–minute drive away. Excellent cuisine, too.

Daphil's Hotel

TAPION REEF HOTEL
PO Box 370
Castries, St. Lucia, WI.
Tel: (758) 452–7471/7470
Fax: (758) 452–7552
Telex: 6216

This hotel on Tapion Bay has 32 self-contained, air-conditioned apartments with cable television (available at a surcharge), and telephone. Facilities: Restaurant: bar; pool; daily bus service to city (except Sundays and holidays) at a surcharge of $5 EC.

Daphil's (Mini) Hotel, situated in Gros Iset on the northwest tip of St. Lucia, comprises 10 guest rooms, a mini restaurant and bar. Each room has its own toilet and bath facilities with hot and cold water. Some rooms are air-conditioned but the units are hardly used because of the coolness of the prevailing sea breeze. Daphil's Hotel boasts close access to 2 miles of white sandy beach, just a half minute walking distance. Within short walking distance of the much talked about "Gros-Islet Friday Night Street Fair." Only 15 minutes drive from Castries.

THE FRIENDSHIP INN

Sunny Acres
PO Box 1475
Castries, St. Lucia, WI.
Tel: (758) 453–6602
Fax: (758) 453–2635

Friendship Inn

This mini hotel features seven units with equipped kitchenettes which include a refridgerator, and three one-bedroom units. All contain air-conditioning, cable television, telephone, and private bath. The Friendship Inn is three miles from Castries on the road to Rodney Bay and is within easy walking distance of the beach, nightclubs, a discotheque, and shopping mall. There's a poolside barbecue on Saturday evenings, and the bar specializes in tropical drinks. Facilities: Restaurant; bar; pool.

HARMONY APARTEL

PO Box 155
Castries, St. Lucia, WI.
Tel: (758) 452–8756/0336
Fax: (758) 452–8677

Facilities: Restaurants, bar, pool, mini-mart and delicatessen. All suites are luxury four-star and five-star standard. Featuring: jacuzzis, Bidets, King and Queen size beds, remote control air-conditioning, mini-bars, mirrored walls, wet-bars, remote control cable color TV, coffee/tea makers, hair dryers, clock radios, room safes, room service, diret dial telephones.

Harmony Apartel

ANSE CHASTANET

PO Box 7000
Soufrière, St. Lucia, WI.
Tel: (758) 459–7000/7350/7353/7354/7355
Fax: (758) 459–7700
Telex: 0398/6370 Anchasta LC

Anse Chastanet

One of the Caribbean's most romantic resort settings, with unrivaled breathtaking views of St. Lucia's famous Pitons and two soft sand beaches. Forty-eight delightful octagonal gazebos and unique individually designed suites are nestled into a lush hillside, and spacious beachside rooms are set within a tropical garden. Facilities include a professional PADI 5-Star scuba centre. Complimentary snorkeling, windsurfing, sunfish sailing, and tennis available; a variety of excursions can be arranged.

LADERA RESORT & DASHEENE REST.
PO Box 225,
Soufrière, St. Lucia, WI.
Tel: (758) 459–7323
Fax: (758) 459–5156

Ladera Resort and Dasheene Restaurant

Small and sophisticated, Ladera has an air of intimacy, and a personal touch. Ladera also offers the luxuries of fine dining, superior service, and a wide variety of leisure activities both in the surrounding countryside and at nearby beaches. Peaceful and secluded, Ladera is set on a hillside amid the lush Pitons of southern St. Lucia. From every point on the property, the incredible panorama stretches out across a green sea of rain forest. Each of the 16 villas and suites has an 'open wall' exposing one of the most breathtaking views in the Caribbean.

THE ISLANDER HOTEL
PO Box 907
Castries, St. Lucia, WI.
Tel: (758) 452–8757
Fax: (758) 452–0958

The Islander Hotel

Experience the convenience of St. Lucia's newest, most modern self-catering and hotel complex. Our 60 air-conditioned junior suites are beautifully decorated: 20 rooms with a fully equipped kitchenette and living/dining area and 40 with breakfast bar and refrigerator. All units feature cable TV. Amenities include a restaurant and terrace bar as well as a freshwater swimming pool. Just a few minutes walk from St. Lucia's finest beach. Complete watersports are available.

THE BLUE LAGOON
PO Box 637
Castries, St. Lucia, WI.
Tel: (758) 452–8453
Fax: (758) 452–4978

The Blue Lagoon

Situated in the Rodney Bay area with a wonderful view of the Marina's tropical sunsets and other beautiful surroundings. The Blue Lagoon accommodates approximately 50 persons in a comfortable atmosphere. Most rooms are self contained with one separate fully equiped kitchen for anyone wishing to do major cooking. Laundry servuce us available on request. Located only 6 miles from the capital city of Castries and Vigie Airport, 25 miles from Hewanorra International Airport.

ATLANTIC BREEZE

PO Box 376 Castries. Gros Islet, St. Lucia, WI.
Tel: (758) 450–2999
Fax: (508) 754–4604
Reservations:
U.S. (508) 792–0449 (day); (508) 756–0448 (night)

Atlantic Resort

For a well deserved vacation where nothing comes between you and nature, this private three unit condo (2 bedrooms each) is built on 1.5 acres of land for peace, quiet, and tranquility. Every balacony, and almost bedroom offers a commanding ocean view. A huge sundeck with grill awaits you for tanning and cookouts. This condo accommodates up to 12 adults and is completely furnished and includes maid service. Close to all the major activities – hotels, night clubs and restaurants. Golfing, tennis, deep sea fishing, horseback riding, parasailing, car rental arranged.

NATIONAL RESEARCH & DEVELOPMENT FOUNDATION

PO Box 1097
La Clery, Castries,
St. Lucia, WI.
Tel: (758) 452–6627
Fax: (758) 453–6389

National Research and Development Foundation

The National Research and Development Foundation has reasonable rates for Bed & Breakfast, and it is located within walking distance to the beach and Castries City Centre. It is one minute from Vigie Airport. Pleasant surroundings and great local cuisine.

PARROT'S HIDEAWAY

PO Box 1820
Castries, St. Lucia, WI.
Tel: (758) 452–0726

The Hideaway is one of the finest restaurants specializing in tasty creole foods, (Continental dishes on request). Here you are in a very romantic atmosphere spiced with music to your taste. We offer a local talent show on Tuesday nights with no cover charge, and every Friday night some of the hottest local bands play at Parrot's

Parrot's Hideaway

Hideaway. Here you get more for less, don't just take our word for it.

SEASCAPE
PO Box 797
Castries, St. Lucia, WI.
Tel: (758) 450–1645
Fax: (758) 452–7967

Seascape is ideal for that quiet holiday you have always dreamed about. Secluded in 3 acres of private grounds sweeping down to the shore but within walking distance of the main highway and mini-bus service; only a few minutes drive to the nearest beach. Located about 4 miles from Castries between the Wyndham Hotel and Windjammer Landing. Suitable for every age; all rooms and the large swimming pool are on one level. Four bedrooms including 1 superior suite with 3 bathrooms and large lounge, and a balcony with panoramic views.

Seascape

SKYWAY INN
PO Box 353
Beanfield Vieux Fort
St. Lucia, WI.
Tel: (758) 454–7111/5
Fax: (758) 454–7116

Skyway Inn

The thirty-two luxury rooms are extremely spacious, and equipped with air-conditioning units, telephone with direct dial capabilities, color television, and ceiling fans. Our main Restaurant and Bar is air-conditioned. Additional facilities include conference rooms, satellite television, gift shop, swimming pool and a shuttle service to and from the airport and beach. Skyway Inn caters to your utmost contentment, so come experience it for yourself.

TOP O' THE MORNE ESTATES
PO Box 376
Castries, St. Lucia, WI.
Tel: (758) 452–3603/2531
Fax: (758) 453–1433

Perched atop historic Morne Fortune overlooking the city of Castries with its beautiful harbor and the French island of Martinque on the horizon. 4 miles from Vigie Airport. Spacious and comfortably furnished one- and two-bedroom apartments with full kitchens and large balconies. Superb views from every balcony apartment in this century old British colonial building. Self-drive cars available at highly competitive rates.

Top 'O' Morne Estates

TROPICAL VILLAS
PO Box 189
Castries, St. Lucia, WI.
Tel: (758) 450–8240
Fax: (758) 450–8089

Tropical Villas

Luxury villas in St. Lucia are available for rent, ranging in size from two to six bedrooms, the majority with swimming pools. Some are located on spectacular hillside while others are on the beach, but all are situated in an acre of landscaped gardens. Villas are staffed with competent housekeepers, who will assist with shopping and preparing delicious Creole meals. Tropical Villas can arrange on request: transfers, car hire and stocking the villa with groceries.

VILLA BEACH COTTAGES
PO Box 129
Choc Bay
St. Lucia, WI.
Tel: (758) 452–2691
Fax: (758) 452–5416

Villa Beach Cottages

Situated on picturesque Choc Bay among the coconut palm trees; 3 miles from Castries and Vigie Airport. All cottages are one bedroom, with a living room, screened porch and dining area and a fully equipped kitchenette. Restaurant and bar on the premises, large shopping mall 5 minutes walking distance. Tennis, tours, watersports and car rentals arranged by our friendly staff.

AUBERGE SERAPHINE
PO Box 390
Castries, St. Lucia, WI.
Tel: (758) 453–2073
Fax: (758) 451–7001

Auberge Seraphine

An elegant, 22-room hotel, Auberge Seraphine overlooks the blue waters of Vigie Cove. The hotel is nestled behnd a mangrove amidst lush tropical vegetation, and yet is only minutes away from the beach, Vigie Airport and the Pointe Seraphine duty-free shopping complex.

Auberge Seraphine offers the discerning traveller spacious luxurious accommodations with air-conditioned bedrooms and patios. Most of the rooms enjoy a spectacular view of the Vigie Marina and cove, while other have the additional advantage of a sundeck – the perfect place to watch the magnificent sunset. All rooms have cable TV and direct-dial telephone. The hotel offers fine international and Caribbean cuisine. Other facilities include a pool, gift shop, and a fully-equipped conference/meeting room. A shuttle service transports guests to and from the nearby beach.

THE FOX GROVE INN
Mon Repos, St. Lucia, WI.
Tel: (758) 454–0271
Fax: (758) 454–0271

The Fox Grove Inn

A real hideaway in the lush countryside, this 12-bedroom country inn has a magnificent view of Praslin bay and the Fregate Islands Nature Reserve. Complete with a swimming pool, great cuisine, horseback riding and nature trail walks, all just a 20-minute drive from the international airport.

THE ORANGE GROVE HOTEL
PO Box GM 702
Castries, St. Lucia, WI.
Tel: (758) 452–0021

St. Lucia's newest small hotel, The Orange Grove caters to visitors wanting complete convenience and comfort at extremely moderate prices. In addition to 11 newly renovated suites, you'll find a swimming pool and a full-service restaurant. The hotel also offers free trips to Reduit Beach.

EAST WINDS INN LTD
La Brelotte Bay,
Gros Islet,
PO Box 1477
St. Lucia, WI.
Tel: (758) 452–8212
Fax: (758) 452–9941

Secluded and tastefully decorated, East Winds Inn is set among eight acres of lush tropical gardens, on the beachfront of one of the best and most sheltered bays on St. Lucia. Informal yet elegant and private, spacious but still romantically cozy, the inn has only 26 rooms. Complete with open-air bar, restaurant and clubhouse.

GLENCASTLE RESORT
Massade, Gros Islet
PO Box 143
Castries, St. Lucia, WI.
Tel: (758) 450–0833
Fax: (758) 450–0837

Situated on a hillside overlooking picturesque Rodney bay Marina, the Glencastle Resort has 17 spacious deluxe rooms, with air-conditioning and private balconies. Located just minutes from the airport, the marina, a golf course, a riding stable and beaches, it also has a swimming pool, gazebo bar and a full-service restaurant as well as conference and meeting facilities.

SANDALS RESORT HALCYON
PO Box GM 910
Choc bay,
Castries, St. Lucia, WI.
Tel: (758) 453–0222
Fax: (758) 451–8435

Sandals Halcyon, the second and newest Sandals hotel in St, Lucia, is laid-back yet upbeat and exciting in true Sandals style. Exclusively for couples, this brand-new beachfront resort has a colourful, bright atmosphere that will make you feel great. Facilities include three gourmet restaurants, and guests receive full exchange privileges with Sandals St. Lucia, including free transfers.

Beach Walk Inn

Beach Walk Apartments are located within walking distance of Choc Beach, a shopping mall and several restaurants. Accommodations include studios and apartments, all with bath/shower, kitchen and air-conditioning or ceiling fans. Cable t.v. is available on request. Beach Walk guests can use the "Waves" restaurant and watersports facilities at Choc Beach. Public transport to nearby Castries and Vigie airport is available.

Sandals Halcyon

CHESTERFIELD INN
PO Box 415
Castries
Tel:/Fax: 758-452-1295

BEACH WALK INN
Sunny Acres
PO Box 464
Castries, St. Lucia, WI.
Tel: (758) 451–7888
Fax: 758-453-7812

Chesterfield Inn

295

Chesterfield Inn is ideally situated at the lower end of Bridge Street overlooking the city of Castries and Castries Harbour. It is surrounded by green lawns, tropically landscaped with three outdoor patios where the cool evening breezes can be enjoyed. The inn offers a choice of comfortable, air-conditioned rooms with private bath, television, private balcony, plus one fully-furnished apartment. At the Chesterfield Restaurant and Bar, one of the best fruit and rum punches, as well as the tastiest creole lunches can be enjoyed, while experiencing the traditional St. Lucian hospitality. Dinner is served amidst a unique setting of outstanding antique furniture.

THE COUNTRY INN
PO Box GM 786
Castries
Tel:/Fax: 758-452-8301

Country Inn

The Country Inn is located just 15 minutes from Castries, in the unspoiled countryside and tranquility of Moulin-a-Vent, Monchy. It is only five minutes from the Rodney Bay beaches and the fishin village of Gros Islet. The inn sits in the center of beautiful tropical gardens with freshwater lily ponds and fruit trees of all kinds. The six air-conditioned rooms have a private bath, king or queen-size beds, private patios, lounge and breakfast area – an ideal place to enjoy a leisurely St. Lucian breakfast.

FRIENDSHIP INN
PO Box 1475
Castries
Tel: 758-452-4201
Fax: 758-453-2635

Friendship Inn

Conveniently located just three minutes north of the capital city of Castries and Vigie Airport, the inn has 10 one-bedroom units. Some rooms have kitchenettes as well as private balconies. Other facilities include a freshwater pool. The property is within walking distance to the Gablewoods Shopping mall, sandy beaches, restaurants and other activities. It is perfect for vacationers who prefer the peace and quiet of a small inn, but want to be close to the city and beach facilities.

GOLDEN ARROW INN
PO Box 2037
Castries
Tel: 758-450-1832
Fax: 758-450-2459

Situated off the John Compton Highway, two miles north of Vigie Airport and Castries, and a 10-minute walk from the beach, this newly built inn has 15 comfortable rooms, all with private bath. Some rooms are equipped with double beds, cooling fans and televisions. Other facilities include a bar, dining room and TV lounge. The inn, which provides panoramic and sunset views, is within walking distance to restaurants, and close to shopping and recreational activities.

Golen Arrow Inn

Marlin Quay

HARBOUR LIGHTS INN
Vide Boutielle, Castries
Tel: 758-452-3506
Fax: 451 9455

Delight in the beautiful white sands of Vigie Beach, splash around in the crystal waters of the Caribbean Sea, or chat and relax in the bar and restaurant offering local cuisine. Harbour Light Inn offers all this and more. With a beautiful panoramic view of the Caribbean, this 16-room hotel is lcoated within two minutes drive from Vigie Airport, and three minutes drive from the capital city, Castries. Also within walking distance are beaches and shopping facilities. All rooms have television and shower, and there is choice of twin, double or queen-size beds. Eight rooms are air-conditioned. All guests have access to a fully-equipped kitchen. The inn has a restaurant that can serve up to 40 persons comfortably, and a bar with covered terrace. Guest parking is available.

MARLIN QUAY
PO Box 2204
Gros Islet
Tel: 758-452-0393
Fax: 758-452-0383

In the magnificent surroundings of Rodney Bay Marina, master builders and craftsmen have created 43 exclusive villa-style residences. The spacious apartments and villas are luxuriously furnished, and provide ideal accommodations for couples and families. All apartments have air-conditioning, cable t.v., full kitchens, ceiling fans and daily maid service. Each also has a private rooftop sun terrace with a plunge pool/jacuzzi overlooking the marina. Marlin Quay's facilities include a restaurant, cocktail bar and a 65-foot freshwater pool, with playground area for children. Guests can also enjoy Rodney Bay's beaches, restaurants and nightlife, plus watersports, scuba, golf, tennis and horseback riding.

SWEET SHAVES
PO Box 161
Castries
Tel./Fax: 758-452-3559

Located atop historic Morne Fortune, ten-minutes drive from the capital, Castries, and Vigie airport, Sweet Shaves is comprised of two two-bedroom apartments with sitting rooms, verandas and fully-equipped kitchens. Other features include cable t.v., private lawn and parking. The apartments are also within close proximity to restaurants and other activities. This peaceful, conveniently located property offers personalized service, and is a lovely setting for an authentic St. Lucian vacation experience.

Harbour Light Inn

The Green Parrot restaurant has a world famous chef, award winning cuisine and an excellent view of Castries

Spinnakers Beach Bar and Carvery, Reduit Beach

Français

STE LUCIE
La beauté pure et simple

Ste Lucie est le dernier trésor des Caraïbes à avoir été découvert: un paradis tropical où des fleurs exotiques caressent les sens. Partout le regard y est séduit par des plages secrètes, des montagnes aux sommets majestueux, et des villages de pêcheurs pittoresques. En effet, la beauté naturelle de Ste Lucie est encore largement intacte. Les visiteurs seront éblouis par l'abondance et la richesse des paysages intérieurs de l'île. Dans les plantations, les bananiers, les cocotiers, les manguiers et les papayers poussent à profusion. Vous pouvez explorer les forêts tropicales humides où prospèrent des orchidées sauvages, des fougères géantes et des oiseaux de paradis, et des espèces telles que le perroquet de Ste Lucie, indigène et très rare, et qui sont jalousement protégées dans leur habitat naturel. C'est également un pays où l'on continue à cultiver la courtoisie d'antan. Que vous visitiez un petit village de bord de mer ou bien la capitale de l'île, Castries, les St Luciens vous accueillent naturellement avec un sourire chaleureux et un "bonjour" amical. Que vous cherchiez le plaisir ou l'émotion, Ste Lucie saura combler votre attente. Vous pouvez faire de la plongée sous-marine ou plongée en apnée à l'ombre des Pitons, le sommet jumelé de l'île qui se dresse de façon spectaculaire à plus de 600 mètres au-dessus de la mer. Ou bien explorer les ruines de la forteresse où les puissances européennes se sont si souvent affrontées pour s'assurer la possession de cette île fertile. Visiter les marchés de plein air en quête de fruits et de légumes tropicaux et des produits de l'artisanat indigène. Pénétrer jusque dans le cratère fumant d'un volcan drive-in unique au monde. Ou simplement se détendre sur une plage et se gorger de soleil.

SITUATION GÉOGRAPHIQUE

Ste Lucie, une des îles du Vent des Petites Antilles, est située entre la Martinique et St Vincent, au nord-ouest de la Barbade. Elle a la forme d'une mangue, un de ses fruits les plus savoureux. Ste Lucie mesure environ 43 km de long sur 22 km en son point le plus large. L'océan atlantique rafraîchit la côte est de Ste Lucie, tandis que la Mer des Caraïbes caresse avec douceur la côte ouest qui offre aux visiteurs le surf le plus calme et les meilleures plages. Ste Lucie abrite deux aéroports, l'aéroport international Hewanorra à Vieux Fort au sud de l'île, et l'aéroport Vigie au nord-ouest, près de Castries. Plusieurs grandes compagnies aériennes américaines, européennes et antillaises assurent un

Deutsch

ST. LUCIA
Eine Insel von bezaubernder Schönheit

St. Lucia ist eine Perle der Karibik, die als solche erst kürzlich entdeckt wurde: Ein tropisches Paradies, wo exotische Blüten die Sinne berauschen. Einsame Strände, majestätische Bergspitzen und malerische Fischerdörfer sind eine Augenweide. Tatsächlich haben die Spuren der Zeit die natürliche Schönheit St. Lucias unberührt gelassen. Besucher werden von dem üppigen Inneren der Insel überwältigt. Auf den Feldern gedeihen Bäume mit Bananen, Kokosnüssen, Mangos und Papayas in verschwenderischer Fülle. Sie können den Regenwald erkunden, wo wilde Orchideen und Riesenfarne wachsen und Paradiesvögel leben; dort werden außerdem seltene Tierarten, wie der einheimische St. Lucia Papagei, in ihrer natürlichen Umgebung sorgfältig geschützt.
Dies ist außerdem ein Land, in dem eine längst vergessen geglaubte Höflichkeit zum normalen Umgangston gehört. Ob Sie ein kleines Küstendorf oder Castries, die Hauptstadt der Insel, besuchen, die Einwohner von St. Lucia werden Sie mit einem herzlichen Lächeln und einem freundlichen Gruß empfangen. In St. Lucia können Sie Ihre Zeit auf vielerlei aufregende und angenehme Art verbringen. Schnorcheln oder Sporttauchen am Fuß der Pitons, den beiden imposanten Berggipfeln, die sich bis 610 Meter oberhalb der See erheben. Oder Sie können die Ruinen der Festung erkunden, wo Europäer mehrmals um den Besitz dieser fruchtbaren Insel gegeneinander kämpften. Bummeln auf den Märkten unter freiem Himmel, wo Sie tropische Früchte, Gemüse und einheimisches Kunstgewerbe erstehen können. Tauchen Sie ein in den dampfenden Krater des einzigen zugänglichen Vulkans der Erde. Oder entspannen Sie sich einfach am Strand in der Sonne.

LAGE

St. Lucia ist eine der Windward Inseln der Kleinen Antillen und liegt zwischen Martinique und St. Vincent sowie im Nordwesten von Barbados. Ihre Form entspricht der einer Mango, die zugleich ihre verführerischste Frucht ist. St. Lucia ist etwa 44 km lang und an der breitesten Stelle 23 km breit. Der Atlantische Ozean grenzt mit seinen kühleren Gewässern an das Ostufer, während die Westküste sanft von der Karibik umspült wird. Hier werden die Besucher die ruhigste See und die schönsten Strände finden. St. Lucia verfügt über zwei Flughäfen, den Internationalen Flughafen Hewanorra in Vieux Fort im Süden und den Vigie Airport

Français

service de vols régulier vers l'île en provenance de douzaines d'aéroports étrangers.

HISTOIRE

Les premiers habitants de Ste Lucie étaient les indiens Arawaks. Ils sont arrivés dans l'île en provenance de l'Amérique du sud vers l'an 200 apr. J.-C. pour échapper à leurs ennemis. Les Caraïbes sont arrivés plus tard, ont vaincu les Arawaks et établi leur domination de l'île. Au 17ème siècle, les Britanniques ont essayé à plusieurs reprises de coloniser celle-ci.

Ste Lucie est restée sous administration anglaise jusque en 1667, date à laquelle l'île a été conquise par les Français, et a été administrée par la Compagnie Française des Indes Occidentales jusque en 1674. A la suite de quoi, et pendant 150 ans, Britanniques et Français ont lutté pour la possession de Ste Lucie. L'île a changé de mains 14 fois et a été définitivement cédée aux Britanniques en 1814.

Ste Lucie est devenue indépendante en 1979 et elle jouit d'un régime parlementaire démocratique et stable.

Bien que les Britanniques aient gagné la lutte pour la possession de Ste Lucie, l'influence française demeure profonde. L'anglais est la langue officielle. Cependant, la plupart des St Luciens parlent aussi un patois français. Lors de votre exploration de l'île, n'oubliez pas de conduire à gauche, comme dans les pays britanniques. Plusieurs villes ont des noms français, par exemple Vieux Fort, Soufrière et Fond St Jacques. En effet, Ste Lucie conjugue les attraits de plusieurs cultures; les St Luciens sont aussi passionnés de leur savoureuse cuisine franco-créole qu'ils le sont d'un bon match de football. Ste Lucie est justement fière du fait d'avoir donné naissance à deux lauréats du prix Nobel. Feu Sir W. Arthur Lewis s'est vu décerné le prix Nobel d'économie en 1979, et le poète Derek Walcott le prix Nobel de littérature en 1992.

Les St Luciens sont également très fiers de la beauté naturelle de leur île. Ils sont très hospitaliers et vous aideront volontiers à découvrir les meilleures plages, restaurants et attractions touristiques.

Le pays possède un grand nombre d'hôtels et de centres de vacances qui répondent à tous les goûts et à tous les budgets. Aucun des hôtels ne comporte cependant de tours d'habitation. La plupart des résidences sont situées à l'écart dans un havre de forêt tropicale, et certaines le sont sur le sommet de collines romantiques avec une vue spectaculaire sur les Pitons.

SPORT

La plupart des hôtels offrent des courts de tennis et des

Deutsch

in der Nähe von Castries im Nordwesten. Eine Reihe von großen amerikanischen, europäischen und karibischen Fluglinien fliegen das Land regelmäßig von dutzenden von Gateways an.

GESCHICHTE

Die ersten Einwohner der Insel waren die Arawak Indianer. Sie kamen etwa 200 Jahre n. Chr. von Südamerika auf die Insel, um ihren Feinden zu entkommen. Später kamen die Caribs, besiegten die Arawak Indianer und übernahmen die Herrschaft über die Insel. Im 17. Jahrhundert unternahmen die Engländer einige Versuche, die Insel unter ihre Kolonialherrschaft zu bringen.

Bis zum Jahr 1667 blieb die Insel unter englischer Herrschaft, dann wurde sie von den Franzosen eingenommen und bis 1674 von der Französischen West-Indischen Gesellschaft regiert. Damit begann ein 150 Jahre lang andauernder Krieg zwischen Engländern und Franzosen um den Besitz von St. Lucia. Die Vormachtstellung auf der Insel wechselte 14 Mal, bis diese im Jahr 1814 schließlich an die Engländer fiel.

Seit 1979 ist St. Lucia ein unabhängiger Staat und ist nun eine stabile parlamentarische Demokratie.

Obwohl die Engländer aus dem Kampf um den Besitz von St. Lucia als Sieger hervorgingen, blieb ein starker unverkennbar französischer Einfluß erhalten. Die Amtssprache ist englisch. Die meisten Einwohner von St. Lucia sprechen jedoch außerdem einen französischen

Français

aménagements de sport nautique, avec planche à voile, ski nautique et petits voiliers de plaisance. Des ports de plaisance avec aménagements très complets à Rodney Bay et Marigot Bay offrent des yachts que vous pouvez louer avec ou sans équipage. Les amateurs de golf peuvent profiter de deux terrains stimulants. Et des stages de formation comme de perfectionnement par instructeurs assermentés sont disponibles dans tous les magasins de plongées de l'île, pour les plongeurs expérimentés comme pour les novices. Aucune visite de Ste Lucie n'est complète sans une randonnée dans la forêt tropicale humide. Et c'est à cheval que l'on peut le mieux apprécier la beauté naturelle de Ste Lucie? La plupart des hôtels peuvent organiser en collaboration avec l'un des centres d'équitation locaux des galops d'essai sur la plage pour leurs clients.

RESTAURANTS

A Ste Lucie, île riche au sol fertile, poussent une grande diversité de fruits et légumes. Elle est actuellement un des plus gros exportateurs de bananes des Antilles. Et à côté de six sortes de bananes, on trouve aussi les papayes et les mangues, les anones et le fruit de la passion, les noix de coco et les goyaves. Les chefs de cuisine de l'île exploitent largement l'abondance naturelle de la terre et de la mer à Ste Lucie. Dégustez le homard grillé, ou du poisson frais pêché et cuit dans une sauce piquante créole, des légumes frais cueillis, suivis de desserts agrémentés de fruits tropicaux. Ste Lucie offre un choix étendu de restaurants antillais, européens et internationaux au cadre romantique où les visiteurs peuvent dîner aux chandelles; des cafés restaurants plus détendus offrent des spécialités du pays, comme le callaloo, les plats au curry, les ragoûts poivrés, et il existe un grand nombre d'établissements intermédiaires.

Pratiquement tous les restaurants de Ste Lucie ont en commun un cadre d'une beauté naturelle incomparable. Ils savent tirer le meilleur parti de cet environnement, avec des salles à manger de plein air donnant vue sur la mer.

ACHATS

Ste Lucie offre toutes sortes d'options, y compris les produits importés hors taxes tels que les parfums de luxe, le cristal et la porcelaine, à Point Seraphin, un nouveau complexe commercial portuaire. Et il y a le jour du marché, lorsque les femmes des agriculteurs se rendent au marché de plein air moderne de Castries pour colporter des fruits et légumes frais, ainsi que des épices et produits artisanaux locaux. Demandez un tamarin ou achetez un panier de fruits tressé pour la table de cui

Deutsch

Dialekt. Wenn Sie die Insel per Auto erkunden, müssen Sie nach britischem Muster links fahren. Viele der Städte haben jedoch französische Namen wie Vieux Fort, Soufrière und Fond St. Jacques. Das Kulturgut von St. Lucia vereint in der Tat das wertvollste Gut mehrerer Kulturen; die St. Lucianer sind ebenso passionierte Anhänger ihrer französisch-kreolischen Küche wie eines guten Fußballspiels. St. Lucia ist verständlicherweise stolz darauf, die Heimat von zwei Nobelpreisträgern zu sein. Der verstorbene Sir W. Arthur Lewis gewann 1979 den Wirtschaftsnobelpreis und der Dichter Derek Walcott erhielt 1992 den Nobelpreis für Literatur.

Der Stolz der Einwohner von St. Lucia ist außerdem die natürliche Schönheit ihrer Insel. Sie vermitteln Besuchern schnell ein Gefühl der Heimat und sind ihnen mit Freude behilflich, die schönsten Strände, die besten Restaurants und die interessantesten Touristenattraktionen zu entdecken.

Das Land bietet eine große Anzahl von Hotels, die für jeden Geschmack und für jeden Geldbeutel das Passende bereithalten. Hochhäuser unter den Hotels finden sich nicht. Die meisten Anlagen fügen sich harmonisch in die üppige, tropische Umgebung ein; einige sind auf romantischen Hügeln angelegt und bieten einen spektakulären Ausblick auf die Pitons.

SPORT

Die meisten Hotels verfügen über Tennisplätze und bieten Wassersportmöglichkeiten, wie Windsurfen, Wasserski und kleine Segelboote an. In den Yachthäfen in der Rodney Bay und Marigot Bay, deren umfassendes Angebot alle Wassersportfreunde auf ihre Kosten kommen läßt, können Sie sowohl bemannte als auch unbemannte Yachten chartern. Für Golfspieler wurden zwei reizvolle Golfplätze angelegt, geübte Sporttaucher und Anfänger können auf der ganzen Insel ihrem Niveau entsprechende fachliche Betreuung und Tauchplätze finden. Bei einem Besuch auf St. Lucia darf eine Wanderung durch den Regenwald nicht fehlen. Und was könnte angenehmer sein, als die natürliche Schönheit von St. Lucia auf dem Rücken eines Pferdes kennenzulernen? Die meisten Hotels arrangieren für ihre Gäste gern einen Proberitt am Strand über einen der heimischen Reitställe.

DIE KÜCHE DER INSEL

St. Lucia ist eine Insel, die mit einer üppigen Vegetation und einem fruchtbaren Boden gesegnet ist, auf dem eine reiche Vielfalt an Früchten und Gemüsen wächst. Die Insel zählt zu den führenden Bananenexporteuren der Karibik. Neben sechs verschiedenen Bananensorten gibt

Français

sine. A Castries et dans les environs, un certain nombre de magasins vendent également des paniers faits sur place, des sculptures sur bois et des poteries. Les vêtements de sérigraphie faits à la main et des vêtements de batik aux couleurs vives sont également des achats excellents. Des studios locaux offrent un grand nombre de tableaux illustrant la flore et la faune de l'île. Ils sont presque aussi beaux que Ste Lucie elle-même.

EXPLORATION

Dans la capitale, **Castries**, visitez Derek Walcott Square où un arbre vieux de 400 ans (un samaan) donne de l'ombre à la Cathédrale de l'Immaculée Conception construite en 1897.

Au nord de Castries, visitez le **Pigeon Island National Park** pour revivre les tribulations de la guerre entre la France et l'Angleterre pour la possession de Ste Lucie. Dans ce monument consacré à l'histoire de l'île, n'oubliez pas de vous rendre au centre d'information dans les casernes et de jeter un coup d'oeil dans les soutes à munitions et sur les remparts de Fort Rodney.

Morne Fortune (Mont bonne chance) qui domine Castries, est le site d'une bataille décisive de la guerre franco-anglaise. Les Français ont commencé à construire une forteresse en ce point stratégique au 17ème siècle. Ce sont toutefois les Britanniques qui en ont terminé la construction après la capitulation des Français en 1796.

Plus au sud, **Marigot Bay** était également une base maritime importante. Un amiral anglais a un jour pris les Français en embuscade dans cette baie pittoresque en camouflant sa flotte avec des feuilles de palmier. Aujourd'hui port de plaisance, Marigot reste une des plus belles attractions de Ste Lucie.

A l'intérieur du pays, le **Mt Gimie**, haut de 930 mètres, est le point culminant de Ste Lucie. Faites une excursion jusqu'au sommet sous la direction d'un guide local.

La **Forêt tropicale humide nationale (National Rainforest)** de Ste Lucie couvre 7 600 hectares de montagnes et vallées à la végétation luxuriante. Une source d'enchantement pour les ornithologues amateurs, les randonneurs et tous les passionnés de la nature. Un guide des Services forestiers vous aidera à identifier le très grand nombre de fleurs, fruits, arbres et oiseaux chamarrés exotiques que l'on rencontre en chemin, et vous apercevrez peut-être le plumage bigarré d'un perroquet de Ste Lucie, qui a reçu le nom affectueux de Jacquot.

Anse la Raye et **Canaries** sont de minuscules villages de pêcheurs. Dans l'après-midi, les bateaux arrivent avec leur prise de la journée. La ville la plus ancienne de

Deutsch

es Papayas und Mangos, Annonenbaumfrüchte und Passionsfrüchte, Kokosnüsse und Guaven, um nur einige Namen zu nennen. Die Küchenchefs der Insel haben ihre Küche auf die natürlichen kulinarischen Reichtümer des Landes und des Meeres abgestimmt. Schwelgen Sie in gegrilltem Hummer oder frisch gefangenem Fisch in einer kreolischen Sauce, in frisch geerntetem Gemüse und in Desserts, die mit tropischen Früchten garniert sind. St. Lucia bietet eine Reihe von romantischen karibischen, europäischen und internationalen Restaurants, wo die Gäste bei Kerzenlicht speisen können; die Karte der einheimischen Speiselokale enthält hauseigene Spezialitäten wie Callaloo, Currygerichte und Paprikaeintöpfe und zahllose andere Varianten.

Die Restaurants auf St. Lucia haben nahezu alle eines gemeinsam: sie sind unvergleichlich reizvoll angelegt und passen sich mit open-air Speiseräumen mit Ausblick auf das Meer der natürlichen Schönheit ihrer Umgebung an.

SHOPPING

In St. Lucia gibt es viele Möglichkeiten zum Einkaufen, u.a. importierte zollfreie Ware wie Designer-Parfums, Kristalle und Porzellan, die am Pointe Seraphine, einem neuen am Hafen gelegenen Einkaufszentrum angeboten werden. Außerdem gibt es einen Markttag, an dem die Frauen der Bauern nach Castries zu dem modernen Marktgelände unter freiem Himmel kommen und frisches Obst und Gemüse, Gewürze und einheimisches Kunstgewerbe anbieten. Suchen Sie nach Tamarinde oder erstehen Sie einen geflochtenen Obstkorb für Ihren Küchentisch. Eine Reihe von Geschäften in und um Castries verkaufen ebenfalls auf der Insel hergestellte Körbe, Holzschnitzereien und Töpferwaren. Handgefertigte Kleidung und farbenfrohe Batikgewänder laden ebenso verführerisch zum Kauf ein. Zahlreiche Entwürfe einheimischer Studios stellen die Flora und Fauna der Insel dar. Diese sind fast ebenso schön, wie St. Lucia selbst.

ENTDECKUNG DER INSEL

Besuchen Sie in der Hauptstadt Castries den Derek Walcott Platz, wo ein 400 Jahre alter Samaan-Baum die Kathedrale der Unbefleckten Empfängnis beschattet, die im Jahre 1897 erbaut wurde.

Im Norden von Castries lädt der Pigeon Island National Park Sie ein, sich in die Tage der Schlachten um St. Lucia zwischen Frankreich und England versetzen zu l

Français

Ste Lucie, *Soufrière*, située au sud, a été fondée par les Français en 1746. La nouvelle place du marché est égayée de peintures murales hautes en couleurs et de fioritures fantaisistes.

L'unique volcan drive-in au monde, la Soufrière, et ses sources sulfureuses **(Sulphur Springs)** offrent une exceptionnelle leçon de géologie. Demandez à des guides locaux de vous conduire à travers les sources fumantes et bouillonnantes de ce volcan actuellement en sommeil.

A **Diamond Falls** et à **Mineral Baths**, où le roi de France Louis XVI a fait construire des bains publics pour ses troupes, les visiteurs peuvent prendre une douche tonifiante dans les cascades naturelles et s'attarder dans les bains riches en minéraux.

Près de Soufrière, les **Pitons** sont devenus le symbole de la beauté indomptée de Ste Lucie. Seuls les randonneurs les plus expérimentés ont gravi ces deux sommets; vus de mer, les Pitons offrent néanmoins un panorama dramatique qui est l'un des attraits des diverses excursions en bateau menant au sud de l'île.

Les amateurs de la nature peuvent également observer la flore et la faune sauvages indigènes au **Maria Islands Interpretive Centre**, le biotope de deux reptiles endémiques, et à Fregate Island, un asile pour les frégates pendant la saison des amours.

La ville de pêcheurs **Gros Islet** se transforme chaque vendredi soir en scène de carnaval. Le soca et le reggae font danser tout un chacun sur la route. C'est une 'sauterie' à ne manquer en aucun cas.

Apprenez à connaître les plantations de Ste Lucie, leur passé et leur présent, à l'occasion d'une visite dans une des plus vastes d'entre elles, la **Marquis Plantation**.

NAUTISME

Il est possible de louer des yachts (avec ou sans équipage) auprès de plusieurs agences de location. Les deux ports de plaisance les plus populaires de l'île, Rodney Bay et Marigot Bay, offrent divers services de location. Ils offrent tous deux un mouillage sûr, des douches publiques, des restaurants et bars, des épiceries et des installations d'entretien de yachts. La plupart des agences de location nautiques sont situées dans ces ports de plaisance.

PLANCHE À VOILE

Il est possible de faire de la planche à voile dans la plupart des hôtels, avec des moniteurs et un équipement de première qualité. Cas en Bas et Vieux Fort sont les endroits les plus populaires pour les véliplanchistes de niveau moyen et avancé. Il est recommandé aux débu

Deutsch

lassen. An diesem Monument der Geschichte der Insel können Sie das Informationszentrum bei den Kasernen sowie Magazine und Schutzwälle von Fort Rodney besichtigen.

Hoch oben über Castries war Morne Fortune (Glückshügel) ein zentrales Schlachtfeld während der französisch-britischen Kämpfe. Die Franzosen begannen im 17. Jahrhundert mit der Errichtung einer Festung an diesem strategisch wichtigen Punkt. Dennoch waren es die Engländer, die diese Arbeit vollendeten - nach der Kapitulation der Franzosen im Jahr 1796.

Im Süden war die Marigot Bay ein zu Kriegszeiten wichtiger Ort. Ein britischer Admiral lockte hier in dieser malerischen Bucht die Franzosen in einen Hinterhalt, indem er seine Flotte mit Palmenwedeln tarnte. Als heutiger Yachthafen ist die Marigot Bay noch immer einer der schönsten Plätze auf St. Lucia.

Im Landesinneren ist der Mt. Gimie mit einer Höhe von 950m die höchste Erhebung von St. Lucia. Sie können den Berg mit einem einheimischen Führer erklimmen.

Der Nationale Regenwald von St. Lucia erstreckt sich über 77km2 üppig bewaldeter Berge und Hügel. Dies ist ein wahres Paradies für Vogelkundler, Wanderer und Naturliebhaber. Ein Führer des Forstministeriums macht Sie auf die vielen exotischen Blumen, Früchte, Bäume und farbenprächtigen Vögel aufmerksam, die Ihnen auf Ihrem Weg begegnen, und vielleicht können Sie einen Blick auf den bunten St. Lucia Papagei erhaschen, der liebevoll Jacquot genannt wird.

Anse-le-Raye und Canaries sind winzige Fischerdörfer. Am Abend laufen die Boote mit ihrem täglichen Fischfang ein. Die älteste Stadt auf St. Lucia, Soufrière, wurde im Süden im Jahr 1746 von den Franzosen errichtet. Der neue Marktplatz wurde mit farbenfrohen Wandmalereien und aufwendigen Verzierungen geschmückt.

Der einzige zugängliche Vulkan der Erde, der Soufrière, bietet mit seinen Schwefelquellen ein einzigartiges geologisches Erlebnis. Schließen Sie sich einem einheimischen Führer an, um die brodelnden dampfenden Quellen dieses nun ruhenden Vulkans zu umrunden.

An den Diamant-Wasserfällen und in Mineralbädern, wo Frankreichs König Ludwig XVI Badehäuser für seine Truppen errichten ließ, können Besucher eine belebende Dusche unter natürlichen Kaskaden nehmen und in Bädern verweilen, die reich an Mineralstoffen sind.

In der Nähe von Soufrière sind die Pitons zu einem Symbol von St. Lucias wilder Schönheit geworden. Während nur geübte Wanderer diese Gipfel erklommen haben, kann Ihnen der Anblick der Pitons ein ebenfalls beeindruckendes Erlebnis vom Boot aus bescheren, bei einer der vielen Rundfahrten auf dem Meer im südlichen

Français

tants de s'essayer sur les eaux plus calmes de la côte occidentale.

PÊCHE HAUTURIÈRE

La pêche hauturière est une activité de récréation populaire à Ste Lucie. Il existe sur l'île un certain nombre d'agences d'affrètement de bateaux à la journée ou la demi-journée. En fonction de la saison, vous pouvez pratiquer la pêche au maquereau, maquereau royal, marlin blanc, barracuda, maquereau espagnol et pèlerin.

CENTRES D'EXERCICE PHYSIQUE

Ste Lucie dispose de plusieurs gymnases bien équipés, dont la plupart offrent des classes d'aérobic. Body Inc, qui se trouve dans le complexe Gablewoods Mall, offre des salles d'haltérophilie, l'aérobic normal et le step aérobic, ainsi qu'un centre d'entraînement cardiologique. Le personnel de Body Inc compte des culturistes de renommée mondiale tels que Rick Wayne et Mae Sabbagh Gonard. Le centre La Borde de Hospital Road dispose d'un équipement de pointe Weider. Caribbean Fitness Expression, situé à Vide Boutielle, Castries, offre des cours de jazzercise, de step, de stretching et de tonus, une vaste salle de poids et haltères ainsi qu'un restaurant. Certains des plus grands hôtels ont également des gymnases bien équipés.

Deutsch

Teil der Insel.

Naturforscher haben die Möglichkeit, einen Teil der natürlichen Wildnis der Insel im Maria Islands Interpretive Centre kennenzulernen, wo sich der Lebensraum zweier endemischer Reptilien befindet; in der Paarungszeit ist Fregate Island eine Zufluchtstätte für Fregattvögel (einheimischer Name Fregate).

Das Fischerdorf Gros Islet verwandelt sich jeden Freitagabend in eine karnevalistische Hochburg. Soca und Reggae-Musik treiben jedermann auf die Straße. Diesem "magnetischen Sog" können und sollten auch Sie sich nicht entziehen.

Über die Plantagen auf St. Lucia, zu vergangenen und heutigen Zeiten, können Sie sich auf einer der größten Plantagen, der Marquis Plantage, informieren.

SEGELN

Bei verschiedenen Bootsverleihern können Sie Segelyachten mit oder ohne Skipper chartern. In den beiden bekannten Yachthäfen, Rodney Bay und Marigot Bay, finden Sie eine Reihe von Bootsverleihen. Beide haben sichere Anlegeplätze, Waschgelegenheiten, Restaurants und Bars, Lebensmittelgeschäfte und Wartungseinrichtungen für Yachten. Die meisten der Bootsverleiher sind in diesen Yachthäfen zu Hause.

WINDSURFEN

Von den meisten Hotels wird Windsurfing angeboten sowie Surflehrer und erstklassige Ausrüstungen. Für bereits etwas geübte und fortgeschrittene Surfer sind Cas en Bas und Vieux Fort die besten Plätze. Anfänger sollten sich eher in den ruhigeren Gewässern an der Westküste tummeln.

HOCHSEEFISCHEREI

Die Hochseefischerei ist eine beliebte Freizeitaktivität auf St. Lucia. Es gibt eine Reihe von Charterorganisationen, die über täglich auslaufende Boote verfügen, die ganztägige und halbtägige Ausflüge anbieten. Je nach Saison können Sie Makrelen, Königsmakrelen, weißen Marlin, Barrakuda, Königsfische und Fächerfische fangen.

FITNESS CENTER

St. Lucia besitzt einige gut ausgestattete Fitness Center, von denen die meisten auch Aerobicgruppen anbieten. Im Body Inc am Gablewoods Mall können Sie sich bei Krafttraining, Step und Aerobic verausgaben, außerdem verfügt es über ein Kardiozentrum. Zum Personal des

Français

GOLF

Ste Lucie a deux terrains de golf, celui de Sandals La Toc et celui de The Cap Estate. Le terrain de The Cap Estate est ouvert au grand public et offre un terrain de 9 trous que l'on peut également utiliser comme terrain de 18 trous. La diversité des trous et des obstacles ainsi que le panorama qui s'y découvre rendent la visite du terrain obligatoire pour tout golfeur de passage dans l'île. Le pavillon renferme un bar bien fourni et un magasin professionnel. Des inscriptions temporaires et des équipements de golf sont disponibles, ainsi que des leçons données par le golfeur professionnel en résidence.

EQUITATION

Le centre d'équitation International Riding Stables à Gros Islet offre des promenades à cheval avec assurance tous risques à tous les niveaux. Il existe une grande variété d'excursions sur sentier battu, plus une randonnée à cheval fantastique avec pique-nique sur une plage de Cas en Bas. Cette randonnée, qui est une excursion idéale pour les familles, comprend une promenade touristique à travers la campagne, ménage le temps d'une baignade, puis une chevauchée le long de la plage. Un autre centre, Trims Riding School, se trouve à Cas en Bas.

PLONGÉE SOUS-MARINE / PLONGÉE EN APNÉE

Ste Lucie est entourée par d'innombrables récifs et une faune et flore sous-marines spectaculaires. L'île a plusieurs centres de plongée indépendants offrant de courtes plongées par bateau, des plongées de nuit et divers stages de plongée sous-marine. Les récifs Anse Cochon et Anse Chastanet comptent parmi les sites sous-marins les plus populaires, avec visite d'épave pour les plus aventureux. L'eau claire et chaude de Ste Lucie constitue un environnement parfait pour les débutants. Un grand nombre d'hôtels offrent des installations de plongée sous-marine et des équipements de plongée en apnée. Il existe également des excursions d'une journée avec plongée sous-marine et plongée en apnée pour les débutants et les plongeurs expérimentés.

SQUASH

Les courts de squash sont situés à proximité du Golf Club de Cap Estate et sur la propriété du St Lucia Yacht Club près de l'hôtel Royal St Lucian. Le St Lucia Racquet Club au Club St Lucia a également un court de squash

Deutsch

Body Inc zählen weltbekannte Bodybuilder, wie Rick Wayne und Mae Sabbagh Gonard. Das Center La Borde in der Hospital Road verfügt über eine hochmoderne Weider-Ausrüstung. Das Carribean Fitness Expression, das am Vide Bouteille in Castries angesiedelt ist, bietet Ihnen Jazzgymnastik, Step, Stretching und Muskeltraining, einen großen Geräteraum sowie ein Restaurant. Auch einige der größeren Hotels haben gut ausgestattete Fitnessräume.

GOLF

Auf St. Lucia sind zwei Golfplätze angelegt, der Platz Sandals La Toc und der Platz Cap Estate. Der Platz Cap Estate ist für die Öffentlichkeit zugänglich und bietet einen 9-Loch-Parcours, der auch als 18-Loch-Parcours gespielt werden kann. Die Vielseitigkeit der Löcher, Hindernisse und Sichtverhältnisse auf dem Platz machen ihn zu einem Muß für jeden Golfer, der die Insel besucht. Im Klubhaus finden Sie eine Bar mit einem breiten Angebot und einen Golfshop. Es gibt kurzfristige Mitgliedschaften und einen Golfverleih, ebenso wird Golfunterricht durch die ansässigen Profis angeboten.

REITEN

Der internationale Reitstall in Gros Islet bietet Reiten für Anfänger und Fortgeschrittene mit einer umfassenden Versicherung. Es gibt verschiedene Reitpfade und einen reizvollen Rundritt, zu dem auch ein Picknick am Strand bei Cas en Bas gehört. Der Rundritt ist besonders als Familienausflug geeignet, da er einen Ritt durch die malerische Landschaft sowie Zeit zum Schwimmen und einen Ritt am Strand beeinhaltet. Eine andere Reitschule, Trims Riding School, liegt in Cas en Bas.

SPORTTAUCHEN / SCHNORCHELN

St. Lucia ist von einer Myriade spektakulärer Riffs und einer faszinierenden Unterwasserwelt umgeben. Auf der Insel finden Sie eine Reihe unabhängiger Tauchzentren, die kurze Tauchgänge vom Boot, Tauchgänge bei Nacht und verschiedene Tauchkurse anbieten. Die beiden Riffe Anse Cochon und Anse Chastanet zählen für Taucher zu den beliebtesten Tauchparadiesen. Die abenteuerlustigeren Taucher können ein altes gesunkenes Schiff erkunden. Aufgrund des warmen, klaren Wassers herrschen ideale Bedingungen für Anfänger. Viele Hotels bieten Tauchmöglichkeiten und sind mit Schnorchelausrüstungen ausgestattet. Es werden außerdem Tagesausflüge zum Schnorcheln für Anfänger und auch zum Tauchen für geprüfte Taucher angeboten.

Français

et un encadrement excellent.

Tennis

La plupart des grands hôtels disposent de courts de tennis. Le St Lucia Racquet Club au Club St Lucia compte 9 courts éclairés par projecteurs. Le St Lucian Hotel a deux courts ouverts au public à des prix raisonnables. On peut également prendre des leçons de tennis.

Ski nautique

Le ski nautique est une activité offerte par la plupart des grands hôtels, avec stages pour les débutants et les skieurs de niveau moyen. La pêche, le yachting ou d'autres sports nautiques peuvent être organisés pour le visiteur par la plupart des bureaux d'activités des hôtels.

Ornithologie pour amateurs

Les visiteurs peuvent observer certaines des espèces rares et indigènes de Ste Lucie: perroquet de Ste Lucie, oiseau moqueur à gorge blanche, vanneau de Ste Lucie, loriot de Ste Lucie et troglodyte de Ste Lucie. Les endroits recommandés pour l'observation des oiseaux sont Bois d'Orange Swamp, la forêt tropicale humide (Piton Flore, Barre de L'isle, Soufrière, Descartiere et Quilesse) et Boriel's Pond (Vieux Fort). Vous pouvez réserver une place pour une excursion tôt le matin ou tard l'après-midi, chaque excursion durant 4 heures et coûtant à partir de US$ 40,00 par personne pour un groupe de 10 personnes au plus et 3 personnes au moins. Les réservations peuvent êtes faites par l'intermédiaire du Service forestier de Ste Lucie (St Lucia Forestry Department).

La Mankote Mangrove à Vieux fort est également un endroit idéal pour l'observation ornithologique. Situé sur la côte du sud-est, la mangrove est la source principale de nutriments pour la zone de reproduction marine naturelle de l'île dans la baie de Savannes (Savannes Bay) à proximité. Tôt le matin et vers le soir, une tour spécialement conçue assure aux ornithologues le meilleur poste d'observation. Des visites guidées peuvent être organisées sur demande auprès du St Lucia National Trust (Tél.: 758-452-5005).

Camping

Bien que l'île ne dispose pas actuellement de terrain de camping officiel, il y aura bientôt un terrain de camping de haute qualité et un centre éducatif sur l'environnement (Environmental Educational Centre) de plein air à Anse Liberté près du village de Canaries. Le complexe

Deutsch

Squash

Plätze zum Squash-Spielen finden Sie in der Nähe des Cap Estate Golf Club und am St. Lucia Yachtclub in der Nähe des Royal St. Lucian Hotel. Der St. Lucia Racquet Club im Club St. Lucia verfügt ebenfalls über einen Squash-Court und bietet darüber hinaus hervorragenden Unterricht.

Tennis

Bei den meisten Hotels finden Sie hoteleigene Tennisplätze. Im St. Lucia Racquet Club im Club St. Lucia gibt es außerdem neun mit Flutlichtanlagen ausgestattete Tennisplätze. Beim St. Lucian Hotel sind zwei der Plätze zu erschwinglichen Preisen für die Öffentlichkeit zugänglich. Es wird auch Unterricht angeboten.

Wasserski

Die meisten größeren Hotels bieten Wasserski an. Für Anfänger und Ungeübte gibt es auch Unterricht. Wenn Sie fischen, segeln oder andere Wassersportarten treiben wollen, können Ihnen die Animationsbüros in den meisten Hotels weiter helfen.

Das Beobachten von Vögeln

Besucher können einige von St. Lucias seltenen einheimischen Vogelarten beobachten, wie den St. Lucia Papagei, eine weißbrüstige Drosselart, den St. Lucia Kiebitz, die St. Lucia Golddrossel und den St. Lucia Zaunkönig. Zum Beobachten von Vögeln müssen Sie sich vor allem in den Bois d'Orange Swamp, den Regenwald (Piton Flore, Barre de l'Isle, Soufrière, Descartiere und Quilesse) und Boriel's Pond (Vieux Fort) begeben. Sie können sich für Ausflüge am frühen

Français

sera intégral, avec pistes de randonnées, refuges, huttes, terrains de camping nus et aires de cuisine. La cuisine en plein air et la production de charbon de bois feront également partie de l'expérience intégrale. Pour de plus amples informations à ce sujet, veuillez prendre contact avec le St Lucia National Trust.

PISTES NATURELLES / RANDONNÉES

La piste de forêt tropicale de Barre de L'isle **(Barre de L'isle Rainforest Trail):** en bordure de la forêt tropicale luxuriante de Ste Lucie, l'attraction principale de cette piste est la pente raide à gravir pour arriver au sommet de Morne la Combe (à 430 mètres au-dessus du niveau de la mer). La montagne se trouve dans la chaîne de Barre de L'isle, et elle offre un point de vue panoramique sur la Vallée du roseau (Roseau Valley) à l'ouest et la Vallée de Mabouya (Mabouya Valley) à l'est. Les forêts entourant Morne La Combe retentissent du chant des perroquets et constituent une attraction supplémentaire pour les visiteurs. Il faut environ trois heures pour boucler la randonnée.

Le circuit forestier éducatif Union **(Union Nature Trail):** un magnifique circuit avec piste recouverte de gravier conduit les visiteurs à travers une forêt secondaire sèche au bout d'environ une heure. De beaux oiseaux tels que les colibris, les fauvettes et les fringillidés peuvent être observés le long de la piste. On y admire aussi des variétés d'arbres spectaculaires introduits dans l'île au cours des trois cent dernières années. Les visiteurs découvrent les merveilles des herbes médicinales et une grande variété d'arbres fruitiers locaux. Un petit zoo, incorporé au circuit permet d'examiner de près certaines

Deutsch

Morgen oder am späten Abend sowie zu vierstündigen Exkursionen für etwa US$ 40,00 pro Person anmelden, die Gruppengröße beträgt höchstens 10 und mindestens drei Personen. Die Anmeldung erfolgt über das Forstministerium von St. Lucia.

Für das Beobachten von Vögeln kann außerdem Mankote Mangrove in Vieux Fort genannt werden. Es liegt an der südöstliche Küste. Der Mangrove ist die Hauptnahrungsquelle für die natürliche Fischzucht der Insel in der nahen Savannes Bay. Der Aussichtsturm bietet Beobachtern am frühen Morgen und am Abend einen hervorragenden Aussichtspunkt. Für von Führern begleitete Touren können Sie sich an den St. Lucia National Trust wenden (Tel. 758-452-5005).

CAMPING

Noch verfügt die Insel zur Zeit über keine ausgewiesenen Campingplätze, doch wird es bald in Anse Liberte in der Nähe von Canaries einen Campingplatz der ersten Kategorie und ein Umweltlehrzentrum geben. Es wird mit Fahrradwegen, kleinen Häusern, Festzelten, Zeltfläche sowie einer Küche vollständig und vielseitig eingerichtet. Kochen unter freiem Himmel und die Produktion von Holzkohle gehören ebenfalls dazu. Für weitere Informationen können Sie sich an den St. Lucia National Trust wenden.

NATÜRLICHE WANDERWEGE / WANDERUNGEN

Der Barre de l'Isle Regenwald Wanderweg: Dieser Wanderweg grenzt an den üppigen Regenwald von St. Lucia. Die Hauptattraktion ist das Erklimmen des Gipfels des Morne la Combe (Höhe 441m). Der Berg gehört zu dem Höhenzug des Barre de l'Isle und von seinem höchsten Punkt sind das Roseau Valley im Westen und das Mabouya Valley im Osten gut sichtbar. Im Wald rund um den Morne la Combe leben zahlreiche Papageien, die eine zusätzliche Attraktion für Besucher darstellen. Für den gesamten Wanderweg benötigen Sie etwa drei Stunden.

Der Union Nature Wanderweg: Ein verwunschener Kiesweg schlängelt sich durch einen trockenen Wald. Diese Wanderung nimmt etwa eine Stunde in Anspruch. Dabei können Sie Vögel wie Kolibris, Waldsänger und Finken beobachten. Außerdem stehen an Ihrem Weg besondere Baumarten, die innerhalb der letzten dreihundert Jahre auf die Insel gebracht wurden. Die Besucher können die Wunder medizinischer Heilpflanzen und eine Reihe von einheimischen Obstbäumen bestaunen. Bei dieser Tour können Sie außerdem in einem kleinen Zoo einige einheimische und exotische Tiergattungen aus der

Français

espèces indigènes et d'autres espèces exotiques. Un centre d'information fournit des renseignements utiles sur les espèces en danger de disparition, les zones de végétation et la forêt tropicale humide de nuit et de jour. Le circuit de la forêt tropicale (**Rainforest Tour**): en guère plus de trois heures et demie, un naturaliste du Service de l'aménagement et des forêts (Forest and Lands Department) guide les visiteurs à travers la réserve naturelle de forêt tropicale. Le sentier est tantôt bordé d'arbres indigènes et tantôt de plantes plus modestes, broméliacées, orchidées et champignons. Tout au long du chemin, vous pouvez également observer de beaux oiseaux, y compris le perroquet de Ste Lucie (Amazona Versicolor). Lorsque sortant de la pénombre de la forêt vous débouchez dans une clairière, une vue magnifique du Mont Gimie, le sommet le plus élevé de Ste Lucie, s'offre à vous. Pour de plus amples informations concernant les randonnées organisées, veuillez appeler le Service de l'aménagement et des forêts au 758-450-2231.

Naturalist Tour: conçu pour ceux qui portent un intérêt particulier à l'horticulture, la biologie, l'entomologie et l'ornithologie, ou qui s'intéressent à la flore et la faune indigènes. Un guide spécialisé conduit les visiteurs dans des régions de l'île qui ne sont jamais fréquentées par la plupart des touristes; la destination et le thème dépendent des préférences exprimées. Cette randonnée spécialisée comprend le trekking en montagne, à travers la forêt et la brousse. Il n'est offert que sur demande. Veuillez par conséquent vous renseigner auprès du Service des forêts. Les prix varient en fonction du type de tour et du nombre des participants.

Fregate Island Nature Trail: cette randonnée mène les visiteurs sur la côte atlantique de Ste Lucie et leur fait découvrir des panoramas fantastiques. La piste naturelle d'un kilomètre et demi fait le tour du parc national et conduit au point d'observation dominant les petites Fregate Islands. La piste traverse également l'habitat de reproduction des magnifiques frégates et de plusieurs autres espèces rares de Ste Lucie, comme le boa constricteur, une région dans laquelle prospère une flore indigène unique. Ces randonnées sont organisées par le St Lucia National Trust.

Morne Le Blanc-Laborie: à 15 minutes de voiture seulement de Vieux Fort, sur la côte du sud-ouest, se trouve la commune de Laborie, à l'ombre de Morne Le Blanc. La crête de Morne Le Blanc offre au visiteur une vue panoramique de toute la plaine sud de Ste Lucie et, la plupart du temps, on peut également apercevoir St Vincent à l'horizon. Une plate-forme d'observation, des kiosques pour pique-niquer à l'ombre, et des installations essentielles permettent de se reposer après une randon

Deutsch

Nähe betrachten. Ein Informationszentrum informiert Sie über bedrohte Tierarten, Vegetationszonen und den Regenwald bei Tage und während der Nacht.

Die Regenwald-Tour: In nur etwa dreieinhalb Stunden führt ein Naturforscher des Forst- und Landwirtschaftsministeriums die Besucher durch das Regenwaldreservat. Die Wanderer sehen alte einheimische Baumarten und beschreiten Wege, an deren Rändern kleinere Pflanzen, Ananasgewächse, Orchideen und Pilze wachsen. Auf dem Weg begegnen Ihnen auch schöne Vögel, wie der St. Lucia Papagei (Amazona Versicolor). Wenn Sie von dem Dunkel des Waldes in das Licht treten, bietet sich Ihnen ein wunderbarer Ausblick auf den Mount Gimie, St. Lucias höchsten Berg. Wenn Sie an organisierten Touren interessiert sind, wenden Sie sich an das Forst- und Landwirtschaftsministerium (758-450-2231).

Die Naturalist Tour: Diese Tour wurde speziell für Besucher entworfen, die ein besonderes Interesse am Gartenbau, an Biologie, Entomologie und Ornithologie sowie der landeseigenen Flora und Fauna haben. Ein fachkundiger Führer eröffnet Besuchern Zutritt zu Teilen der Insel, die den meisten Gästen verborgen bleiben; das Ziel und der Schwerpunkt dieser Tour wird auf das individuelle Interesse abgestimmt. Zu dieser besonderen Tour gehören auch Wanderungen in den Bergen, im Wald und im Busch. Sie wird nur auf Anfrage durchgeführt, wenden Sie sich daher bitte an das Forstministerium. Die Preise variieren je nach Art der Tour und Teilnehmerzahl.

Der Fregate Island Nature Wanderweg: Bei dieser Tour erkunden die Besucher die Atlantikküste und es eröffnen sich Ihnen einige fantastische Ausblicke. Bei diesem Wanderweg von etwa einer Meile Länge umrunden Sie den Nationalpark und erreichen den Aussichtspunkt, von dem aus Sie die kleine Fregate Insel überblicken können. Sie passieren außerdem die Brutstätte der Fregattvögel (einheimischer Name Fregate Birds), die auch die Heimat zahlreicher anderer seltener Arten, wie der Boa Constrictor, sowie der einzigartigen einheimischen Vegetation ist. Wanderungen werden vom St. Lucia National Trust organisiert.

Morne Le Blanc-Laborie: In nur einer Viertelstunde Entfernung von Vieux Fort an der Südwestküste liegt die Gemeinde Laborie im Schatten des Morne Le Blanc. Auf dem Gipfel des Morne Le Blanc bietet sich Ihnen ein Panoramablick auf den gesamten südlichen Teil von St. Lucia und an den meisten Tagen können Sie St. Vincent in der Ferne erblicken. Eine Aussichtsplattform, Kiosks für ein schattiges Picknick sowie einfache Sanitäranlagen laden Sie nach dem 45minütigen Aufstieg zu einer Ruhepause ein. Der Platz kann auch über eine Straße erreicht werden, wenn Sie weniger Zeit

Français

née de 45 minutes. Le site est également accessible par la route, pour ceux qui n'ont pas le temps ou le désir de gravir la montagne à pied. Ces visites guidées sont gérées par le National Trust ou le Bureau du conseil municipal de Laborie (Laborie Village Council Office - numéro de téléphone 758-454-6288).

Southern Safari: les participants voyagent en bus à travers l'intérieur de Ste Lucie, du nord au sud, observant ainsi les paysages divers, la population et la culture du pays. Il y a des arrêts occasionnels dans des sites historiques ou bien pour permettre de prendre un rafraîchissement. Le safari est valorisé par une visite de la vieille plantation de Balembouche où l'on trouve l'un des rares alambics encore en existence sur l'île, les restes magnifiques d'une roue de moulin à eau et d'anciennes cavernes amérindiennes. Un déjeuner délicieux est aussi inclus.

Il existe aussi un circuit safari terre et mer du sud (Southern Safari Land and Sea Tour) qui inclut une vue des Pitons et la visite d'un site à pétroglyphes, avec retour par bateau, le long de la côte est aux paysages sublimes. Pour plus d'informations, veuillez contacter St Lucia National Trust.

Hardy Point Cactus Valley Walking Trek: il s'agit ici d'une randonnée à pied (possible également en bus) qui part de Hardy Point, un promontoire naturel offrant des vues dramatiques sur Esperance Bay, la côte du nord-est et la chaîne de montagnes de La Sorcière. On se rend ensuite à Cactus Valley où on peut admirer diverses espèces de cactus indigènes et un certain nombre d'évents creusés dans la roche par les remous de l'Atlantique et particulièrement photogéniques. Après avoir traversé Donkey Beach, la marche se poursuit vers Pigeon Island pour une visite de ce site historique, y compris son centre d'informations multimédia. Ceux qui le souhaitent peuvent faire le tour de la partie basse de l'île et poursuivre jusqu'à Fort Rodney ou jusqu'au point d'observation. Le reste du groupe peut se détendre et se baigner sur l'une des deux petites plages de l'île. Tout le

Deutsch

haben oder das Klettern Ihnen beschwerlich ist. Nach geführten Wanderungen können Sie sich beim National Trust oder dem Informationsbüro der Gemeinde Laborie erkundigen (Tel. 758-454-6288).

Die Südsafari: Bei dieser Safari reisen die Gäste im Bus durch das Landesinnere der Insel von Norden nach Süden und entdecken verschiedene Landstriche mit ihren Einwohnern und Kulturen. Sie machen gelegentlich Halt bei historischen Stätten oder um sich zu erfrischen. Bei der Safari besuchen Sie zudem das alte Plantagenhaus in Balembouche, wo eine der wenigen Brennereien der Insel und die reizvollen Reste eines Wasserrades sowie eine alte indianische Höhle erhalten sind. Außerdem wird Ihnen ein köstlicher Lunch serviert. Eine andere Variante der Südsafari bietet eine Tour zu Land und zu Wasser, bei der Sie die Pitons und einen Ort mit Steinskulpturen besuchen und dann mit dem Boot an der atemberaubenden Westküste entlang zurückkehren. Für weitere Informationen wenden Sie sich an das St. Lucia National Trust.

Hardy Point Kakteental Wanderung: Diese Wanderung (auch als Busrundtour möglich) beginnt beim Hardy Point, der eine natürliche Felsnase ist und einen spektakulären Blick auf die Esperance Bay, die nordöstliche Küste und den Höhenzug La Socière eröffnet. Dann geht es zum Kakteental, wo Sie zahlreiche einheimische Kakteen und einige sehr photogene Erdlöcher besichtigen können, die durch die Brandung des Atlantik entstanden sind. Sie passieren Donkey Beach und kommen nach Pigeon Island, wo Sie diese historischen Wahrzeichen besichtigen sowie das Multimedia-Informationszentrum besuchen können. Auf Wunsch können Sie den unteren Teil der Insel besuchen und die Tour bis nach Fort Rodney oder zum Aussichtspunkt fortsetzen. Der andere Teil der Gruppe hat Zeit, sich zu entspannen oder an einem der kleinen Strände der Insel ein Bad zu nehmen. Der ganzen Gruppe werden dann ein köstliches Essen oder kühle Getränke in Pigeon Island im neu eröffneten Restaurant Jambe de Bois serviert.

DAS BEOBACHTEN VON WASSERSCHILDKRÖTEN

An der Nordostküste am Grande Anse Beach, wo der Nistplatz der Lederpanzer-Seeschildkröten ist, können Sie Wasserschildkröten beobachten. Diese Aktivität wird von der St. Lucia Naturforschergesellschaft organisiert. Der Zeitraum, in dem Sie diese Tiere beobachten können, reicht von Mitte März bis Ende Juli. Die Teilnehmer zelten am Strand von 16.00 bis 6.30 Uhr (Zelte werden gestellt).

Auch wenn Sie nicht bei jedem Ausflug einen Blick auf

Français

monde prend alors un délicieux déjeuner ou une boisson rafraîchissante au restaurant Jambe de Bois de Pigeon Island, récemment remis à neuf.

OBSERVATION DES TORTUES DE MER

L'observation des tortues, organisée par la St Lucia Naturalist Society, se fait à la plage de Grande Anse sur la côte nord-est, où la tortue de mer vient nicher. La période idéale pour l'observation des tortues va de la mi-mars jusqu'à la fin du mois de juillet. Les observateurs campent sur la plage de 16 heures jusqu'à 6 heures trente le matin suivant (des tentes sont fournies).

Bien que les tortues ne soient pas observées à chaque visite, le camping sous les étoiles et le bruit apaisant du ressac suffisent à justifier l'expédition. Les visiteurs doivent apporter leur propre nourriture, de l'eau et se munir de bonnes chaussures et de vêtements chauds et sombres. Il est permis de faire des photos au flash et de filmer à la caméra. Les observations de tortues n'ont lieu que le samedi soir, et le point de rassemblement est la bibliothèque centrale de Castries à 16 heures.

Pour de plus amples informations, veuillez prendre contact avec Jim Sparks (avant vendredi soir) au 758-452-8100/9951.

STE LUCIE HISTORIQUE

Tour historique de Castries: ce tour comprend une visite de Pigeon Island et un tour de Castries. Il constitue une excellente occasion de découvrir l'histoire de la ville. Les points forts du tour sont la cathédrale et sa décoration incomparable, Morne Fortune, la Batterie La Toc et Bagshaws où vous découvrirez l'art de la sérigraphie et où vous aurez le temps de faire quelques achats.

Il s'avérera également avantageux de faire un tour de Castries de votre propre chef. Le marché, où on vend des fruits frais, des sauces, des légumes, du poisson, des paniers de fabrication locale, des nattes et de la poterie, est digne de visite, en particulier le samedi qui est le jour le plus animé. La ville a également quelques beaux exemples d'architecture, en particulier l'église et la bibliothèque centrale qui se trouvent à Derek Walcott Square.

Choiseul Heritage Sites: à mi-chemin entre Soufrière et Vieux Fort, sur la côte sud-ouest, se trouve le village de Choiseul, riche en histoire et en tradition artisanale, et qui offre des vues spectaculaires. La visite des sites suivants est particulièrement recommandée:

Laybye, situé au coin nord du village, offre une vue panoramique sur les Pitons, la côte, les collines et les vallées. Il y a une plate-forme d'observation pour la prise de photos. Vous pouvez également vous procurer ici des

Deutsch

die Schildkröten erhaschen können, ist das Zelten unter dem Sternenhimmel mit der sanft plätschernden See ein unvergeßliches Erlebnis. Gäste werden gebeten, sich mit Nahrungsmitteln, Getränken, gutem Schuhwerk und warmer dunkler Kleidung auszurüsten. Blitzlichter und Kameras sind gestattet. Das Beobachten der Schildkröten findet nur samstagbends statt, Treffpunkt ist die Zentralbibliothek in Castries um 16.00 Uhr.

Für weitere Informationen wenden Sie sich bitte an Jim Sparks (vor Freitagabend) unter der Nummer 758-452-8100/9951.

DAS HISTORISCHE ST. LUCIA

Eine Tour durch das historische Castries: Bei dieser Tour stehen ein Besuch von Pigeon Island und Castries auf dem Programm. Hier können Sie die Geschichte der Stadt kennenlernen.

Zu den Höhepunkten zählen die einmalig verzierte Kathedrale, Morne Fortune, die La Toc Batterie und Bagshaws, wo Sie die Kunst der Seidenmalerei bewundern können und Zeit zum Einkaufen haben.

Wenn Sie eine Tour durch Castries auf eigene Faust unternehmen, werden Sie ebenfalls auf Ihre Kosten kommen. Der Markt, wo frisches Obst, Saucen, Gemüse, Fisch und vor Ort hergestellte Körbe, Matten und Keramik angeboten werden, ist in jedem Fall einen Besuch wert, vor allem am Samstag, wo ein besonders munteres Treiben herrscht. Die Stadt bietet außerdem interessante architektonische Werke; wie die Kirche und die Zentralbibliothek, die sich am Derek Walcott Platz befinden.

Historische Plätze in Choiseul: In der Mitte zwischen Soufrière und Vieux Fort an der südlichen Westküste liegt das Dorf Choiseul, das reich an Geschichte, Kunstgewerbe und schönen Ausblicken ist. Im folgenden werden einige empfehlenswerte Orte genannt:

Laybye, am nördlichen Ende des Ortes gelegen, bietet einen Panoramablick auf die Pitons, die Küste, Hügel und Täler. Es gibt eine Aussichtsplattform, von der Sie Aufnahmen machen können. Hier finden Sie auch Informationen über die geographischen Gegebenheiten des Gebiets.

Die Steinskulptur: Die auf der Spitze einer Klippe thronende Steinskulptur können Sie von der Straße aus sehen, doch haben Sie einen besseren Blick, wenn Sie sie von Nahem in Augenschein nehmen. Die Skulptur wurde vor Hunderten von Jahren von frühen Bewohnern der Insel in den Stein gemeißelt.

Fort Citreon: Auf der Spitze eines Hügels am südlichen Eingang von Choiseul liegt etwa 10 Minuten entfernt die Stätte einer früheren Festung. Es ist nur eine einzige Kanone erhalten. Die weite Sicht erklärt jedoch, warum

Français

informations sur la géographie de la région.

Le *Petroglyph*. Perché de manière précaire sur une falaise, visible de la route, mais mieux observé à pied, se trouve un pétroglyphe creusé il y a des siècles par les premiers habitants de Ste Lucie.

Fort Citreon. A la crête de la colline, à l'entrée sud de Choiseul, à 10 minutes de marche, se trouve l'emplacement d'un ancien fort. Un seul canon a survécu; néanmoins, la vue spectaculaire explique pourquoi cet endroit a été choisi comme point d'observation de l'approche des vaisseaux. Pour tout renseignement à ce sujet, veuillez appeler le St Lucia National Trust ou le Conseil municipal de Choiseul.

MANIFESTATIONS SPECIALES

Rallye atlantique pour yachts de croisière

Chaque année, au mois de décembre, des passionnés de navigation effectuent un parcours de 4 300 km à travers l'Océan Atlantique, qui les mène de l'île de Grande Canarie aux Iles Canaries jusqu'à Ste Lucie. L'arrivée des yachts se fait au port de plaisance de Rodney Bay où un programme complet de manifestations est prévu pour accueillir chacun des équipages, ainsi que des expositions organisées par diverses sociétés.

CARNAVAL

Le carnaval, qui est un événement annuel inoubliable, est habituellement organisé en février. Ce gala comprend un grand nombre d'activités à travers toute l'île, y compris des spectacles et concours de calypso, l'élection de la Reine du carnaval, et la sélection d'un Roi et d'une Reine des orchestres (King and Queen of the Bands). Des milliers d'enthousiastes et de joyeux convives prennent part chaque année à cette manifestation. Les visiteurs sont aussi invités à prendre part à cette parade musicale annuelle scintillante.

Deutsch

dieser Ort als Aussichtspunkt für herannahende Schiffe gewählt worden war. Für weitere Informationen wenden Sie sich bitte an den St. Lucia National Trust oder das Informationsbüro des Ortes Choiseul.

BESONDERE EREIGNISSE

ATLANTIK RALLYE FÜR SEGLER

Jedes Jahr im Dezember legen begeisterte Segler 4.300 km auf dem Atlantischen Ozean zurück. Sie starten in Gran Canaria auf den Kanarischen Inseln und legen in St. Lucia an. Die Yachten laufen im Yachthafen Rodney Bay ein, wo ein umfassendes Programm sowie Ausstellungen verschiedener Unternehmen jede Crew willkommen heißt.

KARNEVAL

Karneval wird für gewöhnlich im Februar gefeiert und ist ein unvergeßliches Ereignis. Bei der Feier gibt es eine Fülle von Veranstaltungen auf der ganzen Insel, einschließlich Calypso Shows und Wettbewerben, einer Karneval-Queen Show und einen König sowie eine Königin als Gewinner des Musikgruppenwettbewerbs. Tausende von begeisterten Karnevalsfreunden und Feiernde kommen jedes Jahr zu diesem Ereignis. Auch Gäste sind eingeladen, an dieser jährlichen Parade von Musik und Glimmer teilzunehmen, die das Blut der Besucher in Wallung bringt.

KOMÖDIENFESTIVAL

Das Komödienfestival wird vom St. Lucia National Trust organisiert. Es findet im April statt. In dem Programm finden Sie die Namen von weltweit bekannten Unterhaltungskünstlern. Für nähere Informationen wenden Sie sich bitte an den St. Lucia National Trust.

INTERNATIONALER ESSENSMARKT

Bei diesem jährlich stattfindenden Ereignis werden Gelder für wohltätige Organisationen auf der Insel gesammelt. Eine Palette von Speisen aus verschiedenen Ländern - von der authentischen chinesischen Küche bis zur eigenen traditionellen kreolischen Küche von St. Lucia - werden präsentiert und verkauft.

Die Veranstaltung wird durch ein buntes Unterhaltungsprogramm ergänzt und findet normalerweise im Point Seraphine Zentrum während der Tourismuswoche im Oktober statt.

Français

FESTIVAL DE COMÉDIE

Le festival de comédie est organisé par le St Lucia National Trust. Il a lieu en avril, et le programme met à l'affiche des comédiens renommés venus du monde entier. Veuillez prendre contact avec le St LuciaNational Trust pour plus de détails.

FOIRE GASTRONOMIQUE INTERNATIONALE

Les bénéfices de cette manifestation annuelle attrayante sont versés au profit des organisations caritatives de l'île. Une grande variété de mets de différents pays - de la cuisine chinoise authentique à la cuisine créole très typée de Ste Lucie - est présentée et proposée à la vente. La manifestation est rehaussée par diverses spectacles et a habituellement lieu au Complexe de Point Seraphine au mois d'octobre, pendant la Semaine du tourisme.

JOUNEN KWEYOL ENTENASYONNAL (JOURNÉE CRÉOLE INTERNATIONALE)

La "Jounen Kweyol" (journée créole) se fête chaque année le 28 octobre. Ce jour-là, les St Luciens se joignent à des visiteurs venus de divers pays du monde mais parlant tous le créole pour célébrer avec passion leur héritage culturel commun. Les célébrations atteignent habituellement leur apogée dans des activités spéciales telles que la préparation de plats traditionnels, l'exposition d'objets traditionnels et des manifestations folkloriques, le tout organisé le dimanche le plus proche du 28 octobre.

FÊTE NATIONALE

La fête nationale de Ste Lucie est le 13 décembre. Le thème de cette journée est la promotion de la fierté nationale, et elle est célébrée par des manifestations sportives et culturelles spéciales, et par des activités religieuses, sociales et commerciales. Parmi ces dernières, on peut citer le populaire Festival des Lumières avec un concours de fabrication de lanternes, le Festival National des Choeurs et le Festival du Marché. Toutes les villes et tous les villages de Ste Lucie sont illuminés lors de la manifestation.

TOURNOI DE PÊCHE DE STE LUCIE

Le tournoi international de pêche (International Bill Fishing Tournament) a lieu entre les mois de septembre et octobre. Les dates sont choisies de manière à garantir des conditions optimales pour la pêche. Les visiteurs sont cordialement invités à participer au tournoi en s'in

Deutsch

JOUNEN KWEYOL ENTENASYNNAL (INTERNATIONALER KREOLISCHER TAG)

"Jounen Kweyol" wird in jedem Jahr am 28. Oktober begangen. An diesem Tag vereinen sich die Einwohner von St. Lucia mit den kreolisch sprechenden Menschen auf der ganzen Welt und feiern ihre gemeinsame faszinierende Kultur. Die Feiern gipfeln zumeist in besonderen Aktivitäten, zu denen die Zubereitung von traditionellen Speisen, Ausstellungen traditioneller Gegenstände und Folklore gehören. All dies findet am dem 28. Oktober nächstgelegenen Sonntag statt.

NATIONALFEIERTAG

Der 13. Dezember ist der Nationalfeiertag auf St. Lucia. An diesem Tag wird der Nationalstolz hervorgehoben und er wird mit besonderen sportlichen und kulturellen sowie religiösen, sozialen und kommerziellen Veranstaltungen begangen. Besonders beliebt ist das Lichterfestival, bei dem ein Laternenwettbewerb, ein Chorwettbewerb und ein Marktfestival stattfinden. Städte und Dörfer auf ganz St. Lucia werden zu diesem Ereignis mit Lichtern geschmückt.

ST. LUCIA TURNIER DER SPORTANGLER

Der internationale Anglerwettbewerb wird in den Monaten September und Oktober ausgetragen. Es werden Termine festgelegt, um optimale Bedingungen für das Angeln zu haben. Besucher sind eingeladen, an diesem Wettbewerb als Angler auf einem gecharterten Boot teilzunehmen. Besitzer von Hochseefischerbooten sind ebenfalls zur Teilnahme eingeladen. Jedem Mitstreiter werden vier Tage voller Spaß und Anglerfreuden garantiert. Die Fische werden gekennzeichnet und wieder ins Meer geworfen.

ST. LUCIA JAZZFESTIVAL

Auf dem Programm des im Jahr 1992 aus der Taufe gehobenen Jazzfestivals stehen renommierte Künstler und legendäre Jazzgrößen wie Wynton Marsallis, Joe Sample, Ramsey Lewis, Regina Belle, Betty Charter, Herbie Hancock, Luther Francois und George Benson, um nur einige zu nennen. Das viertägige Festival findet jedes Jahr im Mai statt. Die Konzerte finden zum Teil im Freien, zum Teil in Kultureinrichtungen und Hotels statt, welche eine intimere Atmosphäre gewähren. Broschüren mit dem Programm, Veranstaltungsorten und Terminen sind ab Dezember jeden Jahres im Touristenbüro von St. Lucia erhältlich.

Français

scrivant comme pêcheur sur un bateau affrété. Les propriétaires de bateaux de pêche en haute mer peuvent également prendre part au tournoi. Toute personne qui s'inscrit est garantie de passer quatre jours agréables de pêche. Tous les poissons pêchés sont enregistrés et rejetés à la mer.

FESTIVAL DE JAZZ DE STE LUCIE

Organisé pour la première fois en 1992, le festival de jazz rassemble plusieurs artistes de renommée internationale et des grands noms légendaires du jazz, tels que Wynton Marsallis, Joe Sample, Ramsey Lewis, Regina Belle, Betty Carter, Herbie Hancock, Luther François et George Benson, pour n'en citer que quelques uns. Ce festival de quatre jours a lieu chaque année au mois de mai. Ces manifestations se déroulent en plein air, dans des sites culturels et, pour plus d'intimité, dans certains hôtels. La liste des artistes, des lieux et des programmes est disponible auprès du St Lucia Tourist Board (Office du tourisme de Ste Lucie) chaque année à partir de décembre.

COUNTRY MUSIC FESTIVAL

Le St Lucia Tourist Board a lancé un autre festival de musique afin d'ajouter à la gamme des spectacles offerts susceptibles d'attirer les touristes dans l'île en plus grand nombre. Le Country Music Festival a été lancé en décembre 1997 à Pigeon Island. De nombreux artistes de Country & Western, parmi les meilleurs, sont venus chanter à ce festival.
La popularité de la musique Country a considérablement augmenté au cours des dernières années et c'est une forme d'art qui compte parmi les plus populaires aux Etats-Unis.

VISITES ET EXCURSIONS

JARDINS BOTANIQUES

Ste Lucie a deux jardins botaniques: Tropical Gardens au nord, et Diamond Botanical Garden à Soufrière, qui comporte des bains minéraux et une chute pittoresque. Les deux jardins renferment une grande variété d'arbres fruitiers tropicaux, arbustes, vignes et toutes sortes de plantes à fleurs. Pour de plus amples informations concernant les jardins botaniques, veuillez appeler le 758-452-8101.

Deutsch

DAS COUNTRYMUSIK FESTIVAL

Das Touristenbüro von St. Lucia hat ein weiteres Musikfestivals ins Leben gerufen, um die Unterhaltungsveranstaltungen auf der Insel zu bereichern und so den Besucherzustrom auf der Insel weiter zu erhöhen. Das Countrymusik Festival wurde im Dezember 1997 in Pigeon Island ins Leben gerufen. Eine Reihe von erstklassigen Country- und Westernmusikern traten bei dem Festival auf.
Die Countrymusik hat sich in den letzten Jahren zu einer beliebten Musikrichtung entwickelt und erfreut sich vor allem in den Vereinigten Staaten zahlreicher Anhänger.

UNTERWEGS AUF DER INSEL

BOTANISCHE GÄRTEN

Auf St. Lucia gibt es zwei botanische Gärten: einen tropischen Garten im Norden und den Diamond Botanical Garden in Soufrière, in dem Mineralbäder und malerische Wasserfälle angelegt sind. In beiden Gärten finden Sie eine Reihe tropischer Obstbäume, Sträucher, Rebengewächse und jegliche Arten blühender Pflanzen.

Français

TOUR EN BATEAU LOUÉ À LA JOURNÉE

Se promener en bateau le long de la côte ouest de Ste Lucie est une expérience inoubliable. Vous pouvez louer un bateau à titre personnel ou vous pouvez laisser à une agence de voyage locale le soin d'organiser l'excursion. Le voyage vous conduit le long de la côte occidentale, sur la Mer des Caraïbes, et vous fait découvrir des villages de pêcheurs et de petites baies secrètes, jusqu'à Soufrière. Les visiteurs peuvent choisir de s'arrêter sur une plage en chemin ou de continuer le voyage jusqu'à Soufrière pour y visiter les sources sulfureuses (Sulphur Springs), les bassins dits de diamant (Diamond Baths), la grande Chute d'eau et les jardins tropicaux. Ces excursions comprennent aussi un déjeuner et des consommations.

VISITE D'AUTRES ÎLES

Vous pouvez organiser des excursions aux îles Grenadines, à la Barbade, à la Martinique et à la Dominique auprès d'agences de voyage locales. Il est aussi possible de voyager en bateau ou en avion aux îles Grenadines ou à la Martinique. A leur arrivée, les visiteurs sont accueillis par un guide qui leur fait visiter un grand nombre d'attractions naturelles, historiques et culturelles. Les voyages comprennent habituellement un excellent déjeuner et les consommations.

ILES MARIA (MARIA ISLANDS)

Les îles Maria, deux petites îles sur la côte de Vieux Fort, sont une réserve naturelle protégée, et l'habitat de deux espèces qu'on ne retrouve nulle part ailleurs dans le monde. Le serpent Kouwes, qui est considéré comme le serpent le plus rare du monde, s'est réfugié à Maria Major, quittant Ste Lucie, pour échapper à l'homme. Un autre habitant unique des îles Maria est le Zandoli Te, un lézard non arboricole dont les mâles ont une splendide queue d'un bleu brillant. Les excursions en bateau à Maria Major sont organisées par le St Lucia National Trust (tous les participants doivent être de bon nageurs).

VISITES DE MAGASINS

Les visites de magasin sont susceptibles de varier légèrement en fonction de l'agence de voyage qui les organise. Néanmoins, la plupart comprennent Point Seraphine, le centre commercial hors taxes (où les acheteurs devront présenter un billet d'avion et leur passeport pour leurs achats hors taxes), une visite à Castries, à l'usine Caribelle Batik et au studio de sérigraphie de Bagshaws.

Deutsch

Informationen über die botanischen Gärten erhalten Sie unter 758-452-8101.

TAGESTOUREN MIT GECHARTERTEN BOOTEN

Eine Bootsfahrt entlang der Westküste von St. Lucia ist ein unvergeßliches Erlebnis. Sie können auf privater Basis ein Boot mieten oder eine Tour bei einem örtlichen Veranstalter buchen. Bei der Tour gleiten Sie durch die Karibik, entlang der Westküste, Sie passieren Fischerdörfer und versteckte Buchten und erreichen schließlich Soufrière. Gäste haben die Wahl, auf dem Weg an einem Strand zu verweilen oder bis Soufrière zu fahren, um die Schwefelquellen, die Diamant-Bäder, Wasserfälle und die tropischen Gärten zu besuchen. Bei einem im voraus gebuchten Törn werden in der Regel Essen und Getränke angeboten.

VON EINER INSEL ZUR ANDEREN

Bei Reiseveranstaltern vor Ort können Sie Ausflüge zu den Grenadine Inseln, Martinique und Dominica buchen. Sie haben die Möglichkeit, den Reiseweg zu den Grenadine Inseln und nach Martinique auf dem See- oder auf dem Luftweg zurückzulegen. Bei ihrer Ankunft werden die Gäste von einem einheimischen Führer willkommen geheißen, der Sie mit verschiedenen natürlichen, historischen und kulturellen Sehenswürdigkeiten bekannt macht. Bei diesen Ausflügen werden den Gästen in der Regel ein ausgezeichnetes Essen und Getränke serviert.

MARIA INSELN

Zwei kleine Inseln vor der Küste von Vieux Fort sind zum Naturschutzgebiet erklärt worden und sind die Heimat von zwei Tierarten, die es sonst nirgendwo auf der Erde gibt. Die Kouwes Schlange, die als seltenste Schlange der Erde gilt, hat sich von St. Lucia auf die Insel Maria Major zurückgezogen, um sich vor den Menschen in Sicherheit zu bringen. Ein anderer einzigartiger Einwohner der Maria Inseln ist die Zandoli Te, eine Eidechse, deren Männchen einen herrlichen Schwanz in schillerndem Blau besitzen. Bootsausflüge zu den Maria Inseln werden vom National Trust organisiert (alle Teilnehmer müssen geübte Schwimmer sein).

SHOPPING-AUSFLÜGE

Das Programm der Shopping-Ausflüge kann je nach Veranstalter leichte Abweichungen aufweisen. Die meisten Ausflüge führen jedoch zum Point Seraphine, dem zollfreien Einkaufszentrum (hier müssen Besucher ihr

Français

SULPHUR SPRINGS - "DRIVE-IN VOLCANO"

Pas loin des Pitons, dans la ville de Soufrière, se trouve Sulphur Springs (les sources sulfureuses), un cratère d'environ deux hectares et demie, souvent qualifié d'unique volcan drive-in du monde. Une promenade à travers le cratère vous conduit à plus d'une douzaine de bassins et de sources chaudes bouillonnantes émettant une vapeur sulfureuse.

CROISIÈRES AU COUCHER DU SOLEIL (16H30 - 19H00)

Que ce soit en catamaran ou sur le fameux brick Unicorn, une croisière au coucher du soleil est une manière merveilleuse de finir la journée. Naviguez le long de la côte nord-ouest, célébrez la journée avec du champagne et une légère collation, et observez le soleil disparaître à l'horizon. Les activités mentionnées peuvent être organisées par la plupart des bureaux d'activités des hôtels.

ACTIVITÉS NOCTURNES

La plupart des hôtels et un grand nombre de restaurants offrent diverses activités de divertissement, y compris les orchestres locaux de Shak Shak, les orchestres de Steel Pan, les danseurs de limbo, le karaoke, et les danseurs et chanteurs locaux. Les lieux et heures sont indiqués dans le journal local *Tropical Traveller* qui est gratuit partout à Ste Lucie.

Chaque vendredi soir, le village de Gros Islet organise une soirée dansante hebdomadaire, une attraction très populaire auprès des St Luciens comme des visiteurs. Pendant que la musique remplit les rues, on vend du poulet grillé ainsi que des mets locaux et une grande variété de boissons. Cette "soirée dansante" se poursuit habituellement jusqu'aux premières heures de la matinée.

Deutsch

Flugticket und einen Ausweis vorzeigen, um zollfreie Ware einkaufen zu können), nach Castries, zu der Batikfabrik Caribelle und zum Seidenmalereiatelier Bagshaw.

SCHWEFELQUELLEN - "DRIVE-IN VULKAN"

Nicht weit entfernt von den Pitons liegen in der Stadt Soufrière die Schwefelquellen, ein fast 3 Quadratkilometer großer Krater, der als einziger zugänglicher Vulkan der Welt oft als "Drive-in"-Vulkan bezeichnet wird. Bei einem Spaziergang durch den Krater sehen Sie mehr als ein Dutzend Seen und heiße Quellen, aus denen schwefelhaltiger Dampf brodelt.

KREUZFAHRTEN IM SONNENUNTERGANG (16.30 - 19.00 UHR)

Ob Sie auf einem Catamaran oder dem berühmten Brigg, Unicorn, durchs Wasser gleiten - eine Kreuzfahrt in den Sonnenuntergang ist ein wundervoller Tagesabschluß. Sie segeln an der Westküste entlang und lassen den Tag mit Champagner und leichten Hors d'oeuvres ausklingen, während die Sonne am Horizont ins Meer eintaucht.

Die aufgeführten Aktivitäten können in den meisten Hotels vom Animationsbüro organisiert werden.

NACHTLEBEN

Die meisten Hotels und viele Restaurants bieten ihren Gästen ein Unterhaltungsprogramm. Dazu zählen auch Musikgruppen wie Shak Shak Bands, Steel Pan Bands, Limbotänzer, Karaoke sowie Darbietungen einheimischer Tänzer und Sänger. Das Programm und die Termine sind in der lokalen Zeitung Tropical Traveller angegeben, die überall auf St. Lucia kostenlos erhältlich ist.

Jeden Freitagabend herrscht in den Straßen des Dorfes Gros Islet ein buntes Treiben, das die Einheimischen in St. Lucia und auch viele Besucher jede Woche auf die Beine bringt. Die Luft ist von Musik erfüllt, Verkäufer bieten gegrillte Hähnchen und Speisen der einheimischen Küche sowie Getränke an. Die "Party" klingt meistens erst in den frühen Morgenstunden aus.

An Mittwochabenden ist das Restaurant "Lime" in Rodney Bay mit Musik und Tanz bis in die Morgenstunden voller Leben.

Zu den beliebtesten Nachtclubs der Insel gehören das "Indies" und "The Late Lime". Auch diese beiden Nachtlokale sind im Norden der Insel in Rodney Bay angesiedelt. Beide Clubs bieten verschiedene Programme mit Live-Unterhaltung an.

Im Derek Walcott Kunstzentrum, das im Great House

Français

Le mercredi soir, le restaurant "Lime" de Rodney Bay retentit des harmonies de la musique et de la danse jusqu'aux premières heures de la matinée.

"Indies" et "The Late Lime" sont deux des night-clubs les plus populaires de Ste Lucie. Ils se trouvent tous deux au nord de l'île, à Rodney Bay. Les deux clubs ont des soirées thématiques avec interprétations d'artistes sur scène.

Le Derek Walcott Centre For The Arts, situé dans le restaurant Great House, offre des représentations théâtrales.

Heritage Sunday: cette manifestation, qui a lieu pendant les mois d'été, culmine en un spectacle passionnant combinant chanson, théâtre et danse qui célèbre les traditions de Ste Lucie. La manifestation est organisée en plein air, soit dans les ruines historiques et les vastes jardins de Pigeon Island, soit dans le vieux moulin à sucre charmant du village de Anse La Raye. L'atmosphère est proche de celle du carnaval, avec la musique des steel bands, de groupes de violons traditionnels et d'orchestres de percussion de rue. La nourriture est dans le style typique des buffets de plantation, et un mélange égal d'autochtones et de visiteurs viennent savourer les festivités. Pour de plus amples informations, veuillez prendre contact avec le St Lucia National Trust.

Tour historique de Pigeon Island: Pigeon Island est un superbe parc naturel qui reflète mille ans d'histoire. L'île comporte un musée rempli de reliques des activités des premiers habitants humains. Des guides escortent les visiteurs jusqu'à Fort Rodney avec ses vues panoramiques éblouissantes. Les itinéraires marqués le long du chemin sont ponctués de sites historiques intéressants. Une visite au centre d'information de l'île permet d'évoquer la victoire de l'amiral Rodney en 1782, lors de la fameuse "Bataille des Saints". Pour de plus amples informations à ce sujet, veuillez prendre contact

Deutsch

Restaurant untergebracht ist, können Sie außerdem Theateraufführungen besuchen.

"Traditions-Sonntag": Dieses Ereignis, das in den Sommermonaten stattfindet, erhält seinen besonderen Charakter durch die Aufführungen von Musik, Theater und Tanz, die der Tradition auf St. Lucia Tribut zollen. Es findet unter freiem Himmel entweder an den historischen Ruinen, auf dem urwüchsigen Boden von Pigeon Island oder an der reizvollen alten Zuckermühle im Dorf Anse La Raye statt. Die Atmosphäre erinnert mit den Klängen der Steelbands, traditionellen Violinensembles und Percussion Straßengruppen an den Karneval. Das Essen ist im Stil der typischen Plantagenbüffets bereitet und das Publikum besteht aus einer bunten Mischung aus Einheimischen und Gästen. Weitere Informationen erhalten Sie beim St. Lucia National Trust.

Historischer Rundgang auf Pigeon Island: Pigeon Island ist ein zauberhafter Naturpark, der eine tausendjährige Geschichte widerspiegelt. Auf der Insel gibt es ein ansprechendes Museum, in dem Zeugnisse der frühen Menschheit aufbewahrt werden. Führer begleiten die Besucher nach Fort Rodney, von wo Sie einen atemberaubenden Ausblick genießen können. An den beschilderten Wanderwege liegen eine Vielzahl historischer Stätten. Bei einem Besuch des Informationszentrums der Insel können Sie den berühmten Sieg des Admirals Rodney im Jahr 1782 in der legendären "Schlacht der Heiligen" wieder aufleben lassen. Informationen erhalten Sie beim St. Lucia National Trust.

St. Lucia - Rhythmen und Farben: "Rhythmen und Farben" ist eine gesellschaftliche Veranstaltung des National Trust, bei der zur Teezeit die Geschichte von St. Lucia in chronologisch aufgebauten Teilen mit Hilfe von Video und Dias präsentiert wird. Es wird von den Menschen berichtet, die auf der Insel gelebt haben, von der Art und Weise, wie sie gelebt haben sowie von ihrem historischen, kulturellen und botanischen Vermächtnis. Es werden traditionelle Lieder, Tänze und Musik von St. Lucia aufgeführt. Gäste haben die Möglichkeit, sich selbst an einfacheren Tanzschritten zu versuchen. Es werden außerdem Tee, traditionelle Süßigkeiten und andere Getränke serviert.

PLANTAGEN-TOUREN

Errard Plantage: Die Plantage liegt auf dem Land in der Nähe des Dorfes Dennery. Bereits die Fahrt zu der Plantage durch das Landesinnere und entlang des Regenwaldes ist ein spektakuläres Erlebnis. Bei der Ankunft begleitet der Eigentümer die Gäste bei einem Rundgang über die Plantage und erläutert ihnen die verschiedenen Obstsorten sowie die Verarbeitung von

Français

avec le St Lucia National Trust.

Ste Lucie - Rythmes et couleurs: "Rythmes et couleurs" est une activité offerte en fin d'après-midi et organisée par le National Trust. L'histoire de Ste Lucie y est évoquée à travers une présentation chronologique d'enregistrements vidéo et de diapositives. Elle décrit les personnes qui se sont établies à Ste Lucie, leur vie, et présente leur héritage historique, culturel et botanique. Les chansons, danses et la musique de Ste Lucie sont présentées, et les visiteurs ont la possibilité d'apprendre des pas de danse simples. On leur sert également du thé, des friandises traditionnelles et d'autres boissons.

VISITES DE PLANTATIONS

Plantation Errard: la plantation est située dans la campagne, près du village de Dennery. Le voyage vers Errard, à travers l'intérieur de l'île et en bordure de la forêt tropicale, est très spectaculaire. A votre arrivée, le propriétaire conduit le groupe à travers la propriété, explique les différents fruits qui y sont cultivés et le traitement des fèves de cacao, y compris la danse traditionnelle que l'on utilise pour les polir. Le tour se termine par un déjeuner créole accompagné par de délicieux jus de fruits locaux.

La Sikwe - Moulin à sucre historique et expérience de la plantation: la propriété La Sikwe se trouve en bordure du village de Anse La Raye. Les visiteurs sont invités à découvrir un musée et un théâtre culturel et à admirer la roue de moulin géante de 12 mètres qui y a été restaurée. La propriété, d'une superficie de 160 hectares, comporte de beaux jardins botaniques et évoque les années de plantation de canne à sucre du 18ème siècle. Les visites doivent être réservées à l'avance. Les démarches nécessaires peuvent être faites auprès des bureaux d'activités de la plupart des hôtels.

Marquis Estate: la propriété est située sur la côte nord-est, à quelques minutes de Castries. La route traverse la campagne et atteint des hauteurs offrant des vues excellentes. Les visiteurs sont accueillis à la propriété par un des propriétaires. Après une boisson tropicale rafraîchissante vient la visite dont le thème est la production des deux produits agricoles d'exportation principaux de Ste Lucie, la banane et le copra, ainsi que les produits d'exportation principaux du passé, le café et le cacao. La visite d'un vieux moulin à sucre et un voyage en bateau sur le Marquis River sont également compris. La visite se termine par un délicieux déjeuner avec mets locaux dans la résidence de la plantation. Les visites ne sont possibles que si elles ont été organisées à l'avance.

Morne Coubaril Estate: la propriété Morne Coubaril domine la ville pittoresque de Soufrière. La visite comprend une démonstration du traitement du cacao, du

Deutsch

Kakaobohnen einschließlich der traditionellen Reinigungszeremonie. Am Ende des Rundgangs erwartet Sie ein traditionelles kreolisches Essen mit köstlichen Obstsäften aus eigener Herstellung.

La Sikwe - Historische Zuckermühle und Plantage: Der Besitz La Sikwe grenzt an das Dorf Anse La Raye. Die Besucher können ein Museum und eine Kulturspielstätte sowie ein restauriertes 12 Meter hohes Wasserrad besichtigen. Auf dem 1,6 Quadratkilometer großen Besitz wurden wunderschöne botanische Gärten angelegt und es werden die Jahre des Zuckerrohranbaus im 18. Jahrhundert dargestellt. Besuche müssen im voraus angemeldet werden. Anmeldungen werden in den meisten Animationsbüros in den Hotels entgegengenommen.

Marquis' Estate: Der Besitz liegt an der Nordostküste nicht weit von Castries entfernt. Der Weg führt Sie durch das Landesinnere und Sie haben an manchen hoch gelegenen Punkten eine wunderschöne Aussicht. Die Besucher werden von einem der Eigentümer der Plantage empfangen. Nach einem erfrischenden tropischen Getränk beginnen Sie einen Rundgang, der Sie in die Produktion der Hauptexportfrüchte der Insel eingeführt, Bananen und Kopra. Ebenso werden Sie über die Hauptexportgüter früherer Zeiten informiert, Kaffee und Kakao. Sie besuchen eine alte Zuckermühle und sind zu einer Bootstour auf dem Marquis River eingeladen. Zum Abschluß des Besuches wird Ihnen im Plantagenhaus ein köstliches Mahl der einheimischen Küche serviert. Es sind nur im voraus angemeldete Besuche möglich.

Morne Coubaril Estate: Von der Morne Coubaril Plantage haben Sie einen Blick auf die malerische Stadt Soufrière. Bei dem Besuch wird Ihnen die Herstellung von Kakao, Kopra und Maniok demonstriert. Die Besucher wandeln auf den Spuren und den ursprünglichen Wegen der Maultierwagen, besuchen eine Arbeitersiedlung, eine Zuckermühle, ein Maniokhaus und ein Kakaohaus. Auf dem Besitz gibt es zudem einen Aussichtspunkt, der Ihnen einen faszinierenden Ausblick eröffnet.

TOUREN MIT DEM HUBSCHRAUBER

Transfer zum Flughafen: Durch einen Transfer mit dem Hubschrauber reduziert sich die Reisezeit zwischen Flughafen und vielen größeren Hotels um mindestens eine Stunde und es eröffnet sich Ihnen bereits ein spektakulärer Blick auf die Schönheit von St. Lucias Landschaft. Der Flug startet am Point Seraphine und ausgesuchten Hotels und dauert nur 10-15 entspannende Minuten (je nach Abflugort) vom/zum Internationalen Flughafen Hewanorra.

Français

copra et du manioc. Les visiteurs marchent dans une "rue" authentique utilisée jadis pour les transports à dos de mulet et visitent un village de travailleurs, un moulin à sucre, une maison du manioc et une maison du cacao. Un point d'observation sur cette propriété offre des vues spectaculaires.

TOURS EN HÉLICOPTÈRE

Airport Shuttle: la navette en hélicoptère réduit le temps de voyage entre l'aéroport et beaucoup de grands hôtels d'au moins une heure, et permet une vue spectaculaire de la beauté panoramique de Ste Lucie. L'hélicoptère s'envole de Point Seraphine et d'hôtels sélectionnés et il faut seulement 10 à 15 minutes de détente (en fonction du point de départ) pour chaque trajet entre l'aéroport international Hewanorra et l'hôtel.

Tour du Nord de l'île: ce tour, qui dure environ 10 minutes, part du centre commercial hors taxes Point Seraphine à Castries et conduit à la côte occidentale, survolant un grand nombre des hôtels les plus luxueux de Ste Lucie. L'hélicoptère survole le port de plaisance de Rodney Bay et Pigeon Island, puis fait un tour de l'île qui permet d'admirer la côte atlantique accidentée avant de retourner à Point Seraphine.

Tour du Sud de l'île: le tour du sud de l'île dure environ 20 minutes et part de Point Seraphine. Il survole le port de Castries et continue le long de la ligne littorale occidentale jusqu'à Marigot Bay. Ensuite, il conduit vers le sud à Soufrière où les majestueux Pitons semblent surgir directement de la mer. De là, le vol se poursuit vers l'intérieur du pays permettant d'admirer en surplomb les sources volcaniques chaudes et la forêt tropicale humide de Ste Lucie, avant de retourner à Point Seraphine. Vous pouvez réserver un tour en hélicoptère au bureau d'activités de votre hôtel.

Deutsch

Tour über die nördliche Insel: Der etwa 10minütige Flug startet beim zollfreien Einkaufszentrum Point Seraphine in Castries, von wo er Kurs auf die Westküste nimmt und viele der nobelsten Hotels von St. Lucia passiert. Sie überfliegen den Yachthafen Rodney Bay und die Pigeon Insel und umrunden dann die Insel, um die zerklüftete Atlantik-Küstenlinie aus der Luft zu betrachten, bevor Sie zum Point Seraphine zurückkehren.

Tour über die südliche Insel: Der Flug über die südliche Insel dauert etwa 20 Minuten und beginnt am Point Seraphine. Sie überfliegen den Hafen von Castries und die westliche Küstenlinie zu der malerischen Marigot Bay. Dann geht es Richtung Süden nach Soufrière, wo sich die majestätischen Pitons direkt aus dem Meer erheben. Von hier aus nehmen Sie Kurs auf das Landesinnere, um einen Blick auf die heißen Vulkanquellen von St. Lucia und den Regenwald zu werfen, bevor Sie zum Point Seraphine zurückkehren. Rundflüge mit dem Hubschrauber können Sie über das Animationsbüro Ihres Hotels buchen.

Bibliography

Jesse, *Outlines of St. Lucia's History, The St. Lucia Archaeological and Historical Society*, 1994.
Devaux, Anthony, *Saint Lucia Historic Sites, St. Lucia National Trust, No.1*, 1975.
Dyde, Robert, *Caribbean Companion: The A to Z Reference*, Macmillan, London, 1992.
Devaux, Robert, *A Bird Watcherís Guide to Pigeon Island, St. Lucia National Trust*, 1996.
New Definitive Issue, *Postage Stamps of St. Lucia*, 1970.
The Definitive Issue, *Postage Stamps of St. Lucia*, 1996.
St. Lucia National Trust, *Pigeon Island National Landmark: A Brief History and Guide*, 1993.
ECNAMP, *Maria Islands Nature Reserve*, St. Lucia National Trust, 1985.
Charles, George, *The History of the Labour Movement in St. Lucia 1945-1974*, Folk Research Centre, St. Lucia, 1994.
Doyle, Chris, *Sailors Guide Directory 1997-1998*,
Supplement in Sailors Guide to the Windward Islands, 1997.
COLEACP, *The Exotic Vegetables Book*, The Fresh Fruit and Vegetable Information Bureau, London.
Lennox, G.W. & Seddon, *S.A., Flowers of the Caribbean*, Macmillan, Caribbean, 1978.
Barlow, Virginia, *The Nature of the Islands: Plants and Animals of the Eastern Caribbean*, Chris Doyle Publishing and Cruising Guide Publications, 1993.
Philpott, Don, *Caribbean Sunseekers: St. Lucia*, Moorland Publishing Co., 1995.
Bond, James, *Birds of the West Indies: A guide to the species of Birds that inhabit the Greater Antilles*, Lesser Antilles and Bahama Islands, 5th edition, Collins, London, 1985.
Robert J. Devaux OBE, *They Called us Brigands: The saga of St. Lucia's Freedom Fighters*. St. Lucia 1997.
Linda Molloy, *Saint Lucia Past: A Pictorial History*. Linda Molloy, Swanage, England 1996.

Further Information

St. Lucia Tourist Board Head Office, Pointe Seraphine, P.O. Box 221, Castries.
Tel: (758) 452 4094/453 0053   Fax: (758) 453 1121
USA: St. Lucia Tourist Board, New York Office, 820 2nd Ave, 9th Floor, New York, NY 10017
Tel: 212 867 2950   Fax: 212 808 4975
CANADA: St. Lucia Tourist Board, 4975 Dundas St. W, Suite 457, Etobicoke 'D'Islington, ON Canada M9A 4X4
Tel. 416 236 0936   Fax: 416 236 0937
UK: Saint Lucia Tourist Board, 421a Finchley Road, London NW3 6HJ.
Tel: 0171 431 4045   Fax: 0171 431 7920
GERMANY: St. Lucia Tourist Board, Tannenwaldallee 76a, D-61348, Bad Hamburg, Germany.
Tel: 06172 30 44 31   Fax: 06172 30 50 72
FRANCE: St Lucia Tourist Board, 53 rue Francois ler, 75008 Paris, France.
Tel: 47 20 39 66.   Fax: 47 23 09 65

Public Holidays

New Years Day	1 January
2nd New Years Holiday	2 January
Independence Day	22 February
Carnival Day	(No fixed date)
Good Friday	(No fixed date)
Easter Monday	(No fixed date)
Labour Day	1st Monday in May
Whit Monday	5 June
Corpus Christi	15 June
Emancipation Day	7 August
Thanksgiving Day	2 October
National Day	13 December
Christmas Day	25 December

*Hibiscus:
The National Flower of Saint Lucia*